GROUP PERFORMANCE

Group Performance

Bernard A. Nijstad
University of Groningen, The Netherlands

Psychology Press
Taylor & Francis Group

HOVE AND NEW YORK

First published 2009
by Psychology Press
27 Church Road, Hove, East Sussex BN3 2FA

Simultaneously published in the USA and Canada
by Psychology Press
270 Madison Avenue, New York, NY 10016

Psychology Press is an imprint of the Taylor & Francis Group, an Informa business

Copyright © 2009 Psychology Press

Typeset in Palatino by Garfield Morgan, Swansea, West Glamorgan
Printed and bound in Great Britain by TJ International Ltd, Padstow, Cornwall
Cover design by Jim Wilkie

British Library Cataloguing in Publication Data
A catalogue record for this book is available from the British Library

Library of Congress Cataloging-in-Publication Data
Nijstad, Bernard Arjan, 1971–
   Group performance / Bernard Nijstad.
       p. cm.
   Includes bibliographical references and index.
   ISBN 978-1-84169-668-3 (hbk) – ISBN 978-1-84169-669-0 (soft cover) 1. Social
groups. 2. Teams in the workplace. 3. Group decision making. 4. Small groups.
I. Title.
 HM716.N55 2009
   302.3'4–dc22

                                                                        2009005276

ISBN 978-1-84169-668-3 (hbk)
ISBN 978-1-84169-669-0 (pbk)

Contents

Series preface

Social Psychology: A Modular Course, edited by Miles Hewstone, aims to provide undergraduates with stimulating, readable, affordable, and brief texts by leading experts committed to presenting a fair and accurate view of the work in each field, sharing their enthusiasm with students, and presenting their work in an approachable way. Together with three other modular series, these texts will cover all the major topics studied at undergraduate level in psychology. The companion series are: *Clinical Psychology*, edited by Chris R. Brewin; *Developmental Psychology*, edited by Peter Bryant; and *Cognitive Psychology*, edited by Gerry Altmann and Susan E. Gathercole. The series will appeal to those who want to go deeper into the subject than the traditional textbook will allow, and base their examination answers, research projects, assignments, or practical decisions on a clearer and more rounded appreciation of the research evidence.

Also available in this series:

The Social Psychology of Aggression
by Barbara Krahé

Attribution
by Friedrich Försterling

Attitudes and Attitude Change
by Gerd Bohner and Michaela Wänke

Prosocial Behaviour
by Hans-Werner Bierhoff

Social Cognition
by Herbert Bless, Klaus Fiedler, and Fritz Strack

For more information about this series please visit the *Social Psychology: A Modular Course* website at www.psypress.com/socialmodular

Acknowledgments

Writing this book was a lot of fun, not least because of the encouragement and patience of the people at Psychology Press. I thank Miles Hewstone for inviting me to write this book (in the summer of 2005) and for his patience when I failed to meet deadlines. I am indebted to Wolfgang Stroebe, Robert Lount, Andreas Mojzisch, and Scott Tindale for their helpful comments on an earlier draft of this book. Various people commented on different chapters, including Carsten de Dreu, Hamit Coskun, Katherine Stroebe, Astrid Homan, Gerben van Kleef, Michel Handgraaf, and Mauro Giacomantonio. Two students helped me with checking the references, approaching publishers to obtain reprint permissions, and finding suitable illustrations: Thank you Philip Schuette and Hillie Aaldering. On a more personal note, I would like to thank Katherine. Although I was not always happy with your remarks about my progress, they were in fact extremely helpful, as was you just being there.

Studying small groups 1

In 1961, the US President John F. Kennedy and his group of advisors made a disastrous decision: They decided to invade Cuba. Since 1959, Cuba had been ruled by the communist regime of Fidel Castro, much to the dislike of the USA. Kennedy and his advisors therefore took up a risky plan. They used a brigade of recruited Cuban exiles, supported them with weapons and transportation, and dropped them in Cuba, in a place known as the Bay of Pigs. The Bay of Pigs invasion, however, was a complete failure. Within days, all 1,300 troops were killed or arrested.

Later analysis showed that the fiasco was due to faulty decision-making by Kennedy and his advisors. Janis (1972, 1982) analyzed the Bay of Pigs invasion as an example of *groupthink* (see Chapter 7 for a more elaborate discussion). Janis was interested in the question of why a group of smart people, such as Kennedy and his advisors, could make such a bad decision. He reasoned that it was due to certain group processes, and coined the term "groupthink": "A mode of thinking that people engage in when they are deeply involved in a cohesive in-group, when members' strivings for unanimity override their motivation to realistically appraise alternative courses of action" (Janis, 1972, p. 9). The essence of groupthink lies in excessive concurrence-seeking: Group members try to maintain consensus and group harmony, and refrain from criticism or counter-argumentation against the alternative that is favored by the group. Because group members do not critically appraise the alternatives, and everyone appears to agree with the proposed decision, they run the risk of convincing themselves to adopt a course of action that normally would be perceived as inadequate or even dangerous.

Only one year later, in 1962, President Kennedy and his group (Figure 1.1) faced a new crisis. The intelligence agencies had found out that the Soviet Union was shipping nuclear weapons to Cuba. There were air-photographs that showed new missile bases. Also, there were Soviet ships on the way to Cuba, and these ships probably

carried nuclear warheads. Clearly, this presented a great risk to the USA. Furthermore, if not handled carefully, the so-called Cuba crisis might easily end in World War III. President Kennedy and his group considered different alternatives, including a new attack on Cuba. Eventually they decided on a blockade of Cuban ports with navy ships. Their strategy was successful and the Soviet ships turned around, possibly preventing a full-blown nuclear war. Later, the Soviet Union agreed to retract its missiles from Cuba, while the USA would retract its missiles from Turkey. Clearly, President Kennedy and his group had this time made the right decision.[1]

FIGURE 1.1.
President Kennedy with Secretary of Defense Robert McNamara (left) and Secretary of State Dean Rusk (center), three of the main characters during the Cuban Missile Crisis (seen on 10 December 1962, just after the crisis; photograph by Cecil Stoughton).

Political decisions, like the ones described above, are often made in groups, and can have far-reaching consequences (including war and peace). Many other tasks are also done in groups: Groups of students write a paper together, companies structure their work around teams, management teams decide about the future of an organization, friends organize a party, and many sports are played in teams. The topic of this book is performance of these groups. One of the most important questions is what determines group effectiveness. Why do some group decisions lead to complete fiascos (the Bay of Pigs invasion), whereas others are extremely effective (the Cuban missile crisis decision)? Why do some teams perform poorly, whereas others perform very well? How well do groups perform their tasks as compared to individuals: Who is more creative, who makes the better decisions, and who is the better problem-solver? How do individual member capabilities relate to the performance of the group as a whole? How does the environment of groups shape their performance? These questions will be addressed.

In this first chapter, we first clarify what in the context of this book is a "group." Second, we discuss the different functions that groups may have for their members. Third, we go into the ways that groups can be studied scientifically. We close with an overview of the book.

---

1   The 2000 movie *Thirteen Days* (directed by Roger Donaldson; with Bruce Greenwood playing John F. Kennedy and Kevin Costner playing one of his advisors) is based on the Cuba crisis.

Defining groups

Entitativity

Many authors have suggested definitions of groups. Lewin (1948) suggested that common fate is critical: people are a group when they experience similar outcomes. For example, a group in an organization might be collectively rewarded for performing well. Sherif and Sherif (1969) proposed that some form of social structure (status or role differentiation, e.g., a leadership role) is essential, because otherwise the "group" would just be a loose collection of individuals. Bales (1950) emphasized face-to-face interaction, and argued that a group requires that members meet on a regular basis. Tajfel (1981) emphasized shared identity, and argued that groups exist when members identify with their group.

Rather than giving a black-and-white definition of groups, it might be more useful to view "groupiness" as a dimension on which collections of individuals can vary (see also McGrath, 1984; Moreland, 1987): Some groups are more "groupy" than others. Instead of "groupiness," researchers often use the term "group entitativity." Group *entitativity* refers to the degree to which a collection of persons is perceived as being bonded together in a coherent unit (Campbell, 1958). In fact, common fate, social structure, face-to-face interaction, and shared identity may all contribute to group entitativity (see also McGrath, 1984).

This approach assumes that having certain properties makes certain collections of individuals more entitative: The more of these properties it possesses, the more entitative the group is. It is similar to classifying animals as birds. An animal becomes more bird-like when it has certain properties, such as that it can fly, has feathers, has a beak, lays eggs, and so on. However, some birds do not have all these properties (e.g., ostriches cannot fly, penguins have no feathers) and they still are birds, although less bird-like than a robin (which has all these properties and is a very *prototypical* bird). Similarly, some groups may not have certain properties (e.g., they never meet, or they don't experience common fate) but can still be considered groups. But which properties make groups more entitative?

Group properties

Table 1.1 lists some important group properties. Some of these speak for themselves, such as group size and duration. Group structure

TABLE 1.1
Important group characteristics

Characteristic	Description	Relation with entitativity*
Interdependence	The degree to which group members depend on one another to achieve their goals or important outcomes	+
Importance	The degree to which the group is important to its members	+
Interaction	The degree to which group members meet on a regular basis	+
Size	The number of people that are members of the group	−
Duration	How long the group stays together as a group	+
Permeability	The degree to which it is easy to join or leave the group	−
Similarity	The degree to which group members are similar to one another on one or more attributes	+
Group structure	The degree to which the group has developed specific characteristics, such as norms, roles, and status differences	(+)
Cohesion	The degree to which group members feel attracted to the group	(+)

* Based on Lickel *et al.*, 2000; + indicates a positive relation, − indicates a negative relation; group structure and cohesion were not studied by Lickel *et al.* but one might assume a positive relation.

(including status differences and role differentiation) will be discussed in the next chapter. We will discuss the others here.

Interdependence

One property on which groups vary is the degree to which group members are interdependent. Interdependence refers to situations in which a group member's individual performance or outcomes depend not only on the actions of that individual, but also on the actions of other members. *Task interdependence* refers to the degree to which group members are mutually dependent on one another to accomplish their tasks. For example, a forward player in a football team is dependent on the actions of others players: They have to pass the ball to allow the forward to score. *Outcome interdependence* refers to the degree to which group members are mutually dependent to receive valued outcomes (e.g., money or praise). A football team, for example, would receive a better ranking and more praise after winning a game. Winning a game (and thus receiving these outcomes) is dependent not only on a team member's own actions, but also on the actions of the other members. Task and outcome interdependence often co-occur, but this is not always the case (see Chapter 9).

Importance

Importance refers to how important the group is for its members. Groups can be important for members not only because they have a task to perform; rather, being in a group can have a number of consequences for group members. These are discussed in more detail in the next section, on functions of groups.

Interaction

Interaction refers to some form of (verbal or nonverbal) communication among group members. Do they interact frequently, or not so often? Interaction can be face to face, but can also involve discussions on the internet, telephone conversations, and so on (Chapter 11). When group members are highly dependent on one another, usually more interaction within the group is required to coordinate group members' activities.

Permeability

Permeability refers to how easy or difficult it is to enter or leave the group. Is group membership relatively stable, or do frequent changes occur? Further, some groups are elite, or have very high status, and these groups usually are not very permeable. For example, it is very difficult to join the All England Tennis Club – the club that organizes the Wimbledon tennis tournament – which is the tennis club in Britain with the highest status (but winning a singles title at Wimbledon would also win you membership).

Similarity

Group membership is often based on similarity. People form certain groups because they are similar: They all like playing chess and start a chess club, or they all are psychologists and form a psychology department. Further, outsiders tend to categorize similar people together (e.g., they talk about the "people from marketing" as if they were a group) (Campbell, 1958). Finally, it is important to note that people who are similar usually also like one another more than people who are dissimilar (Byrne, 1971; Newcomb, 1956).

BOX 1.1.

Cohesion and performance

One long-standing issue in social psychology concerns the relation between group cohesion and performance (Mullen & Copper, 1994). Often, people think that cohesion will lead to better performance: When group members value their group, they will work hard to perform well! However, results regarding the relation between cohesion and performance are inconclusive. For example, of the 34 studies reviewed by Stogdill (1972), 12 studies indicated that cohesive groups were more productive, 11 indicated that cohesive groups were less productive, and in the remaining 11 studies there was no relation between cohesion and performance. Clearly, things are more complex.

One possibility is that the relation between cohesion and performance depends on other factors. Podsakoff, MacKenzie, and Ahearne (1997) argued that the relation between cohesion and performance would depend on group goal acceptance. They reasoned that if a group accepts their performance goals (they agree with the goals that were given to them by their management) there should be a positive relation between group cohesion and performance, because cohesion will motivate members to work hard towards these performance goals. However, if the group does not accept the performance goals, this relation should not be found, because group cohesion will not motivate people to work toward goals that they do not accept.

Podsakoff *et al.* (1997) tested this hypothesis in a survey study among workers of a paper mill. They asked 218 employees of the paper mill, who worked in 40 different groups, to fill out a questionnaire. In this questionnaire, there were questions about group cohesion (e.g., "We like working in this group") and about goal acceptance (e.g., "We feel that our goals are fair"). Employees were asked to rate the questions on rating scales, making it possible to quantify these variables. Data regarding group performance came from company records. The company kept track of each team's performance as a percentage of machine capacity. Thus, groups could maximally perform at 100 per cent of machine capacity, but lower scores were also possible.

Figure 1.2 shows Podsakoff *et al.*'s findings. Consistent with predictions, there was no relation between cohesion and performance for groups that did not accept the company goals. However, this relation was positive for groups in which goal acceptance was high. Thus, it appears that the relation between group cohesion and performance critically depends on goal acceptance: Only when groups accept performance goals does cohesion motivate members to work hard.

FIGURE 1.2.

Performance as a function of cohesion and goal acceptance. Taken from: Podsakoff, P. M., MacKenzie, S. B., & Ahearne, M. (1997). Moderating effects of goal acceptance on the relationship between group cohesiveness and productivity. *Journal of Applied Psychology, 82*, 974–983. Copyright American Psychological Association. Reprinted with permission.

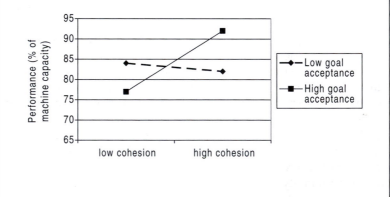

Group cohesion

Group *cohesion* (or "cohesiveness") is the force that binds its members to the group and induces them to stay with the group (Festinger, 1950). Group cohesion is assumed to be important to group functioning, because it helps keep the group together and motivates group members to exert themselves on behalf of the group.

It is useful to distinguish between types of cohesion. *Task cohesion* refers to the shared commitment to the group's tasks, while *interpersonal cohesion* refers to the attraction to the group (e.g., Mullen & Copper, 1994). It is often assumed that cohesion will help performance – this is probably the reason why some companies send their teams to "team building" trainings. However, Box 1.1 describes some research showing that the relation between cohesion and performance is more complicated.

Group properties and entitativity

Using a number of the properties listed in Table 1.1, Lickel, Hamilton, Wieczorkowska, Lewis, Sherman, and Uhles (2000) investigated how possessing certain properties is associated with perceptions of group entitativity. What makes one group "groupier" than another? Lickel *et al.* provided participants in their study (American and Polish students) with a sample of 40 different "groups," such as "members of a family," "Blacks," "members of a jury," and "people in line at a bank." Participants had to rate these different groups on eight dimensions: importance of group members to each other, common goals, common outcomes, degree of interaction among members, size, duration, permeability, and similarity among group members. The groups were also rated on the degree to which the group really was a group (group entitativity). Lickel *et al.* (2000) considered which of their eight group characteristics best predicted group entitativity. They found that the most important predictor was interaction among group members: Higher levels of interaction were associated with higher entitativity. The other characteristics also contributed to entitativity: Importance, common goals and outcomes, group member similarity and duration showed a positive relation (the higher the importance, common goals, etc., the higher perceived entitativity), whereas group size and permeability showed a weak negative relation (larger groups and highly permeable groups were rated lower in entitativity) (Table 1.1). Thus, factors such as common fate and face-to-face interaction indeed make groups more "groupy."

In this book, we mainly consider task groups. These groups are often relatively small, usually (but not always) have face-to-face interaction, and have a common goal: task performance (also Lickel *et al.*, 2000). So, task groups will usually be fairly high in entitativity. Nevertheless, some task groups may be more entitative than others, depending on the amount of interaction that takes place between group members, stability of group membership, and other factors. For example, some groups in organizations might be geographically dispersed, and only communicate through email or teleconferences. Nevertheless, despite the lack of face-to-face contact, to some degree this might still be considered a group. Further, some groups might have relatively unstable group boundaries and quick changes in membership. For example, a project team might temporarily recruit people into the group based on its current need for specialized knowledge (cf. Ancona & Bresman, 2006). Nevertheless, it is still possible to talk about groups in these cases as a more or less coherent unit that has a common task (i.e., finish the project successfully), although the group might be lower in entitativity.

Functions of groups

Task groups have the function to perform a certain task (or a number of different tasks). Sometimes these tasks cannot be done by individuals working alone (e.g., making a feature film; Simonton, 2004). At other times, they might be done by individuals, but doing so would be inefficient (e.g., building a house alone would take too much time). Further, individual group members might specialize in certain tasks, which increases efficiency and effectiveness (e.g., Brandon & Hollingshead, 2004; Liang, Moreland, & Argote, 1995). Even when tasks can be performed adequately by individuals, it might be more fun to perform them in a group (e.g., organizing a party). Thus, there are different reasons to perform a task in a group. However, besides task performance, groups also fulfill other functions for group members. Being a group member has implications for one's view of oneself, for one's view of the world, and for one's wellbeing.

To start with wellbeing, people have certain needs. A particularly important social need is the *need to belong*. This is a human predisposition to form and maintain stable, strong, and positive relationships with others (Baumeister & Leary, 1995). This human need is innate and universal: Across all cultures and situations people have a strong tendency to form stable and positive relations with others, and it probably is evolutionarily "built in" (see also Bowlby, 1958). Positive contacts with fellow group members may serve to satisfy this basic human need. One consequence is that people who lack positive social relations report less wellbeing. It has even been found that positive contacts with other group members, such as members of one's family or church, can prolong life, and that lack of social relations is associated with higher mortality (Berkman & Syme, 1979).

There are other consequences. First, group members will usually have a strong resistance when there are threats to dissolve the group: It would mean a loss of valued social ties. Second, people in general want to be liked and included, which can have important consequences for the functioning of the group. For example, group members might not argue against a position taken by other members, because they fear that this would lead to a negative evaluation and rejection by others (see Chapter 2). Another consequence is that actually being rejected by other group members has a number of negative consequences for people's wellbeing. For example, people who are ignored and excluded by others report (temporarily) lowered feelings of belonging, wellbeing, and self-esteem: Being rejected hurts (Eisenberger, Lieberman, & Williams, 2003; Williams, 2001).[2]

Groups also help us to understand our world. *Social comparison theory* (Festinger, 1954) argues that people want to hold accurate views of themselves and of the world. They can do this by validating their beliefs against "physical reality" (e.g., "I think the ice is thick enough, I will try to stand on it") or against "social reality" (e.g., "I like this music; I wonder what my friends think about it?"). People turn to others especially for beliefs for which there is no physical reality (e.g., preferences, opinions, norms). This has important consequences. For example, when there appears to be a consensus among group members, this is taken as strong evidence that this view is correct – this sometimes is referred to as the "consensus implies correctness" rule (Chaiken & Stangor, 1987). This is not so strange: When several people independently have reached a particular conclusion, it is likely to be valid. As a consequence, other group members might be quick to adopt that conclusion without much thought (even when it is wrong). But also if people evaluate their own

---

2   You can take this literally: Eisenberger *et al.* found that being rejected and ignored while playing a game activates certain areas in the brain that are also active when in physical pain!

abilities, they have to turn to others. Knowing that you can run 100 metres in 13 seconds does not mean much when you do not know how fast others are. Further, seeing that others are faster may in fact be a strong motivator to try harder (see Chapters 4 and 5).

Groups not only help us to understand our world; they also help us to understand ourselves. *Social identity theory* (Tajfel & Turner, 1986) and *self-categorization theory* (Turner, Hogg, Oakes, Reicher, & Wetherell, 1987) argue that people define themselves (and others) partly in terms of group membership. Thus, group membership contributes to our identity as a person, especially when we identify strongly with the group. The part of the self-concept that derives from group membership combined with the value and significance of that membership is called *social identity*. The theory further argues that seeing oneself and others as members of groups helps to reduce uncertainty and make sense of our world (e.g., Hogg & Abrams, 1993). Being a member of a group often provides guidelines for the way we should behave and think, and people who identify strongly with the group will in general behave according to the rules and norms of the group (Turner *et al.*, 1987; also see Chapter 10).

People also derive utilitarian benefits from groups. *Exchange theory* (e.g., Thibaut & Kelley, 1959) argues that social relations (including those within groups) help to fulfill the individual's needs (such as the need to belong), and often take the form of exchange processes. These exchanges might involve material goods (e.g., borrowing a tool, selling your car) or interpersonal helping (helping a friend move to a new house), but also psychological "goods" such as love, friendship, or approval. Enduring exchange relations between two or more people are more effectively organized when people form a (more or less stable) group. Thus, groups facilitate mutually beneficial social exchange. Exchange theory argues that social relations involve costs as well as benefits, and as long as the benefits exceed the costs the relation will yield a "profit." There is much evidence that people are unhappy about relations if they feel that they invest more in them (e.g., time) than they get back (e.g., approval) (e.g., Le & Agnew, 2003). Furthermore, satisfaction with an exchange relationship depends on the degree to which alternative relationships exist that yield more profit. Thus, people join groups because they derive benefits from their group membership. People may leave groups (if possible) when they are unhappy about the benefits relative to the costs of group membership, or when alternative groups exist that have a better cost–benefit ratio (Moreland & Levine, 1982; Rusbult & Farrell, 1983; see also Chapter 2).

How to study groups

This book is concerned with the scientific way of looking at groups. In order to study groups in a systematic and scientific way, researchers employ different methodologies. We discuss three ways to study group performance: qualitative case study, survey, and experiment.

Qualitative case studies

Qualitative research entails that one or a few entities, such as groups or organizations, are extensively studied for relatively long periods of time. Qualitative measures are used, such as interviews with open-ended questions and (participative) observations. The major advantage is that a very rich and detailed picture can be given about particular entities. One can, for example, look into dynamics that occur over time, and collect data from various sources (e.g., from team leaders, team members, observed interactions). The result is an elaborate description that no other method can match in terms of completeness. For example, Sutton and Hargadon (1996) studied group idea generation sessions at a product design company for a period of almost two years. Until then, quantitative studies (such as experiments) had been used to study idea-generating groups (Chapter 6). However, using qualitative methods, Sutton and Hargadon found that idea generation sessions were meant not only to generate ideas, but also to impress clients, learn from one another, and provide information about the expertise of different group members. These alternative goals had until then been neglected by other researchers.

Qualitative case studies have two drawbacks. First, only a few entities can usually be studied so extensively. The consequence is that we do not know whether the conclusions also hold for other entities. In other words, do the results generalize? The second problem is that data can be very rich and complicated and drawing conclusions can be hard. The researcher has much freedom in deciding what to focus on and how to explain what was observed. Perhaps another researcher would focus on something else, and might come to different conclusions. Thus, more than other methods, subjective interpretation of the data is necessary, which sometimes makes it hard to evaluate conclusions.

Taking these pros and cons together, most researchers agree that qualitative research is useful to generate theories and research hypotheses and to find neglected topics. Thus, interesting patterns or dynamics that were observed may lead to new hypotheses. However, observations are less useful when *testing* theories and hypotheses. To test hypotheses, one needs to know whether results generalize to other groups and organizations. This is not possible when studying a limited number of entities. Instead, one has to use quantitative methods, such as surveys.

Surveys and correlational designs

When conducting survey research, researchers approach a large number of entities (people, groups, organizations) and administer structured questionnaires, usually using rating scales (e.g., people are asked to indicate on a scale how much they agree with a statement). These rating scales can be used to quantify variables, such as *how much* group members like each other, *how many* conflicts there are in a team, or *to which degree* group members are interdependent.

Because variables can be quantified, one can compute quantitative relations between variables, using the Pearson product-moment correlation coefficient (abbreviated to *correlation* or the symbol r). These correlations can vary from $r = -1$ (a perfect negative correlation) to $r = 0$ (no correlation) to $r = 1$ (a perfect positive correlation). Negative correlations imply that higher scores on one variable tend to go together with *lower* scores on another variable, and positive correlations indicate that higher scores on one variable tend to go together with *higher* scores on another variable. One can, for example, establish whether there is a correlation between how much group members like each other and how many conflicts there are in a team, and how large this correlation is (one would expect a negative correlation; more conflicts associate with less liking, and the relation would be stronger if the correlation were closer to -1).

Sometimes different sources can be used to collect data, and these sources can be combined with each other. Two possibilities are as follows:

(1) Use different people to measure different variables. For example, team members are asked how interdependent they are, whereas team leaders are asked how well the team performs. One can then compute a correlation between team members' interdependence ratings and team leader performance ratings.

(2) Combine questionnaire data with other data sources, such as archives of a company. Examples include objective performance

indicators (Podsakoff *et al*.'s, 1997, work discussed in Box 1.1 is a good example) or company absenteeism records. One can, for example, establish a correlation between group cohesiveness as measured with questionnaires and absenteeism taken from company records.

Questionnaires can also be administered with the same people at different points in time (*longitudinal* surveys), to establish relations between variables measured at different points in time. If one measures the same variables more than once, one can look at stability or change over time (e.g., did cohesiveness change from time 1 to time 2?). One can further look at correlations between different variables over time. For example, one can study whether cohesion at time 1 correlates with group performance at time 2. Box 1.2 discusses a useful research design: cross-lagged panel correlations.

A strength of survey research, as indicated above, is that one can quantify variables and relations among variables. A second strength is real-world relevance. Podsakoff *et al*.'s (1997) respondents (Box 1.1) were real workers at a paper mill, who produced a real product (paper) for a real company. That Podsakoff *et al*. found that performance differences could be attributed to cohesion and goal acceptance is, in a sense, very impressive.

There are two drawbacks. First, surveys often rely on subjective data. Thus, people are asked to report on their own attitudes, feelings, behaviors, and performance. Sometimes people may not be entirely accurate, for example because they do not really know certain things (e.g., it can be hard to judge one's own performance) or because they want to appear more positive than they really are (i.e., they deliberatively give a high performance estimate). Sometimes this can be solved by combining survey data with other data, such as company records.

The second major drawback of survey studies is that it is not possible to establish causality. The only thing that can be demonstrated is a quantitative relation (or correlation) between certain variables (such as a relation between cohesion and performance). We do not know whether cohesion really *causes* performance. Indeed, the causality might be reversed: Groups that perform well eventually become cohesive. Thus, cohesion might not be the cause of performance, but rather the consequence (Mullen & Copper, 1994, Box 1.2). To some degree, this can be solved through longitudinal surveys and cross-lagged panel designs. However, another problem that prevents conclusions about causality, and that cannot

BOX 1.2.

Cross-lagged panel correlations

If one measures the same variables at different points in time, one can establish cross-lagged panel correlations. Basically, this involves testing whether certain variables measured at time 1 correlate with other variables measured at time 1 and with the same variables measured at time 2.

Figure 1.3 illustrates what can be the result, using data from Mullen and Copper (1994). In particular, when two variables are measured at two times (T1 and T2), in this case cohesion and performance, one can compute a total of six correlations. Two of these are auto-correlations – correlations between the same variables measured at the two times. These reflect *stability*. In Figure 1.3, the stability is reasonably high ($r = .62$ for cohesion, and $r = .64$ for performance). Two of them are synchronous correlation (between cohesion and performance at time 1, and at time 2; $r = .28$ and $r = .41$, respectively). Finally, two correlations are cross-lagged correlations: between cohesion at time 1 and performance at time 2 ($r = .25$) and between performance at time 1 and cohesion at time 2 ($r = .51$).

FIGURE 1.3.

Example of cross-lagged panel correlations. Taken from: Mullen, B., & Copper, C. (1994). The relation between group cohesiveness and performance: An integration. *Psychological Bulletin, 115*, 210–227. Copyright American Psychological Association. Reprinted with permission.

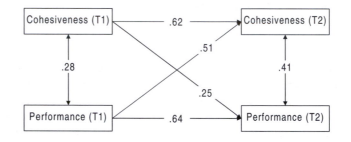

A major advantage of this design is that one can look at causality issues. One prerequisite for causality is that the causal factor should *precede* its consequence (e.g., you first push the button and then the light comes on). When all variables are measured at the same time, for example with one questionnaire, this cannot be established. However, when variables are measured at different points in time, this is possible. For example, one can measure cohesion at time 1 and performance at time 2. When a correlation is found, this *may* imply that cohesion has a causal relation with performance. Indeed, in Figure 1.3 such a relation is found, although it is relatively weak ($r = .25$).

Interestingly one can also look at the reverse: Does performance cause cohesion? Indeed, it is plausible that a group becomes more cohesive after performing well, for example because group members are proud of the group. In Figure 1.3 the relation between performance at time 1 and cohesion at time 2 is $r = .51$. Thus, in the Mullen and Copper (1994) data, the effect of performance on cohesion is stronger than the effect of cohesion on performance! Yet we still cannot be entirely sure about causality, because of the third variable problem (see text).

be solved with longitudinal designs, is the *third variable problem*: The relation between two variables (e.g., cohesion and performance) might be caused by a third variable that we have not measured. Consider the following example. There might be a correlation between computer skills and health: People who have more computer skills are healthier, say. Can we conclude that computer skills lead to better health? That seems unlikely. Instead, what is more plausible is that a third variable, age, accounts for the relation. Thus, people with more computer skills usually are younger, and younger people are healthier. Because younger people both have more computer skills and are healthier, a positive relation between computer skills and health is found. Similarly, a third variable might explain the relation between cohesion and performance. The problem is that we do not know this third variable, and it is impossible to measure *all* possible third variables. The solution to that problem is the experiment.

Experiments

In experiments, a situation is created that is under the control of the researcher. This allows for the use of *manipulations*, in order to see what effects they have. In experiments, one deliberately introduces variations in the conditions under which people or groups work. For example, one can make certain groups cohesive by giving them a team-building exercise, whereas other groups are *not* given that exercise (e.g., Zaccaro & Lowe, 1988). Next one can observe their behavior (e.g., use video recordings) and performance (e.g., have all groups perform a task and see how well they do; Zaccaro & Lowe had them fold paper tents), to see whether the manipulation has certain effects. Importantly, participants in experiments are assigned to different conditions *at random*. Thus, whether groups are in one condition or another (e.g., the low- or high-cohesion condition) is not determined by any characteristic of the group or of people within the group, but only by coincidence.

The advantage of experiments is that one can test causal relations. Because participants are assigned to conditions at random, we can assume that differences among conditions in the behavior or performance that are observed are caused by the manipulations, and not by other characteristics of the group or its members. Indeed, the logic of random assignment is that it is assumed that *all* "third variables" are approximately evenly represented in the different conditions, and therefore cannot account for observed differences between conditions. Thus, in every condition there will be some people who are extraverted and some who are introverted, and the same holds true for any other variable that one can think of (at least, there is no reason to assume systematic differences between conditions).

Sometimes, however, it is not possible to assign people or groups randomly to conditions. For example, companies might not allow that certain teams get a team-building exercise and other teams do not. In such cases, when researchers lack control over the situation, they have to rely on *quasi-experimental designs*. Rather than assigning people to conditions at random, researchers use the existing situation to look for differences between "conditions." Thus, a researcher may compare teams in one department that recently had a team-building exercise with teams in another department that have not had this exercise yet. The problem with quasi-experiments is that one (again) cannot exclude that other third variables are responsible for the effects: The teams in the different department may differ not only in (not) having had the team-building exercise, but in many other ways as well.

The strength of real (as opposed to quasi-) experiments therefore lies in the ability to draw causal conclusions. However, this is achieved by creating an artificial situation, usually in a research laboratory and often with student participants. One can therefore always question whether the observed effects will also be found in less controlled situations. The conclusion should therefore be that experiments are very useful to test theoretically derived causal relations among variables. They do not, however, necessarily correspond with what goes on in the real world.

Conclusion

There are different ways to study groups scientifically. Qualitative research may lead to new insights and new theories, but cannot be used to test theories. Surveys can be used to obtain quantitative relations between variables, and they can provide insight into real-life groups. However, they cannot be used to draw causal conclusions. Experiments can be used to test causal hypotheses, but these results are often obtained in artificial and controlled situations. Thus, the drawback of one method is the strength of another. Therefore, the methods that a researcher chooses should fit the aim of the study. Further, a complete understanding of group performance requires the use of different methods simultaneously.

Overview of the book

This chapter, as well as the next on basic group processes, sets the stage for the chapters to come. Chapter 2 discusses issues of group membership, group development, group structure, and social influence. What are the basic processes going on in most groups? In Chapter 3 a general framework is developed to look at group performance. The basic question underlying the chapter is: How are individual contributions combined into a group product? In Chapter 4 we look at social influence on individual performance. Under the heading of social facilitation, we discuss the performance of individuals working in front of an audience.

In the next four chapters, basic social psychological research on group performance is discussed. In Chapter 5, we consider motivation and group performance. Chapter 6 is on idea generation and creativity in groups. In Chapters 7 and 8 we consider group decision-making, and group problem-solving and judgment, respectively.

In Chapters 9 through 11 we consider some real-life questions. In Chapter 9, the focus is on teamwork and leadership. Chapter 10 is about the social context in which groups work. In Chapter 11 we consider virtual teams.

Chapter summary

(1) Sometimes groups make very poor decisions, when the group is more interested in maintaining group consensus than in an adequate evaluation of alternatives. Janis (1972) has termed this phenomenon "groupthink".

(2) A definition of the word "group" is difficult to provide, and it is more useful to see "groupiness" or "group entitativity" as a dimension on which collections of individuals can vary. Groups are more entitative when there is regular face-to-face interaction, when they are small, have stable membership, and are important, and when group members are dependent on one another for important outcomes.

(3) The relation between group cohesion depends on other factors (such as agreement with group goals), and causality might also be reverse (performance causes cohesion).

(4) Group membership has important consequences for wellbeing, our understanding of the world, and identity, and group members can engage in mutually beneficial social exchange.

(5) Group performance can be studied using a variety of methodologies, including qualitative (case) studies, surveys, and experiments. All methodologies have advantages as well as disadvantages, and the choice of the right method depends on the question the researcher wants to answer.

Exercises

(1) List five groups of which you are a member, and rank these groups according to group entitativity. Then consider the characteristics of these groups: Are they important to you, do they involve face-to-face interaction, are they large, permeable, do you depend on the other group members? Can you see a pattern in these characteristics?
(2) Perhaps you have been part of a group that functioned well and one that did not function well. What were the differences? Why do you think one group performed well and the other not?
(3) Suppose you are interested in groupthink. Which questions could be addressed in qualitative case studies? And which using surveys or experiments?

Further reading

Definition of groups and group entitativity

Lickel, B., Hamilton, D. L., & Sherman, S. J. (2001). Elements of a lay theory of groups: Types of groups, relational styles, and the perception of group entitativity. *Personality and Social Psychology Review, 5,* 129–140.

Functions of groups

Festinger, L. (1954). A theory of social comparison processes. *Human Relations, 7,* 117–140.

Turner, J. C., Hogg, M. A., Oakes, P. J., Reicher, S. D., & Wetherell, M. S. (1987). *Rediscovering the social group: A self-categorization theory.* Oxford, UK: Blackwell.

Studying groups: Research methods

Leary, M. R. (2004). *Introduction to behavioral research methods* (4th ed.). Boston: Pearson Education.

Group processes and social influence 2

Perhaps you have recently joined a group, such as a student society or a sports team. If you have, you might feel insecure in the context of your new group, because you don't know exactly what is expected of you. For example, you might not know whether certain jokes are appropriate or not, or what the customs of the group are. Learning these is called group socialization, and this is the first topic of this chapter.

On other occasions, you might not join an existing group but form a new one. For example, students form groups to work on an assignment, or teams in a company are formed to do a project. These groups will change over time: People get to know one another, certain norms and procedures become accepted, and so on. This is the second topic of the chapter. One other way in which groups develop is that after a while different group members occupy different roles within the group and some members acquire status and influence while others do not. For example, someone in a sports team becomes the team captain. These topics will be discussed in the third section of this chapter.

People who have high status or who have become the group leader usually have a substantial influence on other group members. However, members with less status also constantly influence one another. Some of the most famous research within social psychology concerns these social influence processes among peers. It considers questions such as why people often go along with a majority (even when they think the majority is wrong), when minorities might be influential and bring about change in group norms and practices, and how people in groups may form extreme beliefs or resort to extreme actions (such as terrorist attacks). These forms of social influence are discussed in the last part of the chapter.

Group membership and socialization

FIGURE 2.1.

The Moreland and Levine (1982) model of group socialization. Reprinted from Moreland, R. L., & Levine, J. M. (1982). Socialization in small groups: Temporal changes in individual–group relations. In L. Berkowitz (Ed.), *Advances in experimental social psychology* (Vol. 15, pp. 137–192). New York: Academic Press. Copyright 1982, Elsevier. Reprinted with permission from Elsevier.

Having positive relations with others is very important for people's wellbeing (Chapter 1). An implication is that people who lack social contacts will look for them, and one way to do this is to join a group. This can be observed in the beginning of a new academic year, when new students enter the university. As these students often had to move to a new city, they do not know many people, and it becomes important for them to establish new social contacts. Many of them join groups, such as student societies or sports clubs. In this section we consider the development of group membership over time, from entering the group to eventually leaving it.

Figure 2.1 shows Moreland and Levine's (1982; also Levine & Moreland, 1994) model of *group socialization*. The model distinguishes five stages of group membership: investigation, socialization, maintenance, re-socialization, and remembrance. Moving from one stage to the next involves a *role transition*. Moving from prospective member (the stage of investigation) to new member (the stage of socialization) involves the role transition of entry. Further role transitions are acceptance (from new member to full member), divergence (from full member to marginal member), and exit (from marginal member to

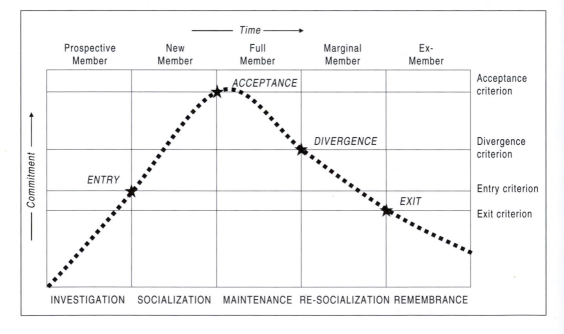

ex-member). Role transitions occur as a result of evaluation processes, in which the group and the individual evaluate one another. When the group is rewarding for members, members will try to enter the group or maintain group membership. Similarly, when a group values a (prospective) member, the group will encourage the person to become or stay a member. The five stages differ in *commitment*: the degree to which a group member identifies with the group and its goals and wishes to maintain group membership. Commitment increases as people become full members, but may later decrease to the point that an individual wants to leave the group.

Investigation and entry

In the stage of investigation, groups look for prospective members who might make a contribution to the attainment of group goals. Task groups will search for members who have the required skills and abilities, but will also be interested in compatibility (e.g., similarity) with the existing membership. Prospective members, on the other hand, will look for groups that may potentially fulfill their needs. For example, they might be interested in obtaining a highly visible position within an important organizational team, in order to help their career. Sometimes prospective members are interested in groups because they expect to like the other members, and joining the group might fulfill their need to belong.

When the level of commitment of the group and prospective member reaches an entry criterion, a role transition occurs: *entry*. Entry is often marked by some ritual or ceremony, such as a welcome speech, that makes it clear that the relation between the group and the (prospective) member has changed. Other examples are various religious rituals such as baptism or circumcision of children. At times, the entry ritual or *initiation* can be quite unpleasant and painful for the prospective member. For example, Lodewijkx and Syroit (1997) describe the initiation into a Dutch sorority (a society for female students). During initiation, the sorority's prospective members are bullied, not called by their real names, and have to endure hardships such as lack of sleep and food. The ritual ends with a so-called integration party, after which it is clear that the prospective members are accepted as new members.

As these unpleasant initiations are widespread and take place in many different groups (e.g., the military, sports teams, student societies), the question arises as to why groups perform these harsh rituals. One reason is that harsh initiation rituals deter prospective members who are not really committed to their new group, and these rituals help to ensure that new members will be valuable to the group. Further, even if harsh rituals do not increase commitment of new members, they often lead to the development of strong relations among new members who had to endure the treatment together (Lodewijkx & Syroit, 1997).

Aronson and Mills (1959) argued, somewhat paradoxically, that harsh initiations increase commitment to the group. Their argument is based on *cognitive dissonance theory* (Festinger, 1957). That theory argues that people find it unpleasant when two cognitions or cognition and behavior are contradictory (or dissonant). Whenever this occurs, individuals are motivated to end the tension caused by dissonance, and will, for example, change one cognition to make it consistent with the other. Suppose a prospective member has undergone harsh treatment, but later it appears that the group is not as attractive as initially believed. This will lead to cognitive dissonance: Members can no longer maintain that they had good reasons to undergo the harsh treatment when they admit that the group is not so attractive after all. Thus, the member will deny that the group is unattractive and will maintain a high level of commitment to the group.

Aronson and Mills (1959) performed an experiment to test this reasoning. They offered female students the opportunity to join a discussion group about sexuality. Some of the prospective members first had to read sexually explicit passages aloud, which was quite embarrassing. Other prospective members did not have to do this. Next, the participants listened to a group discussion that was recorded on tape. This discussion was very boring and was about secondary sexual behavior of lower animals. Participants were next asked to rate the attractiveness of the group. In line with the dissonance explanation, the women who had to read the embarrassing passages rated the group more attractive than those who did not. One reason why groups perform harsh initiations thus seems to be that they increase commitment of new members to the group.

Socialization and maintenance

After entry, the stage of socialization begins. In this stage, new members learn the *norms* of the group: the (unwritten) rules that prescribe the attitudes and behaviors that are and are not appropriate in the context of the group. In addition, new members may acquire the necessary knowledge and skills to function effectively as a group member: They learn their *role* in the group (the set of behaviors associated with a certain position in the group). Thus, the group tries to assimilate the member to fit the expectations of the group. However, new members may also try to influence the group, in such a way that their needs are best met. For example, a new member may try to change the group's norms, customs, or ways of working (e.g., Choi & Levine, 2004). During (successful) socialization, commitment will generally increase. When the acceptance criterion is reached the member will no longer be treated as somebody who needs special attention, the socialization stage is ended, and the new member is accepted as a full member. New members may gain access to information that was previously hidden, may join certain informal cliques, and their behavior is monitored less strictly.

Being accepted as a full member is easier in some groups than in others. It partly depends on the *staffing level* of the group: the degree to which the actual number of group members is similar to the ideal number. Groups can be overstaffed (have too many members) as well as understaffed (have too few members). Understaffed groups will be less demanding of new members (it is easier to become a full member) than overstaffed groups. Indeed, Cini, Moreland, and Levine (1993) found that groups that were understaffed were more open: They were less selective (it was easier to become a new member), and also less demanding for new members (it was easier to become a full member). Solutions to overstaffing, in contrast, were to restrict membership but also to punish deviance from group norms more harshly, hoping that deviant members would leave.

After acceptance, the stage of maintenance begins. This stage is characterized by high levels of commitment (Figure 2.1). Through role negotiation, groups and members try to increase the rewardingness of their relationship: Members try to occupy the role within the group that best satisfies their needs, whereas the group tries to appoint roles to members in such a way that the group's goals are best achieved. One important role within the group is the role of leader (Chapter 9). However, there are other roles that need to be fulfilled, such as the role of "recruiter" (who identifies prospective members) and that of "trainer" (who has a role during socialization of new members). According to the model, the relation between the group and the member will be rewarding, and commitment will remain high, to the degree that role negotiations are successful.

Divergence and exit

After some time, group members may lose interest in the group, for example because they are dissatisfied with their role or because they have identified other, more rewarding groups. On the other hand, the commitment of the group to its members may decline when members fail to live up to the expectations of the group. For example, members may not perform well in their role, or may violate important group norms. This will lead the group to re-label these members as marginal members or deviates. The group might, for example, no longer give marginal members full information, or marginal members may be excluded from informal cliques (e.g., they are no longer asked to come along for a drink after work). Often, considerable pressure is exerted on deviates to realign or even to leave the group (especially if the group is overstaffed). A classic experiment performed by Schachter (1951) on the pressure that is exerted on deviants is presented in Box 2.1.

Divergence might be followed by a period of re-socialization. In this period, the group might try to persuade marginal members not to leave, or might try to accommodate to the wishes of marginal members (e.g., give them a different role). Similarly, group members may try to convince the group not to expel them, and might try to assimilate to the group's expectations again. This might result in re-entry to the group when successful. However, when re-socialization fails, group members may reach an exit criterion and leave the group. As with other role transitions this may involve some ritual, such as a goodbye speech or a party. Alternatively, the group may expel the member, which can be a painful experience: Social exclusion from groups has large negative effects on the excluded member's well-being and self-esteem (also Chapter 1).

The last stage of the Moreland and Levine model is remembrance (Figure 2.1). In this stage, the ex-member and the group retrospectively evaluate each other. Remaining group members will evaluate the ex-member's contributions to the group, and will maintain some commitment to the ex-member if these contributions are seen as positive. Similarly, ex-members look back on their time with the group with either fond or bitter memories. In extreme cases, ex-members may even try to destroy their former group in an act of revenge. Workplace shootings (e.g., in Kansas City, USA in 2004), in which fired employees shoot their boss or former colleagues, are extreme examples. Fortunately, these incidents are rare.

BOX 2.1.
Pressure on deviants

Schachter (1951) performed a classic study on the effects of opinion deviance. He argued that group members first exert pressure on members who deviate from the group norm, but when the efforts to convert deviates are unsuccessful, the group will exclude them. The participants (male college students) supposedly had joined a club, and the experiment took place during their first meeting. During the meeting, all 32 groups discussed a criminal case. Each group consisted of five to seven "real" participants, and three confederates. The confederates were paid to play a specific role during the group discussion: The "mode" accommodated to the group's average judgment, the "slider" initially took an extreme position but then moved toward the group norm, and the "deviate" also took an extreme position but maintained it throughout the discussion. The real participants, of course, did not know that the confederates were playing a role. During the discussion, Schachter recorded how often other group members directed a communication towards the deviate, slider, and mode. Further, after the discussion participants were asked how much they liked each of the group members.

Figure 2.2 shows some of Schachter's findings: the number of communications directed towards the deviate, the slider, and the mode. The number of communications directed towards the deviate was high and increased over time. The number of communications towards the mode was much lower and remained low over time, and the number of communications towards the slider was high in the beginning, but dropped when the slider moved towards the group norm. Schachter argued that the high number of communications directed towards deviates (and towards the slider in the beginning) represent attempts to put pressure on them to change their position. Schachter further found that, after the discussion, the deviates were liked less and rejected more than the slides and modes.

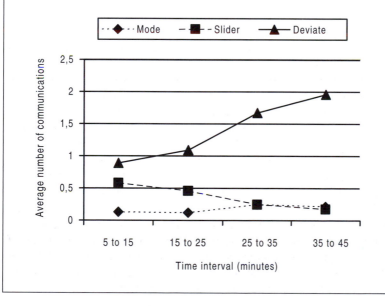

FIGURE 2.2.

Communications directed towards the deviates, sliders, and modes over time (data from Schachter, 1951).

Group development

Groups will generally develop: Interaction patterns among group members change over time. Because every group faces certain challenges and has certain goals and these challenges and goals change over time, there may be similarities in the way different groups develop over time. This is the reasoning behind Tuckman's (1965; Tuckman & Jensen, 1977) model of group development.

These authors distinguished among five stages of group development: forming, storming, norming, performing, and adjourning (Figure 2.3). In the first stage, when the group is *forming*, group members feel insecure because they do not know each other and do not know what is expected of them. As a consequence, interactions are polite and inhibited, and people begin to develop a shared identity as members of the same group. Once people have got to know each other, they enter the second stage (*storming*). The challenge in this stage is to develop a group structure (see later in this chapter). Issues of leadership and influence are at stake, and as group members may compete about different roles in the group, there may be conflicts and disagreements. In the third stage, *norming*, group members come to agree on the group's goals, and develop norms that govern group interaction. Once this has been achieved, the group enters the *performing* stage. Because group structure and norms have been established, efforts can be directed towards achieving the group's task. Although it is still necessary to engage in behaviors to maintain a positive atmosphere in the group, most activities will be task-related. The final stage of group development is *adjourning*. When the task has been accomplished or is abandoned, the group will end. This might be associated either with feelings of accomplishment or with feelings of disappointment (depending, of course, on task success).

FIGURE 2.3.
The five stages of group development (after Tuckman, 1965; Tuckman & Jensen, 1977).

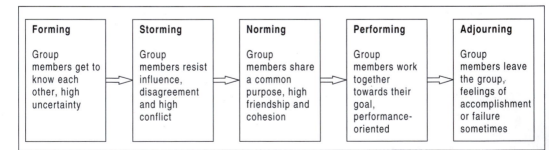

Forming	Storming	Norming	Performing	Adjourning
Group members get to know each other, high uncertainty	Group members resist influence, disagreement and high conflict	Group members share a common purpose, high friendship and cohesion	Group members work together towards their goal, performance-oriented	Group members leave the group, feelings of accomplishment or failure sometimes

According to the Tuckman and Jensen (1977) model, the different stages of group life are characterized by different interaction patterns within the group. To test this idea, it is necessary to observe group interactions, and see which behaviors are more frequent in the early or the later stages of group life. The best-known coding system of group interaction is Bales' (1950) *interaction process analysis* (IPA; also Bales & Slater, 1955). IPA makes the important distinction between *task behaviors* (all behaviors directed at task completion) and *socio-emotional behaviors* (all behaviors directed at interpersonal relations within the group). In the socio-emotional domain it further distinguishes between positive and negative behaviors. According to Bales, task-related behavior is necessary for task completion, but can lead to conflicts when people disagree. In order not to disturb the functioning of the group, socio-emotional behavior is necessary to restore group harmony. The coding system of IPA is shown in Table 2.1. The scheme distinguishes between 12 different categories, divided into socio-emotional behaviors that are positive, task-related behaviors (which are emotionally neutral), and negative socio-emotional behaviors.

According to the Tuckman and Jensen (1977) stage model, these 12 categories of behavior should occur to differing degrees in the different stages of group life. The forming stage should be characterized by positive socio-emotional behavior, whereas in the storming stage more negative socio-emotional behavior should occur. In the norming stage, there should be both positive socio-emotional behavior and task-

TABLE 2.1
The coding scheme of Interaction Process Analysis (after Bales, 1950)

Socio-emotional behavior, positive	(1)	Shows solidarity, raises other's status, gives help, reward
	(2)	Shows tension release, jokes, laughs, shows satisfaction
	(3)	Agrees, shows passive acceptance, understands, concurs, complies
Task behavior, neutral	(4)	Gives suggestions, directions, implying autonomy for other
	(5)	Gives opinion, evaluates, analyzes, expresses feelings, wishes
	(6)	Gives orientation, information, repeats, clarifies, confirms
	(7)	Asks for orientation, information, repetition, confirmation
	(8)	Asks for opinion, evaluation, analysis, expression of feeling
	(9)	Asks for suggestion, direction, possible ways of action
Socio-emotional behavior, negative	(10)	Disagrees, shows passive rejection, formality, withholds help
	(11)	Shows tension, asks for help, withdraws out of the field
	(12)	Shows antagonism, deflates other's status, defends or asserts self

related behavior, and the performing stage should be dominated by task-related behavior. Is this what really happens? In general, the answer is yes. For example, Wheelan, Davidson, and Tilin (2003) found time together to be related to socio-emotional behaviors (the longer the group was together, the *fewer* of these behaviors) as well as to task-related behaviors (the longer the group was together, the *more* of these behaviors).

However, stage models such as Tuckman and Jensen's can easily be criticized. Some groups, for example, may never have a storming stage whereas other groups are always in conflict. Further, the assumption that the different stages are qualitatively different from each other is difficult to maintain. Rather, different activities occur in each stage, although they vary in intensity. Most researchers would therefore argue that there are no abrupt changes in the way group members interact with each other, but that these changes occur gradually, and can be seen as a gradual development of groups over time.

Group structure: Status and roles

Groups have a structure, in which not everyone is identical. Instead, different people have different roles, and people differ in the amount of status and influence they have within the group. Take a football team. Clearly, different players have different roles defined by their position in the field (goalkeeper, defender, forward). Besides these formal roles, there also are informal roles. For example, a more experienced team member (even though not formally the team captain) may have more influence on the other players than a newcomer. Different players may also differ in status. For example, the team captain will usually have more status, and perhaps players who have been in the team longer or who have some special talents are more influential.

Bales' (1950) IPA is a useful tool for looking at status and roles inside a group. One can keep track of the 12 different types of behavior (Table 2.1) for each group member, to see whether there are differences among members. Research using IPA (or other coding systems) to code behavior in freely interacting groups has revealed a number of important insights (see McGrath, 1984, for an overview).

First, some group members talk more than others, and the discrepancy increases with the size of the group. Thus, groups develop a *speaking hierarchy* (Bales, 1953) in which members higher in that

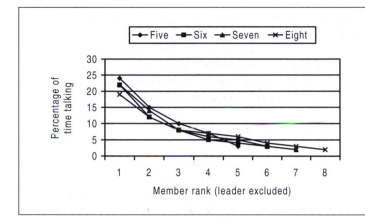

FIGURE 2.4.

Speaking hierarchy for groups of five, six, seven, and eight members (data from Stephan & Mishler, 1952). Reprinted from: Stasser, G., & Vaughan, S. I. (1996). Models of participation during face-to-face unstructured discussion. In E. H. Witte & J. H. Davis (Eds.), *Understanding group behavior: Consensual action by small groups* (Vol. 1, pp. 165–192). Mahwah, NJ: Lawrence Erlbaum Associates. Copyright Lawrence Erlbaum Associates. Reprinted with permission.

hierarchy talk more than those lower in the hierarchy (Figure 2.4). Further, people who talk more are usually seen as more influential. Research has also shown that group members do not distribute their participation evenly throughout the discussion, but that contributions are concentrated in periods of high activity (Dabbs & Ruback, 1987). Thus, a person who has recently spoken is more likely to speak again. Often this takes the form of a dyadic exchange, in which two group members alternate speaking turns (Parker, 1988). Parker found that these dyadic exchanges occur much more frequently than would be expected if all group members contributed equally.

Second, research using IPA has found that some people are consistently more task-oriented (they engage mostly in task-related behaviors, categories 4–9 in Table 2.1), whereas others are more relationship-oriented (they engage more in socio-emotional behaviors) (Slater, 1955). The former type of person has been labeled the task specialist and the latter the socio-emotional specialist: a clear case of (informal) role differentiation. It further appeared that these two group members interacted with each other quite frequently, and much more than would be expected according to chance. Finally, the task specialist was seen as most influential, but was liked less than the socio-emotional specialist.

Who talks most and who takes which role depends on personality and individual ability (also Chapter 9). For example, an extraverted person will probably talk more than an introverted person. However, this is not the whole story. There are other factors that determine who is more and who is less influential. *Expectation states theory* (Berger, Rosenholtz, & Zelditch, 1980) deals with the issue of how status structures emerge in groups, and how they are shaped by the outside

FIGURE 2.5.
Expectation States
Theory.

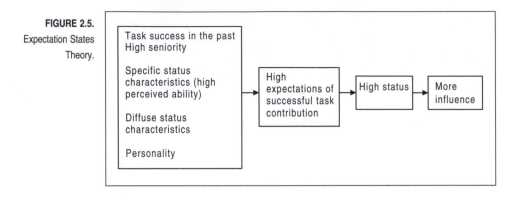

status of group members (see Ridgeway, 2001, for an overview). The theory is summarized in Figure 2.5.

Expectation States Theory assumes that several inequalities within a group, such as inequalities in participation and influence, are all derived from *performance expectations*. Because of certain characteristics of group members, other members form expectations about the usefulness of each member's contributions. These expectations then serve as a self-fulfilling prophecy: The greater the expectations, the more likely a person is to speak up, offer suggestions, and be evaluated positively by the others. The question is: What determines these performance expectations?

The theory assumes that performance expectations are influenced by *status characteristics*. It distinguishes between *diffuse* status characteristics (not necessarily related to the group task) including, for example, gender, age, and race, and *specific* status characteristics, such as skills and abilities (characteristics that are related to the group task). These characteristics carry certain cultural expectations about competencies. For example, women are sometimes seen as less competent than men (especially on tasks that are more "masculine"; e.g., Pugh & Wahrman, 1983) and more senior people may be seen as more competent (up to a certain age) than younger people (Freese & Cohen, 1973). Similarly, higher expectations are formed for people who are more experienced, have a higher status in society more generally, or have a relevant area of expertise. Obviously, these expectations may sometimes be false (i.e., a woman may in fact be more competent than a man), but they nevertheless affect people's status in the group and the amount of influence they have. The reason is that expectations need to be explicitly *falsified* before they lose their influence, and as long as they are not, they continue to have their effect.

There is extensive evidence supporting the theory. For example, Driskell and Mullen (1990) found that characteristics of group members affected their status and power through the expectations of other group members, exactly as the theory would predict (also see Ridgeway, 2001).

Social influence

Two classic experiments

Clearly, some group members are more influential than others. Nevertheless, even in the absence of status differences, group members constantly influence one another. Some of the most famous research in social psychology is concerned with social influence, and social influence is fundamental to all kinds of group processes. Let us first look at two classic experiments.

Sherif (1935, 1936) put people in a completely dark room, in which there was only one small stationary point of light. Because our eyes tend to move involuntarily, the small light seemed to move in the dark room, a phenomenon known as the auto-kinetic effect.[1] Sherif first asked individual participants to estimate how much the light moved. He found that participants were relatively constant in their estimates, but that large differences existed between people. He then put participants in the room with one or two other participants, and asked them to give their responses aloud. After a while, their responses became more and more alike, and the group members eventually gave very similar responses. Apparently, a group norm was gradually established, which indicated what the "correct" estimate was.

Asch (1952) argued that Sherif's results might have been due to the fact that his stimulus, the apparent movement of the small light, was ambiguous: As there was no real movement, participants could not give a "correct" or "wrong" answer. Asch therefore studied social influence with stimuli that were not ambiguous, but where a clear correct answer existed. He asked his participants to give line judgments: They had to indicate which of three test lines was similar in length to a standard (see Figure 2.6). As can be seen, the stimulus

---

1   In a room with enough light this does not happen, because our brain adjusts for the involuntary movements of our eyes. However, in a dark room this adjustment is impossible, because the adjustment depends on seeing surrounding objects (e.g., a stationary wall).

FIGURE 2.6.
An example of a
stimulus used by Asch
(1952, 1955).

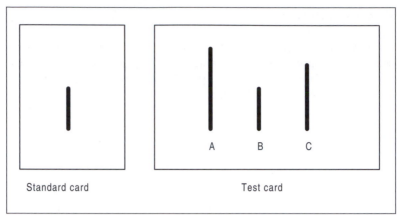

was unambiguous, and everyone could easily identify the correct
answer when asked to do so individually.

Asch had participants perform this task in groups. They sat in a
semicircle and were asked to give their answer aloud on each of 18
trials (each time with a different set of standard and test cards),
starting with the first participant and then moving around the
semicircle. However, the "participants" who were asked to give their
answer first were confederates, who were instructed to deliberately
(and unknown to the real participant, later down the line) give the
same *incorrect* answer on 12 of the 18 trials. Asch then recorded
whether the real participant went along with the unanimous but
incorrect others. Asch initially found that about 76 per cent of participants gave at least one incorrect response, and that 5 per cent went
along in each of the 12 critical trials. Thus, participants were certainly
influenced by the incorrect others, even with an unambiguous task.

Asch further found that when more people initially gave the same
incorrect answer, conformity to the group increased, but this increase
soon leveled out. Three incorrect unanimous confederates were
enough to produce the effect, and adding more had little additional
effect (Asch, 1951; also Latané, 1981). Further, when the real participant had a supporter who did not comply with the rest of the
group, conformity decreased considerably (Asch, 1955). Interestingly,
this even happened when the supporter gave a wrong answer – as
long as it was different from the majority. For example, in Figure 2.6,
when the majority said line A, and one other said C, the participants
were more likely to say B (the correct answer) than when *all* others
said A (also Wilder & Allen, 1977). Thus, unanimity of the majority is
quite important.

Majority influence

The studies of Asch involve conformity to a majority, and are an example of *majority influence*: A larger subgroup produced conformity in a smaller subgroup. But *why* do people often conform to a majority? Deutsch and Gerard (1955) introduced the important distinction between normative and informational social influence. *Normative social influence* occurs when people conform to the *expectations of others*. These others may not necessarily be right, but their influence is accepted because people expect more positive evaluations when they conform to their opinions or norms. *Informational social influence*, on the other hand, occurs when people conform to others because they accept information obtained from others as *evidence about reality*. Normative social influence is thus closely connected to the wish to receive positive evaluations, whereas informational social influence is closely connected to the wish to be accurate about reality (see also Kaplan & Miller, 1987).

Schachter (1951; Box 2.1) has shown that (normative) pressure is exerted on people who do not conform, and that nonconformity might be punished by social exclusion (see also Chapter 1). Deutsch and Gerard (1955), using the line-estimation paradigm developed by Asch, found that normative social influence was *stronger* when participants were part of a group that would collectively be rewarded for performing well. Participants were less likely to deviate from the majority, because they feared negative evaluations of others when their deviating judgments might imply that the group would miss their reward. Deutsch and Gerard found that normative social influence was *weaker* when participants were anonymous, because that made it harder for the others to evaluate the participant.

Informational social influence is related to our need to understand the world. As was argued in Chapter 1, we often validate our beliefs against "social reality," especially if it is hard to evaluate them against "physical reality." For example, opinions, preferences, and norms have no physical reality, and one therefore has to turn to others to validate them (Festinger, 1954). When a majority agrees, we are likely to accept their judgment. Speaking to this, Deutsch and Gerard (1955) included trials in the line-estimation task where the stimuli were removed before participants could give their response, and participants thus had to make their estimates from memory. This increased conformity to the erroneous majority, because it was harder to test one's beliefs against physical reality, and people relied more on social reality.

A more recent study tested the effects of task importance and task difficulty on conformity (Baron, Vandello, & Brunsman, 1996). Participants were told that the study was about eyewitness accuracy. They were shown a series of 13 pairs of slides: first a slide of a perpetrator, and next a slide of a line-up showing the perpetrator and three others. The task was to identify the perpetrator in the line-up. Some participants (high task importance condition) were told that they could receive $20 for accurate judgments, whereas others were told that no money could be earned (low task importance). Further, in the easy task condition, the participants could see both slides for 5 seconds; in the difficult task condition, they could only see them for 0.5 seconds. There always was one real participant and two confederates. On seven of the 13 trials, these confederates deliberately gave the wrong answer. Baron *et al.* recorded how often the real participant went along with these incorrect answers.

Baron *et al.* (1996) argued that increasing task importance would make participants more concerned with accuracy (and less with being liked). As a consequence, when the task was easy they should conform less in the important task condition than in the unimportant task condition. However, when the task is difficult, they will have to rely on others' judgments (and thus on social reality), because it is more difficult to test their own opinions against physical reality. As a consequence, they should conform more when the task is important than when it is unimportant. Figure 2.7 shows their results, which were in line with these expectations. Thus, when a task is important, people will be inclined to follow their own judgments only when judgments can easily be evaluated against physical reality. However, they will follow others even more when the task is difficult.

FIGURE 2.7.
Percentage of conformity as a function of task difficulty and task importance (data from Baron, Vandello, & Brunsman, 1996).

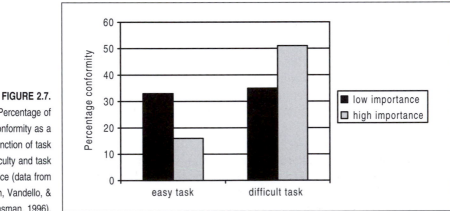

Normative and informational social influence have different effects. Normative social influence leads to conformity, but influence targets do not necessarily believe that the majority is right. This is often called *public compliance*: a change in behavior (e.g., expressing an opinion) without changing one's private beliefs. Informational influence might on the other hand lead to a real change in one's private opinions, for example because one is convinced by new arguments put forward by a majority. This is called *private acceptance* (Eagly & Chaiken, 1993; Kaplan & Miller, 1987). Private acceptance is likely to persist, whereas public compliance will generally disappear when the influence agents (the majority) are no longer present.

Group polarization as anticonformity

By the end of the 1950s, after the impressive studies by Asch and others, researchers generally believed that group pressure would always lead to conformity. This is why a master's thesis by James Stoner (1961) had an enormous impact. Stoner asked groups to respond to a number of scenarios, all involving some degree of risk. In each scenario, participants were confronted with a choice dilemma between an alternative high in probability of success but low in value, and an alternative low in probability of success but high in value. Participants had to indicate the minimum probability of success under which they believed that the latter, more risky alternative should be chosen. For example:

> A low-ranked player in a chess tournament has the choice of attempting or not a deceptive but risky maneuver. This maneuver would lead to quick victory if successful, but to almost certain defeat if it fails. Please indicate the lowest probability of success that you would accept before recommending that the chess player play this risky move.
>
> I would recommend that the chance of success should be at least _____ %

Participants first responded to 12 dilemmas in private, then discussed them as a group and made a group decision, and finally again responded individually. If group members would conform to the group, the group response would be approximately equal to the average of group members' individual (pre-discussion) judgments, and group members would converge around this average judgment. However, this is not what Stoner found: On most dilemmas, the group's judgment (as well as the private judgments after the group decision) was *more* risky than the average of individual judgments. On some items, however, the groups were more cautious than the average individual. The critical factor was whether the individual pre-discussion opinions were on the risky or cautious side: when individual judgments were relatively risky, the group's judgment was even riskier; when they were relatively cautious, the group became even more cautious. Importantly, it is not a conformity effect, because group members do not conform to the group average, but rather become more extreme than they were initially (see Figure 2.8).

Soon it appeared that the phenomenon is not restricted to risky choices. Moscovici and Zavalloni (1969) asked French participants about their attitudes towards the then French President De Gaulle and towards North Americans. As in Stoner's study, attitudes were given individually, then as a group, and individually again. The researchers found that – on average – participants initially had

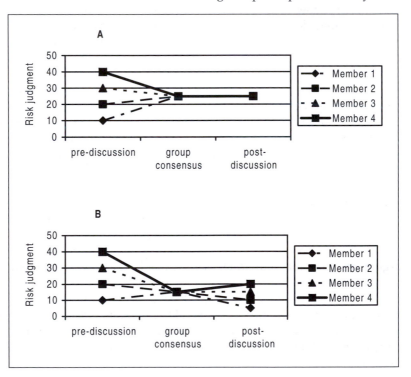

FIGURE 2.8.

Two hypothetical risk judgments of a four-person group. (A) A conformity effect: the group converges on the average risk judgment of the four members, and group members privately agree with that judgment after the discussion. (B) Group polarization: Group judgment and post-discussion judgments become more extreme than the group average.

favorable attitudes about De Gaulle, and these became even more favorable after group discussion. Attitudes about North Americans were slightly unfavorable before discussion, and became even more unfavorable after the discussion. Thus, original attitudes polarized (became more extreme) after group discussion. *Group polarization* has since been shown in a variety of contexts, including stereotypes, gambling behavior, jury decisions, and interpersonal impressions (see Lamm & Myers, 1978): On any judgmental dimension, groups tend to shift to the pole that their members favor initially.

Over the years, a number of explanations have been suggested for this striking phenomenon (see Pruitt, 1971), but research has converged on two major ones: social comparison processes (Sanders & Baron, 1977) and persuasive argumentation (Burnstein & Vinokur, 1977). These explanations fit well with Deutsch and Gerard's (1955) distinction between normative and informational influence, and they both have received substantial support (Isenberg, 1986).

The social comparison explanation argues that people want to put themselves in a favorable light. They want to give their "true" opinion, but also do not want to appear too extreme or deviate too much from other group members. However, before the group discussion they do not know the opinion of others. Firstly, they may therefore give an initial opinion that is less extreme than their true opinion. When during discussion they find out that others' opinions are fairly similar (they engage in social comparison processes), they are more likely to subsequently express their true (more extreme) beliefs. Secondly, group members do not want to be too different from others, but a little bit different is fine. As Brown (1974, p. 469) argues: "To be virtuous . . . is to be different from the mean – in the right direction and to the right degree." Thus, when group members find out the opinions of others, they want to distinguish themselves favorably from these others, and do so by taking an opinion that is slightly more extreme.

The second explanation is *persuasive arguments theory* (Burnstein & Vinokur, 1977). The theory argues that an individual's position on an issue is a function of the number and persuasiveness of pro and con arguments that the individual has available. However, different group members may have different arguments available, and as a consequence a group member may hear *new and valid* arguments during group discussion. When most of these arguments favor one's initial opinion – which is to be expected when group members initially have similar opinions – one becomes more convinced and more extreme.

FIGURE 2.9.

Group polarization may be one reason why some people adopt extremist positions, such as demonstrated by the group committing the 9/11 attacks on New York and Washington. When a group of likeminded people comes together, their attitudes may polarize and perhaps even become extremist. In the case of the World Trade Center attack this cost the lives of thousands of people, including many brave men and women from the New York Fire Department (see www.nyc.gov/fdny). Copyright Todd Rengel. Reprinted with permission.

Both the explanations have received substantial support. In support for the social comparison explanation, it has been found that only giving group members the answers of others is enough to produce group polarization, even without any group discussion. However, in support for persuasive arguments theory, the group polarization effect is stronger when discussion among group members is allowed. Further, the effect depends on the degree to which new and valid arguments come up during this discussion (see Isenberg, 1986, for an overview).

Group polarization is often seen as a cause of extremity in groups. In particular if groups function in relative isolation, group members may convince one another to adopt very extreme positions. This may lead to extreme decisions (see our discussion of groupthink in Chapters 1 and 7) and opinions, including perhaps extreme religious views (Figure 2.9).

Minority influence

So far, we have discussed majority influence and group polarization, both of which occur when most people agree on some issue. However, sometimes *minority influence* occurs: Smaller subgroups produce change in larger subgroups. Indeed, societal change and innovation would not be possible when minorities do not occasionally influence majorities and change the way people look at issues: We would still believe that the sun revolves around the earth if a minority had not successfully argued otherwise.

Among the first to study minority influence were Moscovici, Lage, and Naffrechoux (1969). They argued that minorities will occasionally be influential, because they make other group members less certain about their own opinions. However, minorities must be consistent over time to create enough uncertainty to have an effect rather than being ignored. Moscovici *et al.* performed an experiment in which the Asch situation was basically reversed. In each group, there were four real participants and two confederates. These six people were shown colored slides, and were asked to rate the brightness of each slide and name its color. The slides clearly were blue. However, in one condition the two confederates consistently called the slides green on all trials (36 trials were used). In a second condition, the confederates called the slides green on 24 trials and blue on the other 12 trials. In a control condition there was no minority influence. Moscovici *et al.* recorded how many real participants called the slides green. They found that only a consistent minority had some influence, and caused the real participants to change their color perception in over 8 per cent of the trials. Inconsistent minorities changed the color perception in only about 1 per cent of the trials.

In his *conversion theory*, Moscovici (1980) argued that minority influence is qualitatively different from majority influence. Majority influence will lead to public compliance: Because of normative pressure, people will conform to the majority. However, when asked in private, they might not have changed their opinion. According to Moscovici, people will not necessarily evaluate the majority position very carefully, but will go along to avoid negative outcomes (e.g., rejection). Moscovici argued that minority influence, in contrast, would yield private acceptance. Minorities are not as threatening, and when minorities consistently argue their point they will stimulate others to scrutinize their arguments carefully. When they become convinced, this will yield conversion (or private acceptance). However, people may be reluctant to go along publicly with a minority (and against a majority). Moscovici therefore argued that effects of minority influence would be bigger for private opinions than for public statements. He further argued that people will not always show conversion on the "focal issue" (the issue that was under debate), because they do not want to associate themselves with a minority, but may change on issues related to the focal issue. For example, if a minority argues that homosexuals should have a right to marry, others may not change their opinions on homosexual marriage, but might change on a related issue (e.g., on another liberal rights issue, such as abortion). This is called *indirect influence* as opposed to direct influence (i.e., changing one's opinion on the focal issue).

Over the years, many studies have been performed on minority influence, investigating Moscovici's conversion theory. Wood, Lundgren, Ouellette, Busceme, and Blackstone (1994) summarized these studies. Across 97 different studies, Wood *et al.* found that majorities had a bigger influence than minorities on measures of direct influence, both public and private. However, on measures of indirect influence there was some evidence that minorities had more influence. Finally, consistency of minorities was indeed important, and higher consistency was associated with more minority influence. To conclude, Moscovici (1980) was at least partly right: Minorities create indirect change, and they are more influential when they are consistent. However, majorities are generally more powerful on direct measures of influence, both public and private, whereas Moscovici predicted that they would only be more influential on public measures of conformity.

Nemeth (1986) has argued that minorities and majorities stimulate different *thought processes*. She argued that being exposed to a majority that holds a different opinion causes stress: Minority members will fear that others disapprove of them. Stress, in turn, causes a narrowing of attention, and Nemeth argued that cognitive efforts are as a consequence limited to verifying the majority position ("are they right?"). Being exposed to a disagreeing minority does not cause stress. Rather, people will first assume that the minority is incorrect, but when the minority consistently maintains its position, they will start to think about it. They will not necessarily adopt the minority position, but will eventually consider the issue more thoroughly and with an open mind, because they want to find out why the minority disagrees. Thus, while majorities only stimulate people to consider one side of the issue – the majority opinion – minorities will stimulate people to look at more sides of an issue. Nemeth calls the former "convergent thinking" and the latter "divergent thinking." Divergent thinking, according to Nemeth, leads to better scrutiny of the issue at hand, and also to more creativity.

To test these ideas, Nemeth and Kwan (1985) used a set-up that was similar to the one used by Moscovici *et al.* (1969) described earlier. Participants were shown 20 slides that were blue in color, and were asked to name their color. Prior to seeing the slides, participants were told either that 80 per cent of people judged these colors to be blue and 20 per cent judged them to be green (condition with a disagreeing minority) or the reverse (80 per cent green and 20 per cent blue, condition with a disagreeing majority). Participants gave their color judgments in the presence of another "participant" (a confederate) who consistently called all slides "green." After giving the color judgments, participants were asked to write seven associations to the words "green" and "blue." These associations were coded for originality. Nemeth and Kwan (1985) found that associations of people exposed to a minority were more original than those of people exposed to a majority. For example, they gave original associations to the word "blue" such as "jazz" or "jeans," rather than unoriginal associations, such as "sky."

Conclusion

People are very susceptible to different forms of social influence. They will often conform to majorities (even when wrong), either because they believe that the majority is right (informational influence) or because they fear disapproval or rejection (normative influence). Social influence may also lead to extremity. When group members initially agree about an issue, group discussion can polarize their opinions further. Again, this is caused by both normative influence (social comparison, and simply knowing the position of others) and informational influence (exchanging new and valid arguments). Sometimes minorities can also be influential, but minorities have to be consistent over time. Further, their influence is largely indirect. Finally, minorities may stimulate divergent thinking and creativity.

Chapter summary

(1) Group members move through the different stages of group membership (prospective member, new member, full member, marginal member, and ex-member) separated from each other by role transitions, and these different stages are characterized by different levels of commitment.

(2) The role transition of entry can be marked by a harsh initiation ritual. A classic explanation for these rituals is given by dissonance theory, which argues that harsh rituals increase the commitment to the group.

(3) An important determinant of group openness is staffing level: It is easier to become a full member of an understaffed as compared to an overstaffed group.

(4) When group members deviate from a group norm they are put under pressure to change their behavior or opinion. Group members may be excluded when these influence attempts are unsuccessful.

(5) Groups develop over time, because the challenges they face and the goals they have change over time. The stage theory of Tuckman distinguishes five stages: forming, storming, norming, performing, and adjourning.

(6) Interaction process analysis is a useful coding scheme for group interactions, and makes a basic distinction between socio-emotional and task behaviors.

(7) Groups develop status and role differences. Expectation states theory explains the emergence of status structures in groups. It argues that certain status characteristics lead to performance expectations that subsequently lead to differences in status and influence.

(8) People are greatly influenced by majorities, because they take the majority opinion as evidence about reality (informational influence) or because they conform to the majority to avoid negative consequences (normative influence).

(9) When group members initially agree about an issue, group discussion may lead to group polarization and more extreme opinions. This phenomenon can be explained with social comparison theory and persuasive arguments theory.

(10) Minorities can also be influential, but their influence is often indirect, and minorities have to be consistent over time because otherwise they are ignored. Being exposed to a minority viewpoint can stimulate divergent thinking and creativity.

Exercises

(1) Recall an instance in which you became member of a group. Do you recognize the stages of group membership, and how did you notice that your membership changed over time?

(2) Sometimes there can be power struggles within a group: Different people aspire to the same role (e.g., as a group leader). Can you, based on expectation states theory, predict when such a power struggle is likely to occur?

(3) Several factors increase or decrease the importance of informational or normative influence, such as task importance, anonymity of responding, and task ambiguity. Can you think of other factors that increase or decrease the importance of informational or normative social influence?

(4) On the basis of the discussion of group polarization, what might be done about extremist opinions within society (e.g., extremist right-wing groups or religious fundamentalism)?

(5) Taking a minority position requires courage, because one runs the risk of being rejected. What factors influence the likelihood that someone takes a minority position? Compare your answers to the factors found by De Dreu, De Vries, Franssen, and Altink (2000).

Further reading

On group socialization

Moreland, R. L., & Levine, J. M. (1982). Socialization in small groups: Temporal changes in individual–group relations. In L. Berkowitz (Ed.), *Advances in experimental social psychology* (Vol. 15, pp. 137–192). New York: Academic Press.

On group development

Wheelan, S. A. (1994). *Group process: A developmental perspective*. Boston: Allyn & Bacon.

On status and group structure

Ridgeway, C. L. (2001). Social status and group structure. In M. A. Hogg & R. S. Tindale (Eds.), *Blackwell handbook of social psychology: Group processes* (pp. 352–375). Oxford: Blackwell.

On social influence

Asch, S. E. (1956). Studies of independence and submission to group pressure: I. A minority of one against a unanimous majority. *Psychological Monographs, 70*(9) (whole no. 417).

Isenberg, D. J. (1986). Group polarization: A critical review and meta-analysis. *Journal of Personality and Social Psychology, 50*, 1141–1151.

Moscovici, S. (1980). Towards a theory of conversion behavior. In L. Berkowitz (Ed.), *Advances in experimental social psychology* (Vol. 13, pp. 209–239). New York: Academic Press.

Nemeth, C. J. (1986). Differential contributions of majority and minority influence. *Psychological Review, 93*, 23–32.

A theoretical framework 3

Groups as multilevel systems

In this chapter, a framework is introduced to understand group performance. The framework consists of five elements: group members, group tasks, group interaction, group output, and group context. We will discuss these five elements, and the relations among them. But before we start, it is important to realize that groups are *multilevel systems*. Groups are composed of members, and both the group member and the group as a whole can be perceived as a distinct entity (see also Chapter 1). Groups and members are hierarchically organized: The group member (lower level) is part of the group (higher level). The fact that both members and groups can be seen as distinct entities implies that both have characteristics. Thus, a group member might be extraverted, intelligent, knowledgeable, and so on. At the group level, a group might be small, permeable, cooperative, and so on. Note that group size and group permeability are defined at the group level – they represent group characteristics – and have no meaning at the individual level. Often there also is a third level to take into account, broadly referred to as "context." Indeed, most groups do not function is isolation. For example, a project team is part of an organization, and when you write a research paper in a group, that group probably is part of a larger class (consisting of different groups). Mostly towards the end of this book, we will discuss the context in which groups work, and group context is one of the elements of the general framework.

Acknowledging the different levels is important for several reasons. First, it is important to specify the level one is talking about. For example, one could say about a group that it is "knowledgeable," but what exactly does that mean? It might, for example, mean that it is composed of knowledgeable members (i.e., the group members *individually* have much knowledge). However, it might also mean that the group has the right *combination* of knowledge and group members complement each other's knowledge. Here, the group as a whole has more information than the separate members, and the term "knowledgeable" has another meaning.

Second, realizing that there are different levels makes one sensitive to the fact that there are relations between the levels. These relations may be top-down or bottom-up (Kozlowski & Klein, 2000). *Top-down effects* occur when characteristics at the group level influence group members' behavior, thoughts and feelings. This might be very direct: A group norm that coming late is unacceptable (the norm is defined at the group level) has the direct effect on group members that they do not come late to a meeting (behavior at the individual level). Characteristics at the group level can also influence *relations* between variables at the individual level. This is easy to understand with an example. Extraverted people usually talk more in a group context than introverted people. However, this relation between two variables at the individual level (extraversion of an individual and amount of talking of that individual) will be stronger or weaker depending on group size (a characteristic at the group level). A hypothesis might be that extraversion is associated with talkativeness especially in large groups, and less so in smaller groups, because in smaller groups introverted people are less shy.

Bottom-up effects occur when characteristics at the individual level determine outcomes at the group level. This is very important, because group performance is an outcome at the group level. Indeed, one of the most fundamental issues in group research is the question of *how individual inputs (individual level) are transformed into group outputs (group level)*. The following are examples.

- Individual football players have different qualities (e.g., a good pass, speed, physical strength), but what combination of players yields the best team performance?
- Group members might have different individual preferences, but how are these combined into a group decision (e.g., Davis, 1973)?
- People may differ in problem-solving capacities (e.g., through individual differences in intelligence), but is one smart group member enough to ensure that the group will solve the problem (e.g., Laughlin & Ellis, 1986)?

These bottom-up effects sometimes are quite simple. Take a group that wants to send out a mailing and has to put letters into envelopes. Performance of the group (e.g., how many letters are put into envelopes in one hour) is the sum of individual group members' performances: One can simply add up how many envelopes each member has done. At other times, things will be quite complex. For example, suppose a team in an automobile company has to design a new car. The quality of that design depends on a nonlinear combination of individual contributions (e.g., of mechanical engineers, designers, and marketing specialists) and is much more complicated.

A theoretical framework for group performance

Our framework consists of group members, the group task, group interaction processes, group output, and group context. Four of the five elements of the basic framework, excluding only the group task, are schematically presented in Figure 3.1. Within the group boundary (the dotted rectangle) are three elements: group members, group interaction, and group output. Group context, the fourth element, is everything outside the group boundary. Within the group boundary, at the left-hand side of the figure, are several individual group members (three in this case) who make up the group. These individual group members bring to the group their knowledge, skills, and abilities (*KSAs*), but also their individual motives, emotions, and personalities. Different group members may of course have different

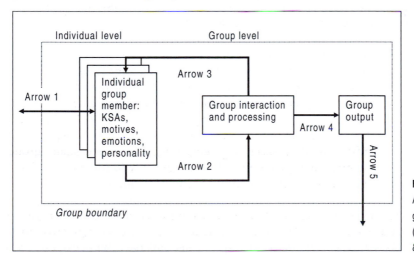

FIGURE 3.1.

A general model of group performance (adapted from Nijstad & Paulus, 2003).

KSAs, motives, and so on. Further, group members have the capacity to learn and can be influenced by people or things outside of the group, and this possibility is represented by Arrow 1. Arrow 1 thus represents one way in which the group context may influence the group, through influencing group members. However, group members can also influence their environment, and therefore Arrow 1 is bidirectional.

Group members can contribute things to the group (Arrow 2 in Figure 3.1). This may be an idea, a piece of information, an evaluation, a filled envelope (when the group was working on a mailing), etc. Once contributed, a contribution will be available to other group members. A contribution made by one group member can subsequently influence other group members, a possibility represented by Arrow 3. Thus, overhearing someone generating an idea might stimulate additional ideas in another group member (e.g., Dugosh, Paulus, Roland, & Yang, 2000), or seeing that someone has already filled 50 envelopes might influence another group member's rate of production ("I am falling behind, I should hurry") (e.g., Seta, 1982). In short, group members will be influenced by what other members contribute.

In the middle of the figure is a box with "group interaction and processing," and this represents group interaction processes (cf. Hinsz, Tindale, & Vollrath, 1997). As argued earlier in this chapter, the contributions of individual group members need to be combined in some way to result in a group output (Arrow 4). The way in which individual contributions are combined often determines the group's success on the task. The group output therefore results from bottom-up processes within the group. According to Arrow 5, finally, group outputs are allowed to influence the context of the group. Thus, the relation between group context and the group is reciprocal: The context will have an influence on the group (Arrow 1), but the group may also affect the context (Arrows 1 and 5). Let us now consider the five elements of our framework, including the group task, in turn.

Group members

In the context of group performance, members provide the necessary *resources* to complete the group task. That is, group members bring to the task their KSAs, and their time and effort. KSAs can vary widely. Take the example of designing a new automobile. Mechanical engineers will have knowledge about engines; designers will have design skills; and marketing specialists will have knowledge about what kind of car will sell best. A right combination of people might therefore lead to a final product – a new car – that is better than any of the individual group members could have created on their own. KSAs might also include skills that are required for effective collaboration, such as communication skills or conflict management skills.

However, group members bring more to the group than their ability to work at the group task. Group members have their own goals that they strive for, and these goals might not always be compatible with the overall group goals. For example, an employee might be interested in getting a promotion, and is therefore motivated to do better than the other group members, rather than for the group as a whole to succeed. Or a member of a decision-making group might have her own reasons for preferring a certain alternative, maybe because she has individual benefits if that alternative is chosen. Thus, besides KSAs, group members also have certain individual motives. Individual group members are characterized by a number of other attributes, such as personality, moods and emotions, attitudes, and so on. These will all have some influence on group processes and thereby on group performance.

Group tasks

For a group to be successful, it needs members who have the necessary resources to contribute to task completion. However, which resources are necessary? This depends critically on the group task. When the group task is to fill envelopes or to pull a rope as hard as possible, one does not need a high IQ or specialized knowledge; rather one needs group members who are motivated to work hard, or who are physically strong. However, if the group task is to design a successful marketing strategy to promote a new product, one needs members who have knowledge about marketing or consumer psychology. Thus, it always is the combination of group members and group tasks that determines whether the group may perform well. This *potential performance principle* was put forward by Ivan Steiner (1972): The potential performance of a group is determined by the resources of the group members in combination with the requirements of the group task. If group members possess the necessary resources to complete the task, potential performance is high. If group members do not possess the necessary resources, potential performance is low:

Potential performance = f (group member resources, task demands)

Note that the term *potential performance* is used. Steiner (1972) explicitly made a distinction between potential performance (what a group could potentially achieve given group member resources and task demands) and actual performance (what the group actually does achieve). Steiner argued that a group might have the potential to perform well but still fail at the task. The reason, he suggested, lies in faulty group processes – an issue we discuss in the next section.

If the group task is so important, it is necessary to distinguish among different types of group tasks. Steiner (1972) used three dimensions to classify group tasks. First, he made a distinction between divisible and unitary tasks. Divisible tasks can be divided into subtasks, whereas this is not possible for unitary tasks. Designing a car is a divisible task (subtasks can be distinguished, e.g., designing the motor versus the exterior), but lifting a piano is a unitary task (there are no subtasks). Second, he distinguished between optimizing and maximizing tasks. This distinction is based on the nature of the performance criterion: Is it about generating the best or a correct response (optimizing), or about generating many responses or doing it fast (maximizing)? Making the best possible decision would be an optimizing task, whereas filling as many envelopes as possible would be a maximizing task.

Steiner's third dimension is concerned with how individual group member input is converted into *potential* group performance. Steiner's classification allows for four task types (Table 3.1): additive tasks, disjunctive tasks, conjunctive tasks, and discretionary tasks. In *additive tasks*, potential performance of the group is determined by the sum or the average of individual performances. An example would, again, be filling envelopes. When we know that, given individual abilities, Andy can fill 200 envelopes in an hour, John can fill 150, and Mary can fill 175, we know that in principle the group as a whole (Andy, John, and Mary together) can fill 525 envelopes in one hour. Making an estimate (of, for example, costs or risks) or a judgment may also be considered an additive task: One can use the average estimates or judgments of group members to compute a group estimate. In *disjunctive tasks* this is quite different: here potential performance of the group is determined by the *best* member. An example would be solving a math problem: If one group member is good at math and can solve the problem, the potential of the group is high and the group as a whole has the potential to solve the problem. In other words, only one person of high ability is needed to have a high

TABLE 3.1
Steiner's (1972) classification of tasks

Task type	Description	Examples	Chapter
Additive	Potential performance of the group is given by the sum or average of individual inputs	Filling envelopes, pulling a rope, brainstorming, making judgments and estimates	5, 6, 9
Disjunctive	Potential performance of the group is given by performance of the best member	Decision-making, problem-solving	7, 8
Conjunctive	Potential performance of the group is given by performance of the worst member	Mountain-climbing, assembly line	5, 10
Discretionary	Potential performance is given by any combination of individual performances, up to the discretion of the group	Making music, designing a car	9

level of potential performance. In *conjunctive tasks*, on the other hand, potential performance of the group depends on the *least* capable member. An example is mountain-climbing. When the mountaineers are tied together with a rope, progress of the group as a whole depends on the slowest member. Finally, in *discretionary tasks*, there is no fixed way in which individual contributions are transformed into outcomes; this is up to (the discretion of) the group. An example would be a rock band: They can choose any way they want to combine their individual contributions.

Many group tasks in the real world might not easily fit this classification. For example, it is hard to say whether designing a new car is an additive task, a disjunctive one, or any other task type. However, when the task is divisible, it will often be possible to break it down in subtasks, and classify each subtask in terms of Steiner's model.

Group processes

Group processes are the vehicle for bottom-up effects: They determine how individual inputs of group members are combined to lead to a group output. Group processes therefore are critical for group performance. Recall that Steiner (1972) distinguished between potential performance and actual performance. Potential performance was a function of group member resources and task demands (the first two elements of our framework). Actual performance, according to Steiner, is a function of potential performance and group processes. More specifically, Steiner proposed:

Actual performance = potential performance − process loss

This formula implies two things: first, that actual performance cannot be higher than potential performance; and second, that group processes (can) lead to *process loss*, which may prevent groups from reaching their potential performance.

Steiner distinguished between two types of process loss: motivation loss and coordination loss. *Motivation loss* occurs when members are not optimally motivated, and therefore exert less effort than would be possible or needed for optimal performance. Take the rope-pulling example again. When group members fail to pull the rope with all their strength, there will be motivation losses. In other types of tasks, group members may fail to contribute other things, such as information that they have when the group is making a decision. Motivation losses therefore are generally related to a failure to contribute (Arrow 2 in Figure 3.1).

Coordination loss occurs when group members do not combine their (potential) contributions in an optimal way. Consider two (quite different) examples. First, take a group that is pulling a rope. If group members do not pull in exactly the same direction at exactly the same time, there will be some coordination loss: The total force exerted will be lower than possible (even when group members pull at their maximal strength and there is no motivation loss). Another example would be a group working at a math task. Suppose one group member has the right answer to the problem, but this member fails to convince the others and the group eventually chooses an incorrect solution; then group performance will fall below what would have been possible. The reason is that individual contributions were not combined in the right way: The group should have chosen the solution of its best member (the one with the correct solution), but failed to do so. Both cases are instances of coordination loss: a failure to coordinate individual inputs adequately. In Figure 3.1, Arrow 4 is closely linked to coordination losses.

It is clear that groups can perform below their potential. However, is it also possible that groups can perform above their potential? To phrase the question differently: Can there, as well as process losses, be *process gains*, due to very effective group processes? The answer depends on the definition of the term "potential performance." If one sees potential performance as *maximum* performance that a group could possibly achieve, then by definition no process gains are possible. However, it might be more fruitful to conceptualize potential performance as a group's potential *given individual member resources and the demands of the group task*. Potential performance in that case is what individuals could possibly achieve (given their individual resources and task demands), and how these possible individual achievements relate to group performance.

Take a disjunctive task. According to Steiner, the group should be able to solve it when at least one member can solve it. Potential performance therefore is closely linked to the best group member's ability. But now suppose that, given their individual resources, not a single member would be able to solve the problem as an individual. Could the group as a whole still solve it? This might be possible, if the group as a whole has more resources than the best individual. In other words, process gains might be possible when the *combination of individual resources* allows the group to perform even better than the best member. This might be seen as an example of coordination gains: Due to a very effective combination of individual resources, the group can outperform the best member.

Besides coordination gains, motivation gains are possible. Motivation gains can occur when group members work harder in a group than they would have done when working alone. In additive tasks, this would imply that $1 + 1 = 3$, in an almost literal way. In conjunctive tasks, where group performance is determined by the worst member, process gains imply that this worst member somehow performs better in a group than he or she would have done alone (see Chapter 5).

Group output

Eventually, the group must produce some output. The important question is: How good is the group's output? In other words, one would like to evaluate the group output on some dimension. Two questions are important: What is the relevant dimension on which to judge the group's output? What standards should we use to judge a group's performance? There are several possible answers to this, and the right answer depends on the situation, such as the group's task.

Performance dimensions

First, it might be useful to distinguish between three types of outcome: performance outcomes, affective outcomes, and learning (cf.

TABLE 3.2
A two-way classification of outcomes

Outcome	Level of analysis	
	Individual	*Group*
Performance	*Individual-level performance:*	*Group-level performance:*
	Amount of influence	Quality of decision
	Personal production	Correctness of solution
	Speed of performance	Group productivity
		Time required
Affective	*Individual-level affective responses:*	*Group-level affective responses:*
	Satisfaction	Group cohesion
	Respect and status	Group affective tone
	Mood	
	Motivation	
Learning	*Individual learning:*	*Group learning:*
	Task proficiency	Transactive memory
	Interpersonal skills	
	Knowledge	

Hackman, 1987). Performance outcomes can be judged in terms of success with regard to task completion. Affective outcomes are reactions of entities (people, groups) toward other entities or toward the task. Learning is related to potential future task performance. All these outcomes can, in principle, occur at the individual or group level of analysis. Table 3.2 gives an overview, including some examples of outcomes that can be looked at.

First, one may look at performance-related output of individual group members. An example would be to look at individual productivity per group member. Another example would be the amount of influence an individual group member has had. For example, in a group decision-making task, was an individual successful in convincing the others to adopt his or her preferred alternative? Second, one might look at affective responses of individuals: Is the individual happy, satisfied, does s/he feels included and respected, and so on. Third, one may look at learning at the individual level. Indeed, sometimes the goal of a group performance exercise is for group members to learn (e.g., when students write a research paper). Thus, a relevant outcome dimension might be learning, or the extent to which the individual is capable of future task performance.

At the group level, the first outcome dimension refers to how well the group has performed on the group task. Has the group made a high-quality decision, has it reached the correct conclusion, was it productive? The second outcome relates to group-level affective responses. One of these outcomes is, for example, group cohesion: In Chapter 1 we have seen that high-performing groups also tend to become more cohesive over time (Mullen & Copper, 1994). The third outcome is group learning. Learning at the group level can, for example, lead to a *transactive memory* system. A transactive memory refers to a situation in which group members may not have certain knowledge or skills, but they do know which other members have it. As you can imagine, knowing whom to turn to for specific information or skills can greatly benefit future task performance (Liang *et al.*, 1995; Wegner, 1986; see also Chapter 9).

Comparison standards

When we know on what dimension the group's performance should be evaluated, we must also determine against which standard it should be evaluated. In other words: When can we call a certain level of performance good, good enough, suboptimal, below average, or give any other type of judgment? To give a judgment, we need a comparison standard against which the group's performance can be evaluated. Three types of standard are possible.

(1) *Absolute or normative standards.* Sometimes it is possible to evaluate performance against an absolute or normative standard. In these cases, we can establish whether a group has succeeded or failed against this external criterion. One example would be an explicit performance goal: When the group has the explicit performance goal to fill 500 envelopes in one hour, we can evaluate whether it has succeeded or failed. Another example would involve group tasks with correct answers: If the group has reached the correct solution it has succeeded; otherwise it has failed.

(2) If it is not possible to evaluate the group against absolute standards, one might use *relative standards*. One could judge the performance of groups relative to each other. This is something that researchers often do. The focus is on explaining why one group performs better than another. An example can be found in Chapter 1, where we discussed the effects of cohesion on group performance. The question was whether we can explain performance differences between groups in terms of differences in cohesion between these groups.

(3) A third possibility is to *compare the group's performance with individual performance*. The question in that case is: Who is better,

individuals or groups? That question can be rephrased as: Does group interaction lead to process losses (individuals do better) or to process gains (groups do better)? Such a comparison may be far from simple, because we need to establish an individual baseline.

The appropriate individual baseline

Much of the research on group performance has considered the question: Who is better, individuals or groups? However, this question is more complex than it might seem, and the reason is the baseline problem. Basically, the question is what one should compare with what. Some possibilities are as follows.

(1) Compare the performance of a group with the performance of a single individual who has worked alone.
(2) Compare the performance of a single group member with the performance of a single individual who has worked alone.
(3) Compare the performance of a group with N members with the performance of N individuals who have worked alone, and then:
   (a) take the sum or the average of the N individuals' performance and compare it with group performance (appropriate for additive tasks)
   (b) take the best individual's performance, and compare it with the group's performance (appropriate for disjunctive tasks)
   (c) take the worst individual's performance, and compare it with the group's performance (appropriate for conjunctive tasks).

One problem with the first option is that this is often not a fair comparison. For example, it is not fair to compare how many envelopes an individual has filled in one hour with how many envelopes a group has filled in one hour. Indeed, the group simply has more resources available (in this example, in terms of person-hours of time), and it would hardly be surprising that the group had filled more envelopes (nor would it be interesting). Thus, in this case, the second option might be better. Indeed, one could compare the performance of an individual with the average performance per group member, which would be fairer and more interesting.

In many cases, however, the third option would be preferable. This option can be described as taking some *statistical aggregate* of individuals and comparing it with a group's performance. In Steiner's (1972) terms, this statistical aggregate of individuals *should present the group's potential performance.* When we compare this potential performance with the group's actual performance, we can see whether there is a process loss or perhaps a process gain. If the group performs better than the (appropriate) aggregation of individuals, there is a process gain. When it performs worse, there is a process loss. The appropriate way to aggregate individual performances should, of course, depend on the group task. In parentheses, therefore, are the tasks for which a particular baseline is appropriate (and these should come as no surprise).

Integration

Evaluating a group's output thus requires determining a dimension on which to evaluate it and a standard against which to evaluate it. In both the cases of choosing a performance dimension and a comparison standard, the choice should first depend on research interests. For example, a researcher who studies performance in ongoing teams might be more interested in learning than a researcher who studies decision-making in an *ad hoc* laboratory group. Second, a choice of performance dimension and comparison standards should, as discussed above, depend on the characteristics of the group task.

Group context

Groups do not exist in isolation, but function in a certain context. Group context is the fifth and final element of our framework. It is a broad term, and consists of the *physical* and *social* environment of the group. The context is important for two reasons. First, the context will influence the group. Second, groups have to manage their contacts with the environment (Ancona & Caldwell, 1988).

If the group context influences the group, we talk about top-down effects (i.e., the higher level influences the lower level). This may happen in a number of different ways, corresponding to the four other elements of the framework.

(1)   The context influences group members. First, the context will determine group membership. Groups often cannot decide for themselves who will be a group member, but rather people are assigned to groups (e.g., by the management of a company, by the teacher of a course). Even when groups can recruit their own members, they are limited in their choice of group members, because of availability of potential members in the environment. Also, members may leave the group because other groups (in

the environment) are more attractive (Chapter 2; Moreland & Levine, 1982). Second, the context may affect group members because it does or does not supply resources to members. A company might, for example, offer training to group members, thereby (it hopes) increasing its resources (arrow 1 in Figure 3.1). The environment may also affect group member motivation (e.g., by offering rewards) or group member moods (e.g., by providing a nice office).

(2) The context will often determine the group task. Group tasks are usually assigned rather than chosen by the group itself. This holds for groups in a company, but also for groups in a laboratory that are given a specific task to perform, or for classroom groups. Even if groups have some leeway in how to perform a task, the context will offer constraints in what they should do and how they should do it.

(3) The context will influence group processes. In fact, much of the work we will discuss in the chapters to follow is about factors outside the control of the group that influence group processes and thereby the output of the group. For example, a group may be put under time pressure, and this will affect group processes: people will start working harder, there will be more pressure to reach quick consensus, and interaction patterns will change (see e.g., Kelly & Loving, 2004; Kruglanski, Pierro, Mannetti, & De Grada, 2006). Organizational culture provides another example. Some organizations (e.g., the military) are more hierarchical than others (e.g., a software firm), and this has implications for the way in which group members interact. A lower ranked soldier might not readily criticize an officer, whereas a starting software developer might be more inclined to criticize his manager. A further example is that often there are other groups in the environment, and the presence of other groups affects group processes (see Chapter 10).

(4) Other people or groups evaluate group outputs. Evidently, because the group context influences group members, the group task, and group interaction processes, the context will affect group outcomes as well. However, usually people outside the group also evaluate group outcomes, and therefore largely determine the degree to which a group has succeeded in its task.

So far, it seems that groups are only passive targets of influence and that they have little control over their environment. However, groups may in fact actively try to influence their environment. For example, group members may try to control which resources the group has (see arrow 1 in Figure 3.1), groups may try to buffer themselves from outside influences (e.g., resist time pressure), and groups may try to control group membership (having a say in who is member of the group and who is not). All these examples are activities that group members perform to manage the environment of the group (Ancona & Caldwell, 1988; see Chapter 10).

Conclusion

We have gone through the five elements of the theoretical framework. These five elements will return to varying degrees in the chapters that follow. To give an overview, the next chapter (Chapter 4, on social facilitation) is about effects of the context on individual performance (arrow 1 in Figure 3.1) and about the way in which individual group members influence each other (arrow 3). Chapter 5 will be on motivation, discussing motivation losses and motivation gains in groups, mostly in the context of fairly simple physical tasks. Chapters 6 through 8 discuss various types of group tasks (group idea-generation, group decision-making, group problem-solving and judgment), and group interaction processes that are relevant to these tasks. Finally, groups are put in a broader context in Chapters 9 and 10, in which we discuss teamwork and leadership (Chapter 9) and the social context of teamwork (Chapter 10). Chapter 11 discusses how group processes change when groups use different communication media (e.g., computers or videoconferencing).

Chapter summary

(1) Groups are multilevel systems, in which members are part of groups and groups are part of the environment. This implies that entities at different levels have characteristics (e.g., individual personality, group permeability, organizational culture), and that there are relations between the levels.

(2) Within groups, there can be top-down effects (when variables at the group level influence group members or relations between variables at the individual level) and bottom-up effects (when individual-level variables influence group-level outcomes). One fundamental question is that of how individual contributions are combined into group outcomes.

(3) There are five elements to a general framework of group performance: group members, group tasks, group interaction processes, group output, and group context.

(4) Group members provide the necessary resources for task performance. Group members also have individual motives, personalities and moods, and these also affect group performance.

(5) Potential group performance is a function of group member resources and task demands. Steiner distinguished among additive, conjunctive, disjunctive, and discretionary tasks.

(6) Actual group performance is a function of potential performance and group processes. Process losses occur when actual performance lies below potential performance, and process gains occur when actual performance lies above potential performance. Process losses (gains) consist of motivation and coordination losses (gains).

(7) Group output can be judged on different dimensions (task-related performance, affective outcomes and learning) at both the individual and group levels. Group performance can be judged against different standards, including objective standards, relative standards, and relative to individual performance. The choice for output dimension and performance standard should be based on research objectives and characteristics of the group task.

(8) Group context consists of the physical and social environment of the group and influences all other elements of the framework (group members, group tasks, group interaction, group output). Groups also perform activities to influence their environment.

Exercises

(1) What kind of top-down and bottom-up processes might occur in a classroom setting?

(2) Suppose you are in a group that has to perform a research project. This task consists of several subtasks and is thus divisible (e.g., developing a research question and hypotheses, developing a research design, writing a report). List the different subtasks, and classify each subtask in Steiner's task classification.

(3) Suppose a team in a company has to develop a new marketing strategy. In what different ways might the performance of the team be judged?

(4) What will happen if two groups simultaneously work on the same task? How will this affect individual outcomes (e.g., motivation, satisfaction) and group outcomes (performance, cohesion)?

Further reading

On multilevel theories and methods

Klein, K. J., & Kozlowski, S. W. J. (Eds.) (2000). *Multilevel theory, research, and methods in organizations: Foundations, extensions, and new directions.* San Francisco: Jossey-Bass.

Theoretical model of group performance

Steiner, I. D. (1972). *Group process and productivity.* New York: Academic Press.

Audience and co-action effects 4

Is a professional baseball player more likely to hit the ball when he is training on his own or when he is playing a game in front of a crowd of forty thousand people? Is a professional piano player more likely to make a mistake while practicing a complicated piece at home or while performing it on stage? How about an amateur piano player who is trying to do the same? Are amateur runners more likely to finish the marathon when they are running alone or when they have a companion who is also struggling to make it? These are the types of question we will deal with in this chapter. They have no easy answers.

Yet these questions are of fundamental importance for group task performance. Indeed, when a group member is performing a task, other group members will often be present. Task performance in the presence of others will be the topic of this chapter. Studies using this *audience paradigm* have participants work on a task while others (may) observe them. Further, when group members perform similar tasks alongside one another, there will be mutual influence among group members. In a *co-action paradigm* participants work on a task in the presence of others who are working on the same task. These others may at the same time be an audience that can observe the participant.

When conceptualized within the framework that was introduced in Chapter 3, the presence of others in the audience paradigm is a contextual factor that influences individual task performance (arrow 1 in Figure 3.1). The co-action paradigm involves a mutual influence of group members who work alongside one another, and thus is linked to arrow 3 in Figure 3.1. We will start the chapter with audience effects that may be obtained in the audience paradigm but also in co-action paradigms. In the second half of the chapter we will consider issues that are only relevant to co-action paradigms.

Audience effects: Social facilitation and inhibition

Zajonc's Puzzle

Social psychology is sometimes defined as the scientific study of how the thoughts, feelings, and behaviors of people are influenced by the actual, imagined, or implied presence of others (Allport, 1954). The study of audience effects is exactly that, and can thus be considered fundamental to social psychology. In fact, the study of audience effects dates back to 1898, when Triplett carried out experiments on the effects of the presence of others on task performance. He noted that adolescents could spin fishing reels more quickly when working in co-acting pairs than when working alone. This effect that people perform better in the presence of others has been termed *social facilitation*.

Let us, however, start our discussion of social facilitation a bit later in time, in 1965 to be precise. In that year, Robert Zajonc published an influential paper in *Science*, entitled "Social Facilitation." In that classic paper, Zajonc noted an interesting empirical puzzle, and proposed a solution. The puzzle was that the presence of others, in both audience and co-action paradigms, sometimes led to improved performance (i.e., social facilitation) and sometimes to deteriorated perform-ance (often termed *social inhibition*). Before turning to Zajonc's solution to this problem, let's first consider some examples of early research.

Travis (1925) had participants perform a pursuit-rotor task. Par-ticipants had to follow a revolving target by means of a stylus, and if they were even momentarily off target, the revolution counted as an error. First, participants were trained extensively until they reached a stable level of performance. Next, they performed the same task, first alone and then in front of an audience. Travis found a clear improve-ment in performance when they performed the task in the presence of an audience. Pessin (1933) asked participants to learn nonsense syl-lables either alone or in the presence of an audience. The participants learning alone needed 9.85 trials to learn a seven-item list; those learning in front of an audience needed 11.27 trials on average. Further, participants in the audience condition made more errors than those in the alone condition. Allport (1920) had participants do a number of tasks, including chain word association, multiplication, problem-solving, and judgments of odors and weights. Some of his participants worked alone while others worked in co-action. Allport found that participants working in co-action performed better on some tasks (chain word association and multiplication), whereas participants

BOX 4.1.

Social facilitation in animals

Consider the following experiment that Chen (1937) performed with ants. Chen placed ants in a bottle half filled with sandy soil. The ants were left in the bottle for six hours, and during that time their behavior was watched. The researcher was interested in nest-building, and noted when the insects started to excavate sand, and after six hours carefully weighed how much sand was excavated. Each of the ants was watched in isolation, and performing in pairs. There was very clear evidence of social facilitation: Ants working alone started excavating later, and excavated less sand than when performing in co-action. For example, performance was about 0.25 grams excavated for individual ants and 0.75 grams for ants performing in dyads: clearly a spectacular difference!

However, also in animals the presence of others sometimes interferes with performance. Gates and Allee (1933) compared data for cockroaches learning a maze in isolation, groups of two, and groups of three. They had five trials, and their data are displayed in Figure 4.1. Clearly, the cockroaches learned more effectively (needed less time) in isolation.

The fact that social facilitation and inhibition occurs both in humans and in other animals indicates that it is quite a pervasive and fundamental effect. Indeed, Zajonc (1980) argues that this indicates that the social facilitation effect is primitive and unlearned.

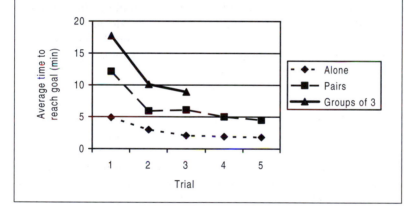

FIGURE 4.1.

Maze learning in isolated and grouped cockroaches (after Gates & Allee, 1933). Taken from: Zajonc, R. B. (1965). Social facilitation. *Science*, *149*, 269–274. Reprinted with permission from AAAS.

working alone performed better on other tasks (problem-solving). In Box 4.1 are some other striking examples, this time with insects.

Zajonc (1965) not only noted that the presence of others yielded inconsistent effects, but also proposed a solution (see Figure 4.2). In his *drive theory* he proposed that the presence of others increases generalized drive or arousal and makes people work harder. Further, he suggested that this enhanced drive especially increases the speed, strength, and probability of the *dominant response* in a particular situation. A dominant response is the response that is most likely to be emitted in a particular situation, for example because it is well-learned, based on habits or routines, or innately likely to be emitted.

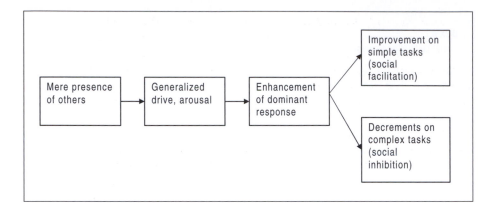

FIGURE 4.2.
Zajonc's (1965)
drive theory.

What Zajonc argued next is that the presence of others will lead to performance improvement if the dominant response is correct or appropriate; however, it will lead to performance deterioration if the dominant response is incorrect or inappropriate. Thus, Zajonc predicted that for well-learned or easy tasks, the presence of others should be beneficial, because it elicits an appropriate dominant response. However, for new and complex tasks, the dominant response will generally be inappropriate, causing performance impairment.

This explanation nicely fits the earlier reported data. Spinning a fishing reel (as in Triplett's, 1898, work) is an easy task, in which the presence of others facilitates task performance. Also, Travis' (1925) results on the pursuit rotor task can be understood. These participants had learned the task so well before they were tested that the correct response had become dominant, and therefore their performance was facilitated in the presence of others. Other simple tasks, such as making chain associations and simple multiplication, also are facilitated (cf. Allport, 1920). However, learning a new task, for which the correct response has not yet become dominant, is impaired when one is scrutinized by an audience, as Pessin (1933) had found. Finally, performing more complex tasks, such as solving problems, is also impaired while one is in the presence of others, because the dominant response is likely to be incorrect (cf. Allport's, 1920, results).

Subsequent tests of Zajonc's drive theory also were supportive. Consider a study performed by Zajonc and Sales (1966). Participants in that study first were confronted with 10 different nonsense words. These words were shown on cards and read aloud by the experimenter. The participant had to repeat each word once. However, the words differed in how many times each was presented (1, 2, 4, 8, or 16 times). After exposure to these words, participants were asked to recognize the newly learned words while they were briefly projected on a screen. On some of the trials, called pseudo-recognition trials, irregular black lines were shown for 0.01 s (too brief to recognize) and on these trials participants had to guess which word they saw. The recognition task was done either while the participant was alone in the room or while two other people were in the same room watching the participant.

What Zajonc and Sales (1966) reasoned was that words that were presented more often would become a more dominant response during the pseudo-recognition trials. Words that were presented only once or twice, on the other hand, should not be a very dominant response. When Zajonc's theory about social facilitation is correct, the presence of an audience should enhance the emission of dominant responses: Words that were presented more often during learning should be given more often with the presence of an audience as compared to when participants were working alone. The results of the study are shown in Figure 4.3. As you can see, the pattern fits the predictions. For the participants working in front of an audience, the effect of presentation frequency is stronger than for those working alone.

Problems with Zajonc's theory

Zajonc's (1965) theory and subsequent results look very promising. Puzzle solved, one might think. However, nothing is further from the

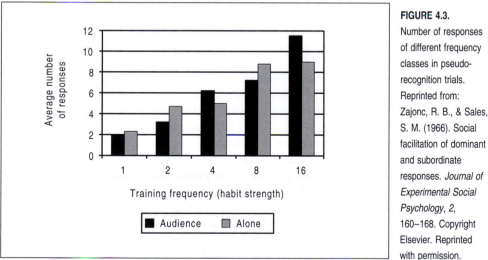

FIGURE 4.3.

Number of responses of different frequency classes in pseudo-recognition trials. Reprinted from: Zajonc, R. B., & Sales, S. M. (1966). Social facilitation of dominant and subordinate responses. *Journal of Experimental Social Psychology, 2,* 160–168. Copyright Elsevier. Reprinted with permission.

truth. In fact, several of Zajonc's ideas have not received unequivocal support, and have aroused fierce debates. Further, a number of alternative accounts have been suggested, and these differ in important facets from Zajonc's theory. We first go into two problems with Zajonc's theory, before moving on to discuss two alternative theoretical accounts of social facilitation.

The role of arousal

Zajonc (1965) originally proposed that the mere presence of others is a source of arousal (or drive), and that presence alone would be sufficient to induce arousal (also Zajonc, 1980). However, Bond and Titus (1983) reviewed the evidence, and concluded that the mere presence of others does *not* necessarily lead to physiological arousal. Instead, this effect was very small and was found only when one was working on difficult tasks, and not on simple tasks. Thus, it appears that the mere presence of others might not be sufficient to lead to physiological arousal.

More recently, Blascovich, Mendes, Hunter, and Salomon (1999) suggested that the term "arousal" is also too broad and unspecific. Instead, they focused on two patterns of physiological responding, called the *challenge* and *threat* patterns. A challenge response occurs when people perceive that they have sufficient resources to meet situational demands (e.g., when people expect that they will be able to perform the task successfully). A threat response occurs when the people perceive that they lack the necessary resources (e.g., when they believe that they will not successfully perform the task). Moreover, both are accompanied by a specific pattern of physiological reactions. In the case of challenge, the pattern is an increase in cardiac reactivity (e.g., higher heart rate), while blood pressure remains the same. In the case of threat, the pattern is an increase in cardiac reactivity in combination with an *increase* in blood pressure. Blascovich *et al.* (1999) reasoned that the presence of an audience should lead to a challenge response on a well-learned task, but to a threat response on a task that was not well-learned. Using measures of cardiac reactivity and blood pressure, this was exactly what they found.

It thus seems difficult to maintain that the presence of others invariably leads to arousal, and that arousal (or drive) is the cause of social facilitation. However, Zajonc was right when he claimed that the presence of audiences does affect physiological responses in meaningful ways. We will return to this issue later.

Mere presence does not always produce social facilitation

There has also been a considerable amount of debate over whether the mere presence of others (i.e., their simply being there) is sufficient to cause social facilitation effects. For example, Cottrell, Wack, Sekerak, and Rittle (1968) repeated the experiment of Zajonc and Sales (1966) we discussed earlier. However, besides a condition in which participants worked alone and a condition in which participants worked in the presence of two people who were watching them, Cottrell *et al.* (1968) added a third condition. In that condition also two people were present but they were blindfolded and could not watch the participant. It appeared that the social facilitation effect only occurred when the audience could watch the participant. Thus, mere presence is not always sufficient.

Based on these results, one might suppose that social facilitation effects occur only when the audience can actually *evaluate* the participants' task performance (Cottrell, 1972). Thus, the presence of (attentive) others might be associated with the expectation of being evaluated, which is often called *evaluation apprehension*, and this evaluation apprehension might be the cause of social facilitation. Social facilitation might then occur primarily in settings that are competitive or evaluative. However, Bond and Titus (1983) found little support for the idea that social facilitation is related to evaluation apprehension. Further, from a review of the literature Guerin (1986) concluded that the mere presence of others who are *not* watching the participant performing the task sometimes leads to social facilitation. According to Guerin, this occurs when there is uncertainty associated with the observer's behavior. For example, social facilitation effects are found when an inattentive observer is sitting behind the participant, and the participant cannot easily monitor the observer (e.g., Guerin, 1983; Innes & Young, 1975). However, they are not found when observers can easily be monitored and behave in a predictable way (e.g., Guerin, 1983; Klinger, 1969). According to Guerin, the reason is that unpredictable observers make people feel unsafe, and threaten the control one has over the situation. These findings are consistent with an alternative account for social facilitation phenomena: Distraction Conflict Theory.

Distraction conflict theory

Distraction conflict theory was proposed by Baron, Sanders, and colleagues (e.g., Sanders & Baron, 1975; Sanders, Baron, & Moore, 1978) and suggests that social facilitation and inhibition result from

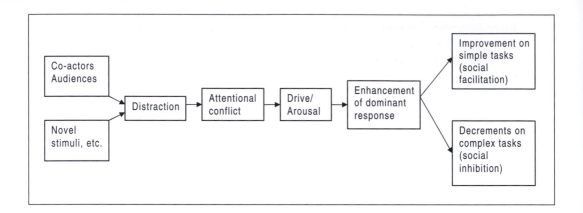

FIGURE 4.4.
Distraction conflict
theory (based on
Baron, 1986).
an *attentional conflict*. It presumes that the presence of an audience or
of co-actors attracts attention. However, at the same time attention is
needed in order to perform the task. When the distraction is hard to
ignore, and when attending to the distracter and the task at the same
time is difficult or impossible, this will lead to an attentional conflict:
People want to attend to two things at the same time, and their
cognitive resources are insufficient. In turn, this attentional conflict
produces arousal and increased drive and effort. As in Zajonc's
theory, this leads to facilitation of simple responses and impairment
of complex responses (see Figure 4.4).

The main difference between Zajonc's drive theory and Distraction
Conflict Theory is that the presence of others has effects only when it
is distracting and leads to an attentional conflict (i.e., *mere* presence is
not enough). For example, an inactive and blindfolded audience
might not be distracting enough to produce social facilitation, which
might explain some of the findings we discussed earlier (e.g., those of
Cottrell *et al.*, 1968). However, the theory is similar to Zajonc's in that
it assumes that the attentional conflict causes elevated levels of
arousal/drive, and that these enhance the dominant response. Distraction Conflict Theory makes several predictions that have received
good support (see Baron, 1986, for an overview). Let's consider three
types of evidence.

The presence of others is distracting

Baron, Moore, and Sanders (1978) had participants perform a paired
associates task. In a learning trial, they were shown pairs of words,
and in a subsequent recall trial they were shown one of the words
and had to give the other. These words were either related (e.g.,
barren – fruitless), making the task easier, or unrelated (e.g., desert –

leading), making it more difficult. The recall trial was done either alone or in front of an audience. After performing the task, participants were asked how much they focused their attention on the task and how much they focused their attention on something else. Further, they were asked to recall features of the task, such as the color of some of the letters. Baron *et al.* found the usual social facilitation effect: As compared to the alone condition, in front of the audience fewer errors were made on the easy recall task but more on the difficult one. More importantly, participants who performed in front of the audience reported less attention for the task and more attention for something else, and they were less accurate in recalling features of the task (also see Strube, Miles, & Finch, 1981).

Non-social distracters produce facilitation and inhibition effects

It is perhaps obvious that distraction produces impairments on difficult tasks: One needs one's attention to perform the task, and distracters make this more difficult. It may be less obvious that distracters produce facilitation on easy tasks. Yet this is exactly what distraction conflict theory predicts: Distraction (arising from both social and non-social sources) increases drive and effort and leads to improved performance on easy and well-learned tasks. One reason is overcompensation: Because people are aware that distracters impair performance, they try harder and overcompensate the negative effects (Sanders & Baron, 1975).

In fact, a number of studies confirm that non-social distracters, such as loud noises or flashing lights, also produce facilitation on easy and inhibition on difficult tasks. For example, Sanders and Baron (1975) asked participants to do either a simple number-copying task or a complex one, in which numbers had to be transformed to other numbers using a complicated coding scheme. While performing this task, participants were distracted or not. When a signal sounded, the distracted participants were asked to look up from their work and look at a painted X on the wall. Not surprisingly, participants in the difficult task conditions performed worse under distraction. In line with distraction conflict theory, however, those in the easy task condition actually performed *better* when being distracted.

The role of attentional conflict

Distraction conflict theory predicts that the presence of an audience only produces social facilitation when attending to it conflicts with task demands. Thus, when no attentional conflict is present, there should be no social facilitation. Groff, Baron, and Moore (1983) investigated this in a clever study. Participants watched a face on a television screen, and occasionally (when a tone sounded) had to rate how positive or negative it appeared. At the same time, they were asked to squeeze a soft plastic bottle with each signal. The main measure of social facilitation was the intensity and latency of the squeeze response, which becomes faster and more intense with increased drive.

There were three conditions. In condition 1 (control condition), there was no audience. In condition 2, participants made the ratings while someone was watching and was presumably evaluating the participants' performance. This person was seated in such a way that the participant had to look away from the television screen in order to see the audience (high-conflict condition). In condition 3, there also was an audience, but the face on the television screen was that of the watching person. In this low-conflict condition, participants could thus watch the audience and perform the task at the same time – they could look at either the audience or the television and see the same face – and there was no attentional conflict. Results showed that participants squeezed the bottle with more vigor and faster in the high-conflict condition than in the other conditions. Note that both in the low-conflict and the high-conflict condition an audience was present, but only when watching the audience conflicted with task performance (i.e., rating the face) did it produce social facilitation. This finding clearly contradicts Zajonc's idea that mere presence is sufficient for social facilitation to occur, but is consistent with Distraction Conflict Theory.

Self-Efficacy Theory

The findings described in the previous section seem to offer good support for distraction conflict theory. However, there is another account for social facilitation and inhibition phenomena, which is *self-efficacy theory*. Self-efficacy theory distinguishes two related expectancies: *efficacy expectancy*, which reflects a person's belief that s/he is capable of performing a required behavior (often referred to as *self-efficacy*), and *outcome expectancy*, which reflects the belief of a person that behavior will result in certain (positive or negative) outcomes (Bandura, 1977). The theory argues that people are motivated to perform a task (and will perform well) to the extent that they believe that they can actually perform the required behavior (i.e., high self-efficacy), and that performing the task will result in positive rather than negative outcomes (i.e., positive outcome expectancy).

Sanna (1992; Sanna & Shotland, 1990) has applied these ideas to social facilitation and inhibition phenomena. He argued that the presence of others is associated with certain positive and negative outcomes (i.e., outcome expectancies), such as approval and disapproval of the audience. Whether one expects positive outcomes (approval) or negative outcomes (disapproval) depends on efficacy expectations. With high self-efficacy, one will generally expect to succeed at the task, and consequently the presence of others leads to the anticipation of positive outcomes (e.g., praise). This will motivate people to perform the task. However, with low self-efficacy, one will generally expect to fail, and the presence of others will lead to negative outcome expectancies, which makes people less motivated to perform the task and will lead to performance decrements. Thus, it is not evaluation apprehension *per se* that is important (i.e., just the expectation of being evaluated); rather it is the *valence* of these expected evaluations that drives social facilitation (positive outcome expectancies) and inhibition (negative outcome expectancies).

Two types of evidence support Self-Efficacy Theory. First, some studies have manipulated efficacy expectancy, by giving participants false feedback about task performance. For example, in one study (Sanna & Shotland, 1990), participants had to memorize a list of 20 words, and were subsequently asked to recall as many words as they could. There first was a practice trial, after which some participants received false failure feedback (they were told that they scored below average), some received false success feedback (they were told that they scored above average), and some received no feedback. Next, they were asked to do two more recall tasks. During recall, some participants were observed by an evaluator, while others worked alone. Failure feedback was found to lead to lower efficacy expectations and to negative outcome expectations, whereas success feedback led to higher efficacy expectations and positive outcome expectations (as compared to the "no feedback" condition). Performance feedback did not affect recall of participants who worked alone. However, the expectation to succeed led to improved performance when watched by an audience, whereas the expectation to fail led to deteriorated performance when watched by an audience (Figure 4.5). Note that neither Zajonc's drive theory, nor distraction conflict theory can explain these findings. Both these theories argue that audiences enhance the tendency to give a dominant response. However, in Sanna and Shotland's experiment, all participants performed the exact same task, and there were no differences between the conditions in what the dominant response would be.

FIGURE 4.5.

Recall performance as
a function of (false)
feedback and the
presence of an
audience (data from
Sanna & Shotland,
1990).

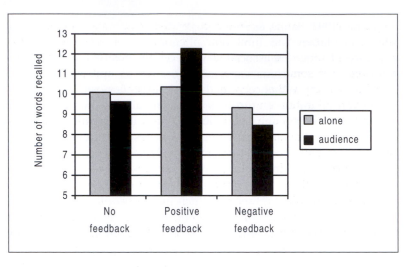

The second line of evidence concerns the effects of easy and difficult tasks on outcome expectancies and performance. Sanna (1992)
has shown that (1) easy tasks lead to expectations to succeed, whereas
difficult tasks lead to expectations to fail; (2) the presence of an
audience leads to positive outcome expectancies when one is working
on an easy task, but to negative outcome expectancies when working
on a difficult task; and (3) high efficacy expectations as well as positive
outcome expectations are associated with better performance. Thus,
according to these results, audiences enhance performance on easy
tasks because on these tasks people believe that they will succeed,
believe that they will be evaluated positively, and thus perform better.

As a final note on self-efficacy theory, consider again the results
found by Blascovich *et al.* (1999). They found that the presence of an
audience led to a challenge response when participants performed a
well-learned task, but to a threat response when participants performed a novel task. These findings nicely fit self-efficacy theory. A
well-learned task should be associated with expectations of success,
and people should believe that they will be able to perform the task –
and feel challenged rather than threatened. However, on a novel task,
participants should expect to fail, and show a threat rather than a
challenge response.

Taking stock

What should we make of all of this? Literally hundreds of studies
have examined social facilitation and inhibition over the course of

more than 100 years, and we have discussed three theories that attempt to account for them. There are inconsistencies, debates, and the issue of social facilitation versus inhibition still is not completely resolved. Yet some conclusions can be drawn, and perhaps these conclusions imply that there are two different types of social facilitation and inhibition effects.

First, the presence of others is often associated with distraction. When being watched, people have a tendency to monitor the behavior and reactions of the audience. Further, they perhaps worry about what the audience thinks, they may attempt to make a good impression on the audience (e.g., Bond, 1982; Carver & Scheier, 1981), and they may start thinking about their own behavior (e.g., Baumeister, 1984). All of this may distract them from the task that they are performing. The effects of distraction on task performance depend on characteristics of the task. Thus, distraction directly interferes with task performance on some tasks, because one needs full attention to perform these tasks. However, at the same time distraction can motivate people to work harder to compensate for the distraction, and people may narrow their attention to some task aspects. When the task is relatively simple, a narrow range of attention and increased effort may lead to superior performance while being watched (also see Huguet, Galvaing, Monteil, & Dumas, 1999).

Second, audiences often have the capacity to evaluate performance. In itself, this may be distracting, but it also implies that it becomes more important to perform well. The reason is that task performance will be associated with positive and negative outcomes, such as praise or criticism. This will make people work harder (in order to receive praise instead of criticism) in situations in which they believe they are capable of performing well (i.e., with high self-efficacy). However, audiences may cause a threat response and deteriorated performance in situations where people have low self-efficacy: they "choke" under pressure.

Co-action effects: Social comparison processes

The co-action paradigm differs from the audience paradigm in one important way: People working in co-action potentially have information about how well others are performing. As a consequence, they can compare their own performance with that of others. How does knowing the performance of others impact one's own performance? This issue is central to social comparison theory (Festinger, 1954), which we discussed briefly in Chapter 1.

Social comparison theory assumes that people are motivated to compare their performance with that of others. Indeed, often there are no objective standards of performance, and the only way to assess how well one is doing is by comparing one's own performance with that of others. For example, if you are asked to finish as many anagrams as possible within 10 minutes and you finish 12, does this mean that you have done well? The only way of answering that question is by comparing your performance with that of others.

Social comparison information as distraction

One way in which social comparisons might affect performance is that social comparison information (i.e., information about how another person is doing) is distracting. Presuming that people are motivated to engage in social comparisons, one has to monitor the performance of co-actors to see how well they are doing. This may be a source of distraction, in which case distraction conflict theory would predict that it leads to social facilitation and inhibition phenomena.

Sanders *et al.* (1978) asked participants to do a simple or a complex digit-copying task. In one condition participants worked alone, in another condition there was a co-actor who performed the same task, and in a final condition there was a co-actor who supposedly performed a different task. Of course, social comparison information is relevant only if a co-actor performs the same task. Sanders *et al.* found that, as compared to the alone condition, participants copied more digits in the simple task condition when their co-actor worked on the same task, but not when the co-actor worked on a different task. In the complex task condition, more errors were made when a co-actor performed the same task, but not when a co-actor performed a different task. Finally, there was evidence for distraction only when the co-actor performed the same task: participants remembered fewer details of the task, and they were quite accurate in estimating the performance of the co-actor. Thus, this study indicates that social comparison information can be a source of distraction.

Social comparison information and competition

Festinger's (1954) social comparison theory makes two other assumptions. The first is that people are especially motivated to compare their performance with that of *similar* others. Thus, a female runner will compare her lap times with those of another woman, rather than with those of a man; an amateur piano player will compare her performance with that of another amateur, rather than with that of a professional concert pianist. The reason is (at least in part) that comparisons with similar others are more informative (e.g., *of course* a professional pianist makes fewer errors). Second, the theory argues that people are motivated to perform upward social comparisons, and compare themselves with others who are slightly better than we are: "an individual is oriented toward some point on the ability continuum slightly better than his own" (Festinger, 1954, p. 126). Thus, when a co-actor is performing slightly better than oneself, one will tend to compete with that co-actor, and try harder to perform as well or better. However, this competition will not occur when a co-actor performs worse (i.e., one does not have to exert more effort to beat the co-actor) or much better (i.e., the co-actor would be too dissimilar and it would be impossible to beat him or her).

Seta (1982) asked participants to press four buttons in a left-to-right sequence as often as they could for 30 min (quite a boring task, really). After seven completed sequences, a tone sounded, giving participants performance feedback. Participants worked either alone or in co-acting pairs. However, for the co-actor a (different pitched) tone sounded (depending on condition) after seven, four, or two completed sequences (the FR7, FR4, and FR2 conditions, respectively). Participants did not know the feedback frequency of the co-actor, and therefore assumed it must be identical to their own. Thus, they should come to the conclusion that the co-actor performed similarly to them in the FR7 condition (where the feedback frequency was similar). They should conclude that their partner was slightly better (FR4 condition) or much better (FR2 condition) when he or she received performance feedback more often. Seta predicted that participants should be especially motivated to compete with the co-actor when the co-actor was slightly superior (in the FR4 condition), but less so when the co-actor was highly superior (FR2 condition). As you can see in Figure 4.6, the participants indeed completed most sequences (a full 1,119) when they thought that their co-actor was slightly superior (in the FR4 condition).

Thus, co-action may stimulate competition and better performance especially when one's co-actor is slightly superior (also Munkes & Diehl, 2003). It should be noted, though, that this effect has been observed in fairly simple tasks, in which the main determinant of behavior was effort. It is unlikely that competition leads to improved performance on tasks in which effort is less crucial.

FIGURE 4.6.

Number of completed
sequences by
condition (data from
Seta, 1982).

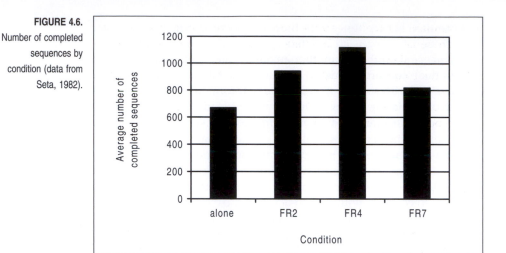

Chapter summary

(1) Performance in the presence of others can lead to performance improvements (social facilitation) and to performance decrements (social inhibition).

(2) Zajonc's drive theory assumes that the presence of others causes an increase in generalized drive and arousal, which in turn leads to a tendency to give a dominant response. When the dominant response is appropriate (e.g., with simple and well-learned tasks), the presence of others leads to improved performance; when it is inappropriate (with difficult and novel tasks), it leads to performance decrements.

(3) Distraction conflict theory argues that the presence of others attracts attention, and that the resulting attentional conflict increases generalized drive and the emission of the dominant response. In support of this theory, it has been found that the presence of others is distracting, and that it leads to social facilitation/inhibition only when there is an attentional conflict.

(4) According to self-efficacy theory, the presence of others is associated with outcome expectancies. With high self-efficacy, outcome expectancies are positive and these lead to performance improvements. With low self-efficacy, outcome expectancies are negative and lead to performance decrements. The theory is supported by data showing that task difficulty associates with

(positive versus negative) outcome expectancies, and by data showing that social facilitation is found when self-efficacy is high, while social inhibition is found when it is low.

(5)   In the co-action paradigm, social comparison information can be available. This may serve as a source of distraction, but can also stimulate competition. This might lead to improved performance especially in situations in which co-actors are slightly superior.

Exercises

(1)   What do you think, after reading this chapter, about the examples we started out with? Is a baseball player more likely to hit the ball and is a piano player more likely to make a mistake when playing in front of an audience? And how about the amateur runner who has a co-actor who is also struggling to make it?

(2)   Do you think there are two types of social facilitation, or just one?

(3)   Can social facilitation in animals (such as insects; see Box 4.1) be explained with the same theories as social facilitation in humans?

(4)   Have you ever experienced that your performance was facilitated or inhibited because of the presence of others? Can you explain why this happened?

Further reading

Zajonc's original paper on social facilitation

Zajonc, R. B. (1965). Social facilitation. *Science, 149,* 269–274.

Distraction conflict theory

Baron, R. S. (1986). Distraction-conflict theory: Progress and problems. In L. Berkowitz (Ed.), *Advances in experimental social psychology* (Vol. 19, pp. 1–40). New York: Academic Press.

Self-efficacy theory

Sanna, L. J. (1992). Self-efficacy theory: Implications for social facilitation and social loafing. *Journal of Personality and Social Psychology, 5*, 774–786.

Social comparison theory

Festinger, L. A. (1954). A theory of social comparison processes. *Human Relations, 7*, 117–140.

Motivation and group performance: Individual effort on collective tasks

5

Have you ever worked on a group project and felt that you were clearly putting in more effort than other group members? What was your reaction? Did you put in extra effort to compensate for the lack of effort of others, or did you also start to work less hard? Alternatively, have you ever been tempted, while working in a group, to let other group members do most of the hard work? The topic of this chapter is motivation of group members, and it considers the situations in which group members do or do not work hard.

The research in this chapter is about individual effort while working on collective tasks. Mostly, the research described in this chapter has compared what group members are in principle capable of given their individual abilities (i.e., the individual's potential performance) with the actual performance of these individuals when they work in a group (see Chapter 3). In the first part of the chapter we consider situations in which group members work less hard when in a group as compared to when working alone. We thus consider motivation losses. In the second part we will consider motivation gains, and discuss the conditions under which group members actually work harder than individuals working alone. As in Chapter 4, we begin with one of the earliest experiments in social psychology.

Motivation losses in groups

The Ringelmann effect

In the 1880s, Ringelmann, a professor working in France, carried out experiments about the relation between group size and performance. He had groups of different sizes pull a rope as hard as they could. Ringelmann (1913) noticed that group performance was not simply

FIGURE 5.1.

The Ringelmann effect:
Decreasing
performance as a
function of group size
(after Ringelmann,
1913).

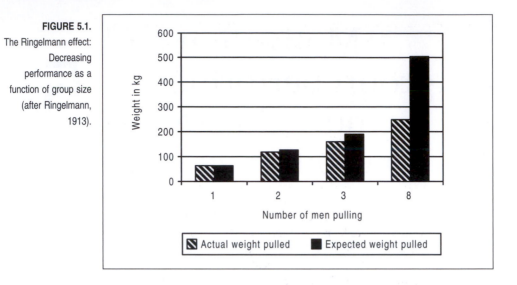

the sum of individual performance of the group members. Instead, while an individual pulling alone could on average manage 63 kg, a dyad managed only 118 (instead of $2 \times 63 = 126$). Further, the difference increased with group size. A group of three pulled only 160 kg (instead of $3 \times 63 = 189$), and a group of 8 only pulled 248 kilos (whereas $8 \times 63 = 504$!). This inverse relation between group size and individual performance is known as the *Ringelmann effect* (Figure 5.1). The Ringelmann effect is by no means limited to rope-pulling. Instead, it has been found on tasks such as pumping air (Kerr, 1983), clapping and cheering (Latané, Williams, & Harkins, 1979), and folding papers (Zaccaro, 1984).

The Ringelmann effect represents a case of process loss: The actual performance of a group is below its potential performance (see Chapter 3). The question is: How can this be explained? Why do eight men pulling a rope pull at only half their potential? When you remember Chapter 3, you will probably say: motivation and coordination loss. And indeed, these effects can be explained by a loss of motivation of group members and/or inadequate coordination among group members.

Distinguishing between coordination and motivation losses

Motivation losses occur when group members exert less effort when they are in a group as compared to when they are working alone.

Coordination losses occur when the input of different group members is not optimally transformed into group output. In the case of rope-pulling, coordination loss would occur when group members do not at exactly the same time pull in exactly same direction. Both motivation and coordination losses contribute to the Ringelmann effect.

Ingham, Levinger, Graves, and Peckham (1974) considered the question of why the Ringelmann effect occurs. They first replicated Ringelmann's (1913) original findings that groups do not pull as much weight as their combined individual members could, and that the difference increased with group size. Next, they added a different experimental condition. In that condition, called the pseudo-group condition, they only used one real participant in each group, and replaced the other group members with confederates. These confederates only *pretended* to be pulling the rope. In order to prevent the real participant from finding out, everybody wore blindfolds and the confederates made realistic grunts indicating physical exertion. In this way, Ingham *et al.* could estimate how much weight individual group members would pull if they only *thought* that other group members also were pulling. Because only one member was really pulling, there can be no coordination loss due to different members not pulling at the same time or in slightly different directions. Thus, if a group member pulled less weight than when pulling as an individual, this would be evidence for motivation loss. The pseudo-groups were compared with performance of real groups, in which all group members were real participants, and all were really pulling the rope; in these real groups there can be motivation as well as coordination losses.

Ingham *et al.*'s (1974) results are shown in Figure 5.2. First, note that there was process loss in the pseudo-group condition. Thus, the Ringelmann effect seems partly due to motivation losses. Further, the process loss was larger in the real group condition, indicating that in real groups there also is process loss due to ineffective coordination (members not pulling at the same time, or pulling in different directions). Finally, the process loss appears to increase with group size, but at a decelerating rate. Motivation losses in the pseudo-group condition do not seem to increase beyond a group size of three.

Similar experiments were reported by Latané *et al.* (1979). Instead of rope pulling, they used shouting and clapping loudness as their dependent variable. Groups of six were put in a room, seated in a semicircle, and given a microphone. Then they were asked to shout or clap alone, in pairs, in groups of four, or in groups of six. As was found by Ingham *et al.* (1974), Latané and colleagues found that

FIGURE 5.2.

Group process loss for real and pseudo-groups. Taken from: Ingham, A. G., Levinger, G., Graves, J., & Peckham, V. (1974). The Ringelmann effect: Studies of group size and group performance. *Journal of Experimental Social Psychology*, *10*, 371–384. Copyright Elsevier. Reprinted with permission.

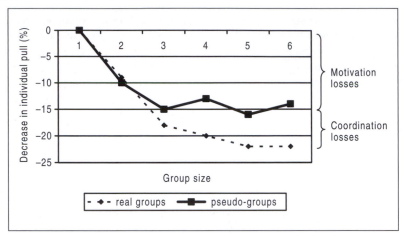

cheering and clapping loudness per person decreased with group size in a decelerating rate: Dyads performed at 71 per cent of their individual capacity, four-person groups at 51 per cent and six-person groups at 40 per cent. This replicates the Ringelmann effect.

In a second experiment, participants came to the lab in groups of six, were seated in a semicircle around a microphone, and were requested to shout as loudly as they could. All participants were wearing blindfolds and headsets (so they could not see or hear each other). Via their headsets, participants were instructed to shout as loudly as they could into the microphone. On some trials, participants were told that they would be shouting alone, and on other trials they were told that they were shouting as a group. However, on some of these "group trials" participants were really shouting alone, while they thought that they shouted as a group (the pseudo-group condition). Because they were shouting alone in that condition, any reduction in loudness would be due to motivation loss. When really shouting together, there could be both motivation and coordination loss. Results of this study are shown in Figure 5.3. As you can see, results were similar to those found by Ingham *et al.* (1974). Thus, there was evidence for motivation loss in pseudo-groups. In real groups there also was some coordination loss, presumably because people did not shout at exactly the same time.

Social loafing and evaluation

Social loafing is defined as a reduction of effort when one is working in a group as compared to when working alone. But why would people

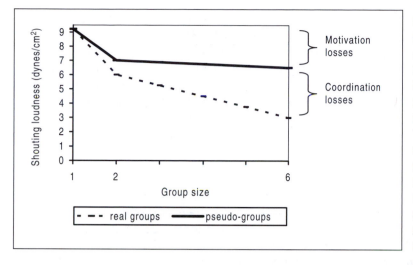

FIGURE 5.3.

Performance per group member. Taken from: Latané, B., Williams, K., & Harkins, S. (1979). Many hands make light the work: The causes and consequences of social loafing. *Journal of Personality and Social Psychology, 37*, 822–832. Copyright American Psychological Association. Reprinted with permission.

reduce their effort when working in a group? In the studies of Ingham *et al.* (1974) and Latané *et al.* (1979), it is easy to understand why coordination loss occurred. In both cases, coordination loss is due to group members not pulling or shouting at exactly the same time. However, what is the reason that group members pulled less hard or shouted less loudly when they merely *thought* they pulled or shouted as a group? Research has shown that lack of identifiability and the inability to evaluate individual contributions is an important factor underlying this motivation loss.

In the shouting experiment of Latané *et al.* (1979), social loafing occurred when groups shared one microphone. It may be that participants failed to work hard because their individual efforts could not be identified (by the other group members or by the experimenter). Shouting loudly or less loudly therefore had no consequences in terms of rewards or punishments. Williams, Harkins, and Latané (1981) tested whether social loafing could be ascribed to lack of identifiability of individual contributions, and whether it could be eliminated by giving participants individual microphones. In experiment 1, Williams *et al.* found that the social loafing disappeared when group members were given individual microphones and when they believed that their individual contributions could always be monitored (regardless of whether one was shouting alone or in a (pseudo-)group).

This first experiment showed that social loafing can be eliminated by making individual contributions identifiable. Next, Williams *et al.* (1981) reasoned that, if lack of identifiability really causes social loafing, than making people believe that their outputs can *never* be monitored, even when they perform alone, should lead to a low level of performance across all group sizes. They set up an experiment with three conditions. Groups of four came to the laboratory, and were given headsets and blindfolds. In condition 1 they were told that their individual contributions were identifiable only when they shouted alone, but not when they shouted in a group. In condition 2 they were told that their individual contributions would always be identifiable, both when shouting alone and when shouting in a group. In condition 3, participants were told that their individual contributions would never be identifiable, either when shouting alone or when shouting in a group. Then all participants shouted alone, in pseudo-dyads, and in pseudo-four-person groups. The sound pressure they produced in the different conditions is shown in Figure 5.4. As is clear, social loafing occurred only when individual contributions were not identifiable. Thus, social loafing occurs when members cannot be held responsible for their individual contributions to the group's performance.

Harkins and Jackson (1985) refined this conclusion by showing that it is not identifiability *per se* that causes social loafing, but rather that it occurs when individual contributions cannot be *evaluated*. Besides being identifiable, evaluation requires that there is some

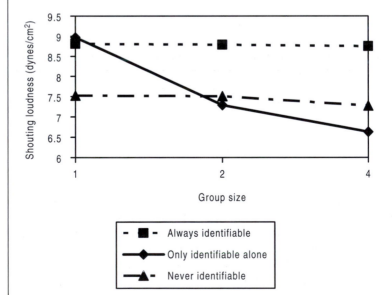

FIGURE 5.4.

Sound pressure as a function of the size of the pseudo-group and identifiability. Taken from: Williams, K. D., Harkins, S., & Latané, B. (1981). Identifiability as a deterrent to social loafing: Two cheering experiments. *Journal of Personality and Social Psychology, 40,* 303–311. Copyright American Psychological Association. Reprinted with permission.

standard against which performance is judged. Harkins and Jackson had participants generate uses for a common object (e.g., What can you do with a brick? What can you do with a newspaper?). Participants sat together in a four-person group at a table and individually wrote down as many uses as they could.

The experiment had four conditions. First, identifiability was manipulated. For some participants, the lists of uses were individually collected, making these participants identifiable. Other participants, however, could put their lists of uses in a common box, so individual contributions could not be identified. This manipulation of identifiability was crossed with a manipulation of evaluation potential. In half the groups, all participants generated uses for the same object. Here evaluation potential is high, because participants can directly compare their performance with the performance of other group members to see whether they have done well or poorly. In the other half, however, each participant had to generate uses for a different object, making evaluation potential low – the performance of others is less relevant when they are generating uses for different objects. The four conditions thus were: identifiable/same object; identifiable/different objects; not identifiable/same object; not identifiable/different objects. Harkins and Jackson expected that social loafing would be prevented only when participants were individually identifiable and when evaluation potential was high, and not when individual performance was identifiable and evaluation potential was low.

Results are shown in Figure 5.5. As you can see, when generating uses for the same object, there clearly was a social loafing effect: Identifiable participants worked harder than those who were not identifiable. However, this effect was not observed for participants working on different objects. Instead, their performance was low regardless of identifiability. The reason appears to be that their contributions could not readily be evaluated. Indeed, doing worse than another group member is not very informative when working on different tasks. Thus, these participants all loafed, because they could not easily be evaluated.

However, even when contributions cannot be evaluated, social loafing does not always occur. The reason is that, besides external reasons (e.g., performance evaluation by the experimenter), there are *internal* reasons to work hard. Thus, social loafing can be attenuated or eliminated when the task is attractive, involving, or interesting (e.g., Brickner, Harkins, & Ostrom, 1986; Smith, Kerr, Markus, & Stasson, 2001; Zaccaro, 1984). Indeed, why loaf and let others do the work when the task is interesting?

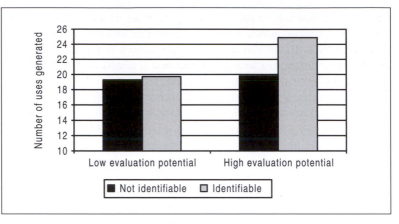

FIGURE 5.5.

Number of uses generated as a function of identifiability and evaluation potential (data from Harkins & Jackson, 1985).

Another reason to work hard (and not loaf) is that one values the performance of the group (also see Karau & Williams, 1993; Williams & Karau, 1991). In Chapter 1 the possibility was discussed that group cohesion is positively associated with performance, because group members would be motivated to work hard for the group (Podsakoff *et al.*, 1997). As was described there, groups performed well when cohesion was high and group members accepted the performance goals given to the group. In that case, group members will be motivated to work toward the group goals, because group performance is important to them (see also Everett, Smith, & Williams, 1992).

Social loafing and social facilitation

Chapter 4 showed that on simple tasks people often work harder and perform *better* while in the presence of others (social facilitation). Yet we see here that people work less hard and perform *worse* when in the presence of others, even though the tasks we discussed were also fairly simple (e.g., shouting, rope-pulling). How can this be explained?

The answer to that question is evaluation potential (e.g., Harkins, 1987; Sanna, 1992). In typical loafing studies, individuals who *can* be evaluated (and in most studies work in a co-action setting) are compared with group members who *cannot* be evaluated; the individuals work harder, and on simple tasks perform better. In typical social facilitation studies, individuals who *cannot* be evaluated (i.e., who work alone) are compared with individuals who *can* be evaluated (i.e., those who work in co-action or in front of an audience), and the latter participants work harder and perform better on simple tasks.

Thus, it might not be working in the presence of others that matters, but rather whether or not one's performance can be evaluated.

Consistent with this idea, Sanna (1992) has proposed that both social loafing and social facilitation can be explained with self-efficacy theory (see Chapter 4). Self-efficacy theory predicts that people will be willing to work hard and perform well when they expect favorable outcomes, such as praise. However, they "choke" when they expect unfavorable outcomes, such as criticism. These outcome expectancies depend on two things, namely the potential to be evaluated and self-efficacy (i.e., the belief that one is able to perform the task). If one can be evaluated but has low self-efficacy (e.g., because one has failed in the past, or because the task is difficult) performance will be low (and lower than in a situation in which one cannot be evaluated). However, if one can be evaluated and has high self-efficacy (e.g., when one has succeeded in the past or when the task is easy) performance will be high (and higher than in a situation in which one cannot be evaluated).

This raises the question of what will happen in a social loafing situation when a difficult task is being used. According to self-efficacy theory, an individual who can be evaluated might develop negative outcome expectancies and will choke under the pressure. However, a group member can hide in the crowd, will not expect negative evaluations, and will thus perform better. If this is true, a reversed social loafing effect can be expected when tasks are difficult: Group members who cannot be evaluated (no outcome expectations) perform better than individuals who can be evaluated (and expect negative evaluations). Both Jackson and Williams (1985) and Sanna (1992) have found exactly this. Thus, on a simple task, participants who could be evaluated performed better than participants who could not be evaluated (both those working alone and those working in groups). However, on a difficult task, participants who could be evaluated performed worse than those who could not be evaluated (again, both those working alone and those working in groups).

Free-riding and the sucker effect

Social loafing occurs because individual performance cannot be evaluated. However, motivation loss sometimes occurs even though individual contributions can be evaluated. Besides social loafing, researchers sometimes distinguish another type of motivation loss, called *free-riding*. Free-riding occurs when group members work less hard because they perceive that their contribution is *dispensable* (Kerr

& Bruun, 1983; Olson, 1965). For example, a woman in a male rope-pulling team might see her contribution as dispensable, because of the greater physical strength of males. This might lead her to exert less effort, because her efforts will not contribute much to the group's success anyway. Or take a situation in which a group is solving a math problem (see also Chapter 8): If group members perceive that other members are better at math, they may have a tendency to sit back and let them solve the problem because they feel that their contribution is not needed. Of course, this may lead to process losses if the contribution of the free-riders (those who do not exert themselves) in fact is *not* dispensable.

The idea of free-riding is closely linked to an economic analysis of *common good dilemmas* (Olson, 1965; Orbell & Dawes, 1981; Stroebe & Frey, 1982). In common good dilemmas, members of a social collective (such as a group, or a society) can contribute resources to establish a common good. If enough people contribute, the common good will be provided to all members of the collective, regardless of whether they contributed or not. An example in society is tax paying. If enough people pay their taxes, the government has enough resources to provide certain common goods, such as an adequate infrastructure. However, tax evaders profit from that infrastructure to the same extent as tax payers. This poses a dilemma, because it would lead people to evade their taxes; however, should too many people do so, the common good cannot be provided, which is detrimental to all members of society. Similarly, in many groups all members profit when a group succeeds at its task, regardless of how much each member has contributed. Further, group members may believe that their contribution (e.g., their effort) is not needed for the group to succeed, and will free-ride on the effort of others, assuming that the others will work hard to assure successful task completion. Of course, if all group members act this way, the group will surely fail.

Kerr and Bruun (1983) applied this analysis to motivation losses in groups. They noted that all social loafing research had used maximizing, additive tasks (Steiner, 1972; Chapter 3): Groups were instructed to pull a rope as hard as they could, shout as loudly as they could, or produce as many uses as they could. In all cases, the performance of the group is given by the sum of individual members' performance. However, there are other task types, including disjunctive tasks (the group's performance depends only on the best-performing member) and conjunctive tasks (the group's performance depends on the worst member). Kerr and Bruun (1983) reasoned that task type (disjunctive vs. conjunctive) in combination with perceived ability (high vs. low) would determine the effort that group members put into a task. When a task is disjunctive, members who perceive themselves to be low on ability will believe that their contribution is not needed, because the group's performance depends only on the best group member. As a consequence, they will work less hard. In contrast, when the task is conjunctive, members who are high on ability might believe that their performance is dispensable: As long as their performance does not drop below the performance of the less able group members, their contribution is not needed for the group to succeed. These effects should occur even when the individual performance of group members is fully identifiable.

Kerr and Bruun (1983) asked participants in one study to blow air into a mouthpiece during a 30 s trial. The amount of air blown was the measure of effort and task performance. After a practice trial, participants received false feedback about their performance, and were told that they either did much better than average or much worse. Next, participants were asked to blow as much air as they could during a group trial. Group members could earn a $10 bonus when their group performed best of all groups in that study. However, for some groups only the performance of the best member counted (disjunctive task) while for other groups only the performance of the worst member counted (conjunctive task). The results are shown in Figure 5.6. Participants who believed that they were not very able reduced their effort for disjunctive tasks; participants who thought they were relatively able reduced their effort for conjunctive tasks. It should be noted that these effects occurred despite the fact that all contributions were identifiable. Thus, the effect is not so much

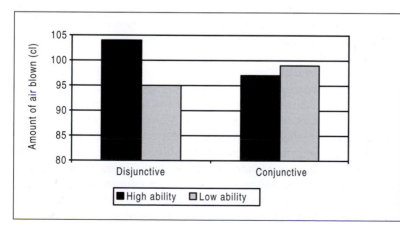

FIGURE 5.6.

Amount of air blown for members of different abilities and under different task types (data from Kerr & Bruun, 1983).

that people "hide in the crowd" (as with lack of identifiability); it is that they perceive their effort to be dispensable.

This might also in part be responsible for the Ringelmann effect. In larger groups, it is more likely that members perceive their contribution to be dispensable. For example, the larger the group, the greater the chance that another group member is better at the task (vs. worse), which would lead to free-riding in disjunctive tasks (vs. conjunctive tasks). Indeed, Kerr and Bruun (1983) found that group members worked less hard when in a four-person group than when in a dyad, even when contributions were perfectly identifiable.

Now suppose that a group member free-rides on the effort of others. How do you think other group members would react? Certainly most people would not like this very much. Free-riding violates important norms, such as the equality norm (everyone should put in similar amounts of effort). These norm violations may lead to anger and to retaliatory behavior to punish the free-rider (e.g., Stouten, De Cremer, & Van Dijk, 2005). However, what kind of effects would a free-rider have on the amount of effort that the other group members put into the task? Would they work harder, or less hard? According to Orbell and Dawes (1981), these other members will feel that the free-rider is taking advantage off them, and are in a situation they called the "sucker role." Kerr (1983) argued that people find this sucker role aversive, because they dislike being exploited. People will therefore withdraw effort when they note that others are free-riding. Thus, they are willing to accept the possibility of negative consequences (worse performance of the group) in order to prevent being pushed into the sucker role. This is what Kerr has called the *sucker effect*: a reduction of effort to prevent being exploited by free-riding fellow group members.

Kerr (1983) reasoned that a sucker effect should only occur when another group member fails to contribute enough even though s/he is *capable* of contributing. When a group member fails to contribute enough because of lack of ability, the sucker effect will not occur. In the latter case the group member is not a free-rider, but simply does not have the ability. Kerr therefore set up an experiment in which he manipulated whether or not another group member contributed enough, and whether this group member did or did not have the capability to contribute (due to personal abilities). Participants supposedly worked in dyads (in reality participants worked alone) and received false information about the capabilities of their partner (either able or unable) and about their partner's task performance (either the partner succeeded or failed on most of the trials). Kerr found that participants reduced their own effort only when the partner was capable but failed to work hard enough. When the partner failed but was unable, participants did not reduce their efforts. In sum, Kerr found evidence for a sucker effect.

Motivation gains in groups

The previous section gave a pessimistic view on group member motivation: People loaf, free-ride, or avoid being the sucker; in any case, they don't work hard when in a group. However, this is not the whole story. Take for example some military teams, in which group members literally are prepared to die for one another. Clearly, they are not "hiding in the crowd" or free-riding on the effort of others. So, can there be situations in which people work extraordinarily hard, precisely because they work in a group? And which situations are those?

Indeed, research has shown two types of motivation gains that can be found in groups: "social compensation" and the "Köhler effect." *Social compensation* occurs when people work hard on a task when they expect that other group members will perform poorly (Williams & Karau, 1991). By working harder, these group members try to compensate the lack of ability or motivation by others, thereby insuring adequate or high task performance of the group. The *Köhler effect*, on the other hand, occurs when group members work harder because they fear that the group would otherwise fail because of them (Köhler, 1926). In this case, the low-ability people especially work harder.

Social compensation

Williams and Karau (1991) describe the following incident. As part of a course, students had to work in groups. A student, who had done exceptionally well before, approached the instructor after class and, fighting back tears, stated that she knew that she would end up doing all the work for the others in her group. She feared that the others would loaf, and that the only way she could possibly get a high mark was to compensate the lack of motivation and ability of the others – which would mean that she would have to work double merely to share an A.

This probably sounds familiar to some students. But is it true? Do group members sometimes work harder to compensate for other members? Williams and Karau (1991) argue that they do, under the following conditions. First, group members have to expect others to perform insufficiently for the group to succeed. Second, these group members must feel that performing well is very important. When these conditions are satisfied, group members may work harder in groups than when working alone.

Williams and Karau (1991) did an experiment in which they varied coworker ability (high vs. low), work condition (individual vs. dyad) and task meaningfulness (high vs. low). What they expected was, first, that people would loaf (or free-ride) when the task was not meaningful, and when the task was meaningful but the coworker had high ability. However, they predicted that in one situation people would work harder in a group than when alone: When the task was meaningful and the coworker was of low ability, because under those conditions group members would compensate the lack of ability of their coworker by working harder.

Participants supposedly worked in dyads (in reality, one dyad member was a confederate and the other was a real participant) and had to generate as many uses as possible for a common object. Either their performance was individually monitored (individual work condition) or the ideas of the two dyad members were put together in one bin, and only group performance was monitored (group condition). Further, the task was made either meaningful, by stating that performance on this task was related to intelligence, or not meaningful, by saying that it was just an unimportant experiment. Finally, the confederate said to some of the real participants that she was very good at the task (high coworker ability) and to others that she was not very good at it (low coworker ability). The number of uses generated in each of these conditions is shown in Figure 5.7. Indeed, in all conditions there was a social loafing effect (people performed better in the individual than the group setting) except in the high meaningfulness/low coworker ability condition. In that condition group members actually worked harder than individuals.

Thus, there is indeed a social compensation effect, and people work harder when a task is meaningful or important to them and when they expect that their coworkers will not be able to perform well (because of either motivation or ability; see also Karau & Williams, 1997; Todd, Seok, Kerr, & Messé, 2006). However, it should be noted that there are some limits to the effect. For example, it might not occur in larger groups, because in that case it is hard to compensate for many other group members. Further, after some time an individual will probably refuse to compensate for others, and

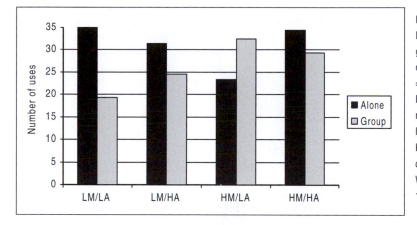

FIGURE 5.7.
Number of uses generated in the different conditions. LM = low meaningfulness; HM = high meaningfulness; LA = low ability of coworker; HA = high ability of coworker (data from Williams & Karau, 1991).

Williams and Karau (1991) speculate that the effect will disappear after some time (because people will refuse being the "sucker" for ever). Finally, individuals who compensate for others might leave the group and join a group in which members are more able or willing to perform (see also Chapter 2).

The Köhler effect

There is evidence for motivation gains in groups that is quite old, but has long been ignored (Witte, 1989). Köhler (1926, 1927) had participants lift weights as often as they could either alone (using a weight of 41 kg) or in dyads (using 82 kg). He systematically varied the ability of each of the dyad members, and studied situations in which their ability (as measured in the trials on which participants worked alone) was quite similar, moderately dissimilar, or highly dissimilar. He then looked at how often dyads could lift the weight as compared to what could be expected based on the average ability of the dyad members. Figure 5.8 shows the results. In that figure, a performance of 100 is expected based on the average performance of the two dyad members while lifting the weight alone, and a score above 100 would thus indicate process gains. As can be seen, dyads with members similar or very dissimilar in ability showed no process gains. However, dyads in which members were moderately dissimilar actually showed a process gain of about 15 per cent! While process losses in this situation might have been due to both motivation losses and coordination losses (i.e., dyad members not lifting the weight at exactly the same time), the process gains seem entirely due to motivation gains.

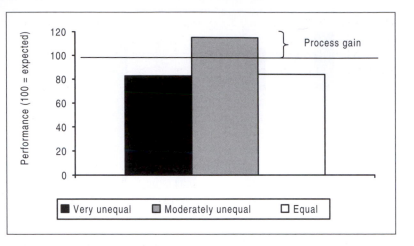

FIGURE 5.8.

Dyadic performance at
the weight-lifting task
as a function of
equality in ability
(based on Köhler,
1926; data from Witte,
1989).

Hertel, Kerr, and Messé (2000), however, reasoned that Köhler had actually used the wrong comparison. Köhler (1926) compared the performance of dyads with the average performance of the dyad members on individual trials. Such a comparison would be appropriate for *additive tasks* in which the performance of the group depends on the sum (or average) of individual performances (Chapter 3). However, lifting a weight together in Köhler's set-up is a *conjunctive task* in which the performance of the worst group member determines the performance of the group: If the weaker dyad member can no longer lift the weight, the stronger member cannot lift it alone (with an 82 kg weight). This implies that one should compare the performance of the dyad with the performance of the weaker member. If such a comparison were made, the motivation gains found by Köhler would be even more dramatic. Further, when seeing the task as a conjunctive task, the higher performance of the dyad must be due to the *weaker* dyad member who works harder in a dyadic situation than alone, because that person is critical for group performance.

Now, why should a less able member work harder in a group situation than when working alone? There may be two reasons (see also Hertel *et al.*, 2000). First, a co-action situation such as that of Köhler might lead to upward social comparisons and competition among participants. In that case, the findings would be consistent with those in Chapter 4: When people perceive their performance as slightly inferior to that of another, they will have a tendency to match the other's performance (see also Seta, 1982). This could account for the Köhler effect, because the weaker group member would work harder to compete with the stronger member. However, there is another possibility, which is that people do not like the idea that their group will perform poorly because of them. Indeed, being the weaker member in a conjunctive setting implies that one's contribution is *indispensable*. In that case, the Köhler effect would be a kind of reversed free-riding effect. The social comparison effect is based on individualistic motives (*individually* being better or no worse than the other), while the indispensability effect is based on social motives (not letting the *group* fail).

Hertel *et al.* (2000) reasoned that if competition underlies the Köhler effect, it would also be found in a co-action setting where the task is additive, because social comparisons will lead to competition as long as people can directly compare their performance with that of others. However, if indispensability underlies the effect, it should only occur when the task is conjunctive, because only in that situation are the contributions of the weaker member truly indispensable. Hertel *et al.* (2000) performed an experiment in which female participants had to hold a heavy bar in front of them with straight arms and measured how long participants could do this. People performed this task both alone (with a 0.69 kg bar) and in dyads and under either additive or conjunctive task conditions. In the additive condition, the members of the dyads each had to hold a bar of 0.69 kg, and the performance of the dyad was defined as the sum of the members' performance (summing the number of seconds the two dyad members could individually hold the bar). In the conjunctive condition, the two dyad members together held a 1.38 kg bar. Hertel *et al.* (2000) found motivation gains only in the conjunctive condition, supporting the indispensability explanation. Further, they failed to obtain an effect for dissimilarity in ability: The motivation gain effect did not depend on the relative ability of the dyad members, as Köhler (1926) had found. Messé, Hertel, Kerr, Lount, and Park (2002) did replicate Köhler's original effect of dissimilarity in ability, but only in situations in which these dissimilarities were made very explicit with performance feedback about each of the dyad members' individual abilities.

In a quantitative review, Weber and Hertel (2007) found that both social comparison processes and indispensability contribute to the Köhler effect. However, the social comparison effect was found especially for males, whereas the indispensability effect was especially pronounced for females. As the previously discussed study (Hertel *et al.*, 2000) was performed only with females, this probably is the reason why they did not find motivation gains in the additive task condition. Weber and Hertel argued that this gender difference might be because females generally are more concerned with collective welfare (social motives), whereas males are more concerned with competition and status (individualistic motives; see also Kerr *et al.*, 2007; Nijstad, Van Vianen, Stroebe, & Lodewijkx, 2004).

Integration: Expectancy-value theory

We have seen that group members socially loaf when their contributions cannot be evaluated, that they free-ride on the effort of others when they perceive their contribution as dispensable, and that they refuse to be the sucker who compensates for the lack of effort of others. Yet when the task is important to them, group members sometimes compensate for the lack of ability and effort of others, and when they perceive themselves to be a less able group member they put in more effort, because of either individualistic (social comparisons and competition) or social motives (indispensability). How can all these findings be explained? Several authors (e.g., Hertel *et al.*, 2000; Karau & Williams, 1993; Shepperd, 1993; Shepperd & Taylor, 1999) have suggested that these findings can be accommodated within an expectancy-value framework.

Expectancy-value theory (Vroom, 1964) assumes that motivation is a multiplicative function of three factors: expectancy, instrumentality, and value (see Figure 5.9, top panel). Expectancy refers to the belief that effort will result in performance, and is closely related to self-efficacy. With high expectancy (or high self-efficacy) a person believes that s/he is capable of performing well at the task. Instrumentality refers to the belief that performance will result in certain outcomes. Instrumentality is high when a person believes that certain outcomes (e.g., praise or criticism, financial rewards) are closely linked to performance. Value, finally, refers to the value attached to these outcomes on a positive–negative dimension. The theory assumes that motivation is high when (1) expectancy is high *and* (2) instrumentality is high *and* (3) value is positive. Only under those situations will exerting effort eventually pay off.

In a group context, things are more complicated (Figure 5.9, bottom panel). The eventual individual outcome depends not only on one's own performance, but also on the performance of other group members, and on how outcomes are distributed among group members. Thus, there are two extra steps: the relations between own performance and group performance and between group outcomes

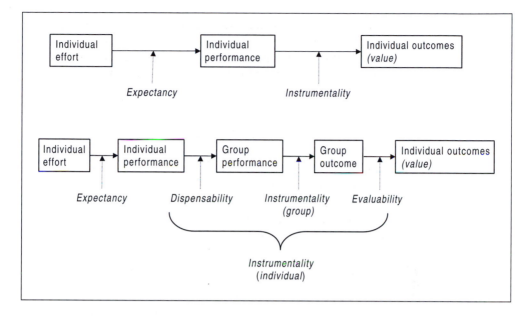

and own outcomes. The first is closely related to dispensability: When individual contributions are dispensable (as in the free-rider effect), there is no or a weak relation between individual performance and performance of the group. However, if individual contributions are indispensable (as in the Köhler effect), this relation is very strong. Further, when individual contributions cannot be evaluated people may loaf, because group members cannot receive individual credit or blame for group performance, and outcomes are divided among group members. However, when the eventual outcome is very important, and when it cannot be assumed that others will contribute enough to obtain it, people may put in extra effort to obtain these outcomes (the social compensation effect). Finally, social comparison effects can be accommodated when we assume that the ability to compare one's performance to that of another member increases the consequences of performance, because it increases the degree to which performance can be evaluated (by either oneself or an audience). Consistent with this, it has recently been found that the Köhler effect is stronger when performance of the weaker member can be evaluated by the stronger coworker (Lount, Park, Kerr, Messé, & Seok, 2008).

The expectancy-value account is hedonistic and individualistic: It assumes that people are motivated only to the extent that they receive valued outcomes. However, sometimes people perform a task because they enjoy it, and the theory will not be applicable. Indeed, most of the

FIGURE 5.9.

Expectancy-value theory for individuals (top; based on Vroom, 1964) and group members (bottom; based on Karau & Williams, 1993).

research we discussed here used tasks of low intrinsic interest (pulling ropes, blowing air, holding a bar), and findings may not generalize to tasks that are more interesting. Further, the theory assumes that only individual outcomes are valued. However, sometimes people also value the outcome of their group. This seems to be more true for women than for men (e.g., Karau & Williams, 1993; Weber & Hertel, 2007), for highly cohesive groups (see Chapter 1), but also in some non-western cultures. For example, some cultures are more collectivist (e.g., in South-East Asia and South America) and value collective outcomes more than cultures that are more individualistic (e.g., North America and Northern Europe) (see Hsu, 1970; Triandis, 1989). For collectivist cultures, the outcome of the group is more important. Indeed, it has been shown that social loafing is less common in these cultures (Karau & Williams, 1993).

Chapter summary

(1) The Ringelmann effect (process losses increase with the size of the group) is due to both motivation and coordination losses.

(2) Motivation losses can be shown when group members perform worse when they merely think that they perform in a group while actually they perform alone.

(3) Social loafing is a reduction in effort when working in a group as compared to working alone. One major factor that causes loafing is that individual contributions to the group product cannot be identified and evaluated.

(4) Free-riding occurs when group members perceive their efforts to be dispensable, for example when a high-ability member works at a conjunctive task or a low ability member works at a disjunctive task. The sucker effect occurs when group members reduce effort because they want to avoid having others take advantage of them through free-riding.

(5) People are willing to put in extra effort to compensate other group members' low performance when they believe that the group would otherwise fail on an important task. This type of motivation gain is called social compensation.

(6) Low-ability group members sometimes work harder when working with high ability coworkers. This Köhler motivation gain effect occurs for individualistic (social comparisons and competition) and social reasons (indispensability for group success).

(7) Expectancy-value theory argues that people are motivated to work hard when expectancy and instrumentality are high and when they value eventual outcomes. It can be used to integrate the findings reported in this chapter.

Exercises

(1) Think of situations in which you have not worked as hard as you could in a group context. Can your behavior be understood in terms of social loafing, free-riding, or the sucker effect?
(2) Similarly, have you ever worked harder than usual in a group setting, and was this because you feared that the group might otherwise fail or because of competition?
(3) Some researchers believe that social loafing can be distinguished from free-riding. Others think that such a distinction is not very useful, because both refer to a reduction in effort while working in a group. What do you think?
(4) Both social compensation and the Köhler effect occur (at least partly) because group members fear that the group might fail when they do not put in more effort. What exactly are the differences between the two effects?
(5) Conceptually, what is the relation between self-efficacy theory described in the previous chapter and expectancy-value theory?
(6) Most of the studies described in this chapter have used fairly simple tasks. Would the findings of the present chapter also be applicable to more complex tasks?

Further reading

The Ringelmann effect and social loafing

Williams, K., Harkins, S., & Latané, B. (1981). Identifiability as a deterrent to social loafing: Two cheering experiments. *Journal of Personality and Social Psychology*, *40*, 303–311.

Free-riding and the sucker effect

Kerr, N. L. (1983). Motivation loss in small groups: A social dilemma analysis. *Journal of Personality and Social Psychology*, *45*, 819–828.

Social compensation

Williams, K. D., & Karau, S. J. (1991). Social loafing and social compensation: The effects of expectations of co-worker performance. *Journal of Personality and Social Psychology, 61*, 570–581.

The Köhler effect

Weber, B., & Hertel, G. (2007). Motivation gains of inferior group members: A meta-analytic review. *Journal of Personality and Social Psychology, 93*, 973–993.

Expectancy-value theory

Shepperd, J. A. (1993). Productivity loss in performance groups: A motivation analysis. *Psychological Bulletin, 113*, 67–81.

Group idea generation and creativity 6

Suppose you are a member of a student society, and you participate in a committee that organizes the yearly party. Each year, the party has a different theme, such as The Wild West, Pirates of the Caribbean, or The Mafia. Your committee has to come up with an interesting theme for this year's party. How would you approach this problem?

Alex Osborn, an advertising executive, suggested a method that could be used to solve these kinds of problems in a creative way (Osborn, 1953). He called this technique *brainstorming*, because people should "use their brain to storm a problem." Brainstorming can be applied to "problems" with many potential solutions that cannot clearly be classified as "wrong" or "right" (although solutions may vary in quality). Brainstorming quickly became very popular, and it still is one of the most common methods of creative problem-solving. Brainstorming has also been a much-studied research topic, and a number of interesting findings have emerged.

Brainstorming is based on two principles: "deferment of judgment" and "quantity breeds quality." Osborn argued that there are two reasons why people fail to be creative: Because they prematurely criticize their ideas and because they give up too quickly. First, he suggested that idea generation should be strictly separated from idea evaluation: Evaluating and criticizing ideas too soon would kill creativity. Second, people should generate as many ideas as possible, because most people will start out with conventional ideas and then give up. Generating many ideas would increase the chance that some good and creative ideas will eventually be generated. Thus, participants in a brainstorming session are instructed to generate as many ideas as possible, and should refrain from evaluation and criticism. Note that the emphasis on idea quantity makes brainstorming an *additive and maximizing task* (group performance can be established by summing the number of ideas generated by each group member). However, researchers have also evaluated idea quality, and had ideas judged on different quality dimensions such as originality (novelty, uncommonness) and feasibility (the degree to which an idea might be realized).

Research has confirmed Osborn's principles (e.g., Parnes & Meadow, 1959). First, people are less creative when they are being evaluated (Bartis, Szymanski, & Harkins, 1988; Camacho & Paulus, 1995), supporting the "deferment of judgment" principle. Second, consistent with the "quantity breeds quality" argument, researchers usually find very strong correlations between the number of ideas and the number of good ideas contained therein, with good ideas defined as ideas that are *both* original and feasible (e.g., Diehl & Stroebe, 1987). A final suggestion made by Osborn (1957) was that brainstorming would be best performed in groups – he suggested 12 as the optimal group size – because group members could build on each other's ideas. This is usually referred to as the potential for *cognitive stimulation* (e.g., Lamm & Trommsdorff, 1973; Dugosh *et al.*, 2000). Precisely this statement, that groups would be more productive, was soon picked up by group researchers.

Productivity of brainstorming groups

In 1958 the first study appeared that tested Osborn's (1957) idea that groups would be more productive than individuals (Taylor, Berry, & Block, 1958). Taylor *et al.* introduced the methodology that many subsequent studies have used. They argued that it would not be fair to compare the performance of a group with the performance of an individual. The group could use the resources of all members, whereas the individual would only be able to use his or her own resources. Taylor *et al.* (1958) therefore compared the performance of "real" groups to the performance of *nominal groups*. Nominal groups are groups in name only, with no interaction among group members. Nominal groups consist of members who work individually and whose ideas are pooled. Because brainstorming is an additive task, the performance of a nominal group can be used to estimate the potential performance of groups (what groups would be capable of when there are no process losses or gains; see Chapter 3). Taylor *et al.* used groups of four, and compared their performance to that of nominal groups of four. Importantly, only non-redundant ideas were counted: Identical ideas that were mentioned by several people were counted only once.

Before their results are revealed, what do you think came out of this study? Who did better, the real or the nominal groups? Was there a cognitive stimulation effect, or was there a process loss? Exactly that question was asked of a number of American students: Is brainstorming best done in a group or as an individual (Paulus, Dzindolet, Poletes, & Camacho, 1993)? About 80 per cent of the students thought the groups would do better. Similar studies in Germany (Stroebe, Diehl, & Abakoumkin, 1992), the Netherlands (Nijstad, 1995) and Japan (Homma, Tajima, & Hayashi, 1995) yielded the same result: Most people think groups do better.

You probably feel it coming: This is not what Taylor and colleagues found. Instead, they found that nominal groups outperformed interactive groups and in fact were twice as productive! This was true for both the number of ideas (productivity) and the number of good ideas (idea quality). This finding is not an exception. Diehl and Stroebe (1987) listed 22 experiments in which the performance of real and nominal groups was compared. No single study found that real groups were more productive: In 18 studies the nominal groups did better, and in four there was no difference. The last four studies all were done with dyads. Indeed, the productivity loss of brainstorming groups is a robust and large effect, and the loss increases with group size (Mullen, Johnson, & Salas, 1991). Of course, the latter finding reminds us of the Ringelmann effect (Chapter 5).

This leaves us with three questions. First, why are groups less productive? Second, is there no cognitive stimulation effect, and can overhearing ideas of others not help one's own idea generation? Third, why do people believe that groups are better, when this seems to be wrong?

Causes of the productivity loss

There may be a number of reasons why groups suffer this productivity loss. Could it be a case of social loafing or free-riding (see Chapter 5)? Could it be that, despite the instruction not to criticize ideas, group members still feel evaluated and do not mention all their ideas? Could it be that overhearing others' ideas is not stimulating, as suggested by Osborn (1957), but distracting? These are a few plausible causes of the process loss. Let us consider the evidence.

Motivation losses
First, the productivity loss of brainstorming groups might be due to motivational factors, such as the ones we discussed in Chapter 5.

Diehl and Stroebe (1987) considered the possibility that the productivity loss is due to free-riding. Group members may feel that their contribution is not really needed (i.e., dispensable) in order for the group to succeed. For example, they may feel that other members are more creative, and leave the work to them. Indeed, some earlier evidence was consistent with that interpretation. Collaros and Anderson (1969) manipulated perceived expertness, and told some group members that the other members had more experience with brainstorming. Groups in which members were told that the others were more experienced were less productive than groups in which this was not told. One interpretation is that group members thought that their individual contributions were more dispensable when the other members were experts, and that they therefore did not work hard (see Chapter 5).

To test this, Diehl and Stroebe (1987) had participants generate ideas in real and in nominal groups. In addition, they made some group members individually accountable for their own performance, and explicitly told them that their *individual* performance would be evaluated. Other group members were told that the researchers were only interested in the performance of the group as a whole. Should free-riding (or social loafing) be responsible for the productivity loss, then the real groups in which members were held individually accountable should do as well as the nominal groups. However, this was not what happened. Although the groups in which people were individually accountable did slightly better than those in which the groups would be evaluated as a whole, the productivity loss still was there, and the difference between real and nominal groups was much larger than the difference between accountable and non-accountable groups.

Paulus and Dzindolet (1993) also investigated motivation losses. They reasoned that group members, unlike people who brainstorm alone, have the opportunity to compare their performance with the performance of other members (social comparison; see also Chapters 4 and 5). Group members will generally not be motivated to do most of the work (they do not want to be the sucker, Chapter 5). As a consequence, they will adjust their performance in order to be about as productive as the least productive group member. Paulus and Dzindolet called this *downward matching*. This implies that the more productive group members will produce fewer ideas, and the performance of the group will suffer.

The evidence for downward matching, however, is mixed. On one hand, Paulus and Dzindolet (1993) found clear evidence that group members over time become more similar in how many ideas they produce: Group members do match one another's performance. Paulus and Dzindolet further found that this performance level acquired normative properties. For example, they had groups perform multiple brainstorms on different topics, and found that performance in one session was predictive of performance in the next. Also, if the groups started out on a difficult topic and then worked on an easy topic, they generated fewer ideas on the easy topic than when they started out working on the easier topic and did the difficult topic later. Apparently, they could not generate many ideas on the difficult topic, and this low level of performance became normative and carried over to the easier topic. However, Paulus and Dzindolet have not clearly shown that group members match performance of the least productive group member, only that they converge around a common standard. Further, they did not clearly show that downward matching contributes to the productivity loss of groups (Stroebe & Diehl, 1994).

All in all, therefore, the evidence that the productivity loss of brainstorming groups is due to motivational factors is not so strong. Probably the reason is that most people find idea generation an enjoyable task. As was noted in Chapter 5, motivation losses mainly occur when the task is not intrinsically interesting.

Coordination losses

Thus, it seems likely that *coordination loss* underlies the effect. One possibility is evaluation apprehension: the fear of being negatively evaluated by fellow group members (see also Chapter 4). Group members, despite the instruction not to evaluate or criticize ideas, might still be anxious to share all their thoughts. Individuals who cannot be evaluated by fellow group members would therefore mention more ideas (including ones that are a bit strange or unusual). Because evaluation apprehension is not due to a reduction in effort, but rather occurs because group members fail to contribute their ideas, it is a case of coordination loss (Stroebe & Diehl, 1994; Chapter 3).

Diehl and Stroebe (1987) considered evaluation apprehension as a possible cause of the productivity loss. Diehl and Stroebe (1987) used both real and nominal groups, and told half of them that there were judges behind a one-way screen who would evaluate their ideas. Diehl and Stroebe reasoned that in real groups high levels of evaluation apprehension will already be present (stemming from fellow group members), so the additional evaluation of the judges will not have a big effect. Individuals are not evaluated by fellow group members, so there the presence of judges should have a bigger effect. However, no support was found for evaluation apprehension as an important cause of the productivity loss. The presence of judges did have a small negative effect on performance, but this was true for both real and nominal groups. Moreover, there still was a large difference between the real and nominal groups, indicating that evaluation apprehension could not explain the productivity loss.

Camacho and Paulus (1995) also studied evaluation apprehension as a possible cause of the productivity loss of groups. Instead of manipulating evaluation apprehension, they used a personality measure. Their participants filled out the *Interaction Anxiousness* Scale (Leary, 1983), which measures the degree to which various interaction situations (talking to a stranger, having a job interview) arouse anxiety and stress. Camacho and Paulus (1995) reasoned that individuals high in interaction anxiousness would suffer more from evaluation apprehension. Hence, these people should perform poorly when brainstorming in a group, and more poorly than people low in interaction anxiousness. However, when brainstorming alone in a nominal group, high-anxious people should do as well as low-anxious people. Camacho and Paulus (1995) thus composed interactive and nominal groups of four people who were low in interaction anxiousness and of people who were high in it. Besides these four conditions (low anxiety/interactive; high anxiety/interactive; low anxiety/ nominal; high anxiety/nominal) they had a fifth condition in which two high-anxious and two low-anxious people brainstormed in an interactive group.

The results of this study are shown in Figure 6.1. The difference between real and nominal groups for participants low in interaction anxiousness was not very big. However, for high-anxious groups there was a big difference, and interactive groups performed much worse than nominal groups. Interestingly, the mixed interactive groups also performed poorly. It might be that in these mixed groups, the low-anxious group members matched the low performance of the high-anxious members, and these groups therefore performed relatively poorly (i.e., downward matching). Finally, high-anxious people reported that they felt more pressure, they more often indicated that they had withheld ideas, they were more nervous, and they were more distracted. All these results indicate that high-interaction-anxious people might suffer more from evaluation apprehension than low-anxious people.

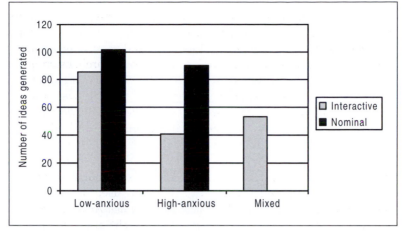

FIGURE 6.1.

Number of ideas generated by interaction anxiousness and type of group. Taken from: Camacho, L. M., & Paulus, P. B. (1995). The role of social anxiousness in group brainstorming. *Journal of Personality and Social Psychology, 68*, 1071–1080. Copyright American Psychological Association. Reprinted with permission.

From the Camacho and Paulus (1995) results, it can be concluded that evaluation apprehension plays a role in the productivity loss of groups, especially for people high in interaction anxiousness. However, there is another important factor. Diehl and Stroebe (1987) hypothesized that *production blocking* might be responsible for the productivity loss in brainstorming groups. The idea is simple: When people are working in a group, usually only one member speaks at any given time. The others have to wait for their turn, and when they are waiting they might not think up new ideas or they might forget their ideas.

It is hard to prevent production blocking in interactive groups, but it is possible to introduce production blocking in nominal groups, and this is what Diehl and Stroebe (1987) did. They created five conditions. Condition 1 was a normal interactive group condition, and condition 2 was a normal nominal group condition. In the other three conditions people worked in separate rooms, like the nominal groups. These rooms were equipped with a "traffic light." When one of the members started talking, a voice sensor was activated, and the traffic light for that person would turn green. At the same time, the lights of the other members turned red. In condition 3, people were instructed that they could not talk when the light was red, thereby creating production blocking. In condition 4, in addition to the traffic light, participants were equipped with headphones, so they could also overhear the other members generate ideas. Finally, in condition 5 the traffic light was present, and people were told how it worked, but they were instructed to ignore it. This last condition therefore was one without production blocking, but could be used to see whether

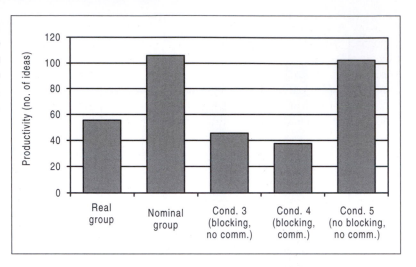

FIGURE 6.2.
Productivity in the
different blocking
conditions (data from
Diehl & Stroebe, 1987,
experiment 4).

the device itself would distract people from idea generation. The results were very clear (Figure 6.2): Groups in conditions with production blocking (the real groups, and the traffic light groups in conditions 3 and 4) were less productive than the groups without blocking (the nominal groups, and the groups that could ignore the traffic light). There were no further differences. Thus, production blocking is a major reason why groups are less productive than individuals. Further, overhearing the ideas of others (in condition 4) does not seem to have a big effect. It neither seems to stimulate people, nor does it distract them.

Later research investigating the blocking effect has found that the reason why blocking has this – rather large – negative effect is cognitive interference (Diehl & Stroebe, 1991; Nijstad, Stroebe, & Lodewijkx, 2003). What is crucial is that ideas cannot be immediately expressed after they have been generated. This leads to the forgetting of some ideas, and also interferes with the ability to generate new ideas (Nijstad et al., 2003). Thus, waiting for one's turn hinders idea generation mostly because it interferes with people's cognitive ability to generate ideas.

Cognitive stimulation and productivity gains

One implication of Diehl and Stroebe's (1987, 1991) findings – that production blocking is an important cause of the productivity loss of brainstorming groups – is that when blocking is eliminated there should be no productivity loss. Further, suppose we can eliminate blocking, but that group members still have access to ideas of others: Would access to ideas of others under those conditions be stimulating? Recent evidence suggests that the answer is "yes."

In groups that sit around a table and express their ideas out loud, it is almost impossible to eliminate blocking: It would require that people talk at the same time. However, one can also share ideas on pieces of paper or through a computer network. In these cases, participants can contribute their ideas in silence and write or type simultaneously, and there is no production blocking. If ideas are distributed to other group members, by passing around pieces of paper or computer files in an internal network, it is still possible to read one another's ideas. Thus, using a writing or typing paradigm might be useful to find out whether, in the absence of blocking, ideas of others can be stimulating.

Several computer systems are available to aid group meetings, and some of these are equipped with an electronic brainstorm system (EBS; e.g., Nunamaker, Applegate, & Konsynski, 1988; see also Chapter 11). In EBS, participants can type simultaneously and can see (all or a subset of) others' ideas on their screens. Some of the earliest studies showed that, because simultaneous typing eliminates production blocking, interactive EBS groups (with idea sharing) did not suffer a productivity loss as compared to nominal groups (Gallupe, Bastianutti, & Cooper, 1991). Further, some studies showed that when production blocking was introduced in EBS groups, for example by having members take turns to type their ideas, a productivity loss was found similar to the productivity loss in traditional brainstorming groups (Gallupe, Cooper, Grisé, & Bastianutti, 1994). Thus, EBS effectively eliminates production blocking, and brings performance of interactive groups to the level of nominal groups.

More interesting was a subsequent finding that access to others' ideas in EBS could also be stimulating. Dennis and Valacich (1993) compared EBS groups with nominal groups, and also varied group size (using groups of six and 12). In groups of six, the nominal groups had a slight advantage over the EBS groups; however, in groups of 12 EBS groups were more productive, for the first time showing a real productivity gain (Figure 6.3)! Later research has replicated this effect, and productivity gains have been reported for groups of nine members and over (Valacich, Dennis, & Connolly, 1994). The authors explain the finding that only for larger groups was a productivity

FIGURE 6.3.
Number of ideas
generated by nominal
and EBS groups of
different sizes (data
from Dennis &
Valacich, 1993).

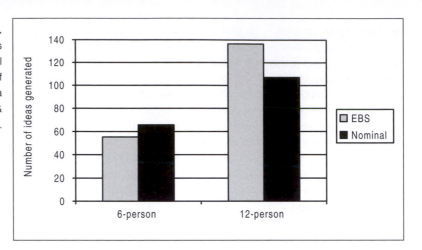

gain found by assuming that the stimulating value of reading other people's ideas increases with group size. However, any direct evidence to support this is missing (see also Dennis & Williams, 2003).

Later research has also found productivity gains in smaller groups. Dugosh *et al.* (2000) used four-person EBS groups. They found that EBS groups in which idea sharing was possible performed better than EBS groups in which people could not read one another's ideas. However, this stimulation effect occurred only when people paid close attention to the ideas of others because they were instructed to remember these ideas. In the absence of this memory instruction, no positive effects were found. Perhaps earlier studies failed to find stimulation in EBS because participants did not pay enough attention to the ideas of others.

Thus, these EBS systems are effective. However, they also are expensive, and require that every group member has a computer and that these computers are interconnected in an internal network. Further, it requires software that most people would not normally have. Isn't there a simpler way? The answer is "yes": use slips of paper. Paulus and Yang (2000) had groups generate ideas on slips of paper. Some of these groups had access to one another's ideas, because the slips of paper were passed around in a round-robin fashion. Paulus and Yang (2000) found that also under these conditions idea-sharing was stimulating and led to productivity gains.

But why exactly are the ideas of others stimulating? Nijstad, Stroebe, and Lodewijkx (2002; also Nijstad & Stroebe, 2006) addressed this question. They argued that ideas cannot be generated from thin air. New ideas usually result from new combinations of existing knowledge (i.e., knowledge that is stored in memory). When one is generating ideas, available knowledge must first be activated in memory (retrieved), after which it can be used to generate ideas. Nijstad *et al.* (2002) argued that once knowledge is activated, it can often be used to generate several ideas, and these ideas should be semantically related, because they are generated using the same knowledge. Several successive semantically related ideas might be called a "train of thought." Ideas within a train of thought can be generated relatively quickly, because no new knowledge has to be activated. However, when switching to a new train of thought, some thinking is required to activate new knowledge, and this takes some time. Nijstad *et al.* (2002) hypothesized that ideas of others aid the activation of knowledge, and that this should help participants switch to a new train of thought. If this were the case, these switches should be quicker when participants see ideas of others as compared to when they do not.

Nijstad *et al.* (2002) performed an experiment in which individual participants typed in ideas at a computer terminal. Some participants were shown stimulation ideas on their screen whereas others in a control condition were not. For each idea a participant entered, it was recorded how long it took to enter it (response latencies). The ideas were later coded as either semantically similar to the previous idea (i.e., fell within a train of thought) or semantically dissimilar to that idea (i.e., a new train of thought was started). Nijstad *et al.* found that participants who were shown stimulation ideas overall were more productive, thus finding evidence for cognitive stimulation. In the control condition, it was found that response latencies were shorter when an idea was semantically similar to the previous idea than when it was different. However, when stimulation ideas were provided, this difference was not found: A switch to a new train of thought was quicker than in the control condition and as quick as staying within the same train of thought (see Figure 6.4). Thus, stimulation led to performance improvements because it helped participants to switch quickly to a new train of thought.

In sum, Osborn in fact was right, and ideas of others are stimulating. However, in a regular brainstorming session, where people verbalize their ideas, factors such as evaluation apprehension (especially for highly anxious people) and production blocking cause large productivity losses. Only when these are eliminated are productivity gains found. These gains probably are due to the fact that ideas of others can stimulate one to come up with ideas that one would

FIGURE 6.4.

Response latencies of
ideas that are
semantically similar to
the previous idea
(within a train of
thought (tot)) and of
ideas that are
semantically dissimilar
to the previous idea
(switch of tot) (data
from Nijstad *et al.*,
2002).

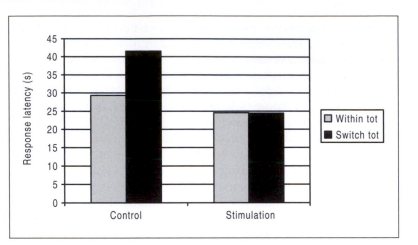

normally not think of, and help one start a new train of thought. Note, however, that this cognitive stimulation effect is much weaker than the disrupting effects of production blocking.

The illusion of group productivity

We have seen that traditional face-to-face brainstorming groups are ineffective, and that their ineffectiveness increases with group size. Further, not verbalizing ideas but sharing ideas on paper or through a computer system eliminates many problems, and can even lead to cognitive stimulation and productivity gains. However, many brainstorming sessions still are conducted in the traditional face-to-face manner, and people seem entirely unaware of the associated productivity losses. For example, a Google search of the Internet (November 2008) yielded almost 7 million (!) hits related to brainstorming, many of which offer advice on how to conduct traditional face-to-face brainstorming sessions. Indeed, most people think that these sessions are more effective than generating ideas individually. Related to this, researchers have frequently found that people are more satisfied with their brainstorming performance after a (traditional) group session than after an individual session (e.g., Larey & Paulus, 1995; Paulus *et al.*, 1993; Paulus, Larey, & Ortega, 1995; Stroebe *et al.*, 1992). Why do people have this illusion that group sessions are effective means of generating ideas?

In fact, there are several explanations. First, Paulus *et al.* (1993) argued that group members have the opportunity to compare their performance with that of other members (social comparisons). Most group members will reach the conclusion that they have contributed about as many ideas as other members. They will therefore generally be satisfied with their own performance. Individuals working alone, however, have no way of telling whether they have done well or poorly. They may consequently feel insecure, and rate their performance more negatively. Indeed, Paulus *et al.* found that giving individual brainstormers information about how well others had performed increased their satisfaction with their own performance.

Stroebe *et al.* (1992) argued that people may overestimate their performance in a group session. They suggested that group members (perhaps unconsciously) take credit for ideas that were actually suggested by another member, because they cannot accurately recall who has generated which idea. You might have had the experience after a group session that several people claim to have generated that particularly useful idea. Indeed, Stroebe *et al.* found that group members were not very good at distinguishing between ideas that they generated themselves and ideas that were generated by others. Further, group members often claimed that many ideas that were suggested by others had also occurred to them.

Nijstad, Stroebe, and Lodewijkx (2006) reasoned that people who work alone often experience difficulties when trying to generate ideas: Sometimes they try but fail to come up with something new. Group members, on the other hand, may sit back and listen to others when they experience these difficulties, and as a consequence, they less often experience them. Indeed, Nijstad *et al.* found that group members reported fewer failed attempts than individuals, and this was associated with higher levels of satisfaction. Thus, subjectively, group brainstorming makes the task of idea generation easier. However, this does not necessarily mean that one really generates more or better ideas; it might also mean that one just has made fewer attempts to generate ideas.

Idea quality and idea selection

Much of the previous discussion was about idea quantity: How many ideas do groups generate as compared to individuals? Does reading the ideas of others lead to the generation of more ideas? This might seem a bit unsatisfactory. Brainstorming sessions are not organized to get large numbers of ideas *per se*; rather one is interested in generating

TABLE 6.1

Idea quality on two dimensions

Feasibility	Originality	
	Low	High
Low	Bad ideas	Crazy ideas
High	Conventional ideas	Good ideas

one or a few ideas that are of high quality and that nobody has thought of before. So, how about idea quality?

The two dimensions most often used to evaluate the quality of ideas are originality and feasibility. An idea can be high or low on both these dimensions, creating four possibilities (see Table 6.1): bad ideas (low originality, low feasibility), conventional ideas (low originality, high feasibility), crazy ideas (high originality, low feasibility), and good ideas (high originality, high feasibility). This closely corresponds to how creativity is usually defined: Ideas are creative to the extent that they are both novel (original) and useful (feasible) (e.g., Amabile, 1983; Paulus & Nijstad, 2003; Sternberg & Lubart, 1999). The quality of a brainstorming session therefore is usually measured by the number of good ideas (both original and feasible). As mentioned earlier, the number of good ideas is strongly correlated with the total number of ideas: As more ideas are generated, more good ideas will be found among them (Diehl & Stroebe, 1987; Parnes & Meadow, 1959).

A question that has received recent research attention is whether groups and individuals are good at *selecting* their best ideas. Indeed, a brainstorming session is effective if it results in a few good ideas that can eventually be used. This implies that after the divergent process of idea generation, a convergent process has to follow in which people select the best ideas among those that have been generated. Rietzschel, Nijstad, and Stroebe (2006) argued that the quality of the ideas that are eventually selected depends on two factors: the quality of the ideas that are generated, and the effectiveness of the selection process (the degree to which the best ideas are chosen). Rietzschel *et al.* further argued that nominal groups will generally have generated more (good) ideas during the brainstorming session, and that they would consequently also have more good ideas to choose from. However, it might be the case that interactive groups are better at selecting their ideas (see also Chapter 7).

Rietzschel *et al.* (2006) performed an experiment in which participants first generated ideas and then selected their four best ideas (also Faure, 2004). Participants were psychology students who worked as a group or individually as members of nominal groups (both during idea generation and idea selection), and the topic of the brainstorming session was how education at the psychology department might be improved. Rietzschel *et al.* found that real groups generated fewer ideas than nominal groups, and also that the ideas of real groups were on average less original but more feasible that those of nominal groups. When it came to the quality of the *selected* ideas, however, there was no difference between the real and nominal groups. Most striking was that the average originality and feasibility of selected ideas was not higher than the average originality and feasibility of generated ideas: Although better ideas were available, people did not choose them, neither in nominal nor in interactive groups. In fact, selection effectiveness was so bad that participants might as well have randomly selected their ideas.

Rietzschel, Nijstad, and Stroebe (in press) considered the question of why selection effectiveness was so low. One of the problems that people face when selecting ideas is that originality and feasibility often are negatively related. Thus, many ideas are either original or feasible, but not both. This causes people to focus more on feasibility than on originality when choosing their ideas. Indeed, one could argue that originality does not really matter, as long as an idea works and it is feasible. However, when people completely disregard originality when choosing their ideas, they will end up with only conventional ideas. Rietzschel *et al.* found that people could be persuaded to choose original ideas by explicitly instructing them to do so; however, this led them to be less satisfied with the ideas they selected.

Group creativity

So far, we have mainly focused on the comparison between individual and group idea generation (and selection). However, this is just one way to evaluate group performance (Chapter 3). Another is to study what makes one group more effective (or creative) than another group. This is useful knowledge, because certain creative activities cannot be performed alone. Examples include the making of feature films (Simonton, 2004) and musical performance in orchestras or bands (Sawyer, 2006), but also writing a research report together. Let's consider some recent evidence about what makes one group more creative than another.

In Chapter 2 we have seen that people often conform to (normative) group pressure. However, to be creative means to be unconventional and *non-conforming*. Indeed, in Chapter 2 we have seen that people who deviate and take a minority position stimulate the opposing majority to think in more creative ways (Nemeth, 1986). Recently, some evidence indicates that the creativity of groups depends on the degree to which group members engage in independent thinking rather than conform to group norms or strive for group harmony. Consider the following examples.

- Beersma and De Dreu (2005) first had groups perform either a *competitive* negotiation or a more friendly and *cooperative* negotiation. These groups subsequently performed a creativity task (designing marketing slogans). The groups who just finished the competitive negotiation were more creative than those who just finished the cooperative negotiation.
- Nemeth and Ormiston (2007) had groups perform two idea generation sessions. After the first session, groups either remained intact or experienced a change in group membership. Groups were more creative after they had experienced a change in membership than when membership remained stable (see also Choi & Thompson, 2005; Chapter 10). However, people in the stable membership groups felt more comfortable than those who had experienced membership change.
- Goncalo and Staw (2006) had group members describe either why they were similar to other members (activating collectivist values) or why they were unique (activating individualistic values). Next, the groups had to generate ideas. The authors found that the groups in which individualistic values were activated were more creative than those in which collectivistic values were activated.

These examples vary widely, but seem to have one thing in common: Groups focused either on what members have in common and group harmony or on how members differ and uniqueness. After a cooperative negotiation, after being together longer, and when focusing on similarity, people may be less willing to "stand out" and take a divergent position. Rather, they conform more to group norms or to pressures toward uniformity. However, for creativity, group members should use different approaches and there should be no pressure towards uniformity (see also Chirumbolo, Livi, Mannetti, Pierro, & Kruglanski, 2004; De Dreu, Nijstad, & Van Knippenberg,

2008). This is more likely after a competitive negotiation, after membership change, and when individualistic values have been activated.

Furthermore, for a more complete picture of the factors that make one group more creative than another, it is necessary to take into account that groups are multilevel systems (Chapter 3). Group creativity basically comes about because individual group members are creative – individual members need to generate creative ideas. However, equally crucial are the group processes that transform individual ideas into creative group products (Nijstad, Rietzschel, & Stroebe, 2005). However, few studies have looked into the multilevel nature of group creativity, one exception being a study by Taggar (2002).

Taggar (2002) studied 94 groups of five to six members who participated in a business course. The groups had to complete different exercises, and the resulting group reports were rated for creativity by expert judges (e.g., one group exercise was to design a plan to manage diversity within a particular company). Taggar measured individual-level characteristics, such as personality and general cognitive ability. Further, group members rated each other on individual-level creativity, and on behaviors that would contribute positively to effective group functioning, such as providing positive feedback, communicating effectively, and coordinating group activities (e.g., assigning specific roles and tasks to group members). Taggar predicted that individual-level characteristics would be associated with individual-level creativity (as rated by fellow group members). Further, average individual-level creativity was predicted to affect group level creativity (the creativity of the group reports). However, Taggar predicted that this would only be the case when group members displayed effective group behaviors. Figure 6.5 shows the basic predictions. The model shown in that figure received good support. Individual characteristics were related to individual creativity. However, individual-level creativity was related to group-level creativity only when group members showed effective group behaviors.

In sum, researchers have begun to analyze why some groups are more creative than others. It appears that creativity in groups might benefit more from an atmosphere in which individuality and uniqueness are valued, because this affects the likelihood that group members take divergent perspectives rather than conform to group pressures. Further, translating individual creativity into a creative group product requires effective group processes.

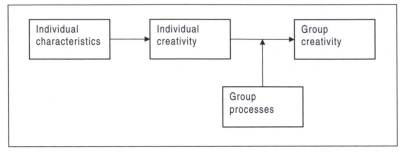

FIGURE 6.5.

Taggar's (2002)
research model. Note
that group processes
affect the *relation*
between individual
creativity and group
creativity (a strong
relation with effective
group processes, a
weak relation without
effective group
processes). Therefore,
the arrow from group
processes is directed
at the arrow linking
individual creativity to
group creativity. When
one variable affects the
relation between two
other variables, we call
it a *moderation* effect.

Chapter summary

(1) Brainstorming is an effective technique for creative problem-solving, in which the emphasis is on quantity rather than quality of ideas.

(2) Groups show a large process loss in idea-generation tasks, and this loss increases with group size. Motivation loss contributes to this, but coordination losses seem more important. The major coordination losses are evaluation apprehension (especially among group members high in interaction anxiety) and production blocking (turn-taking in groups).

(3) When production blocking is eliminated (when ideas are shared through computer systems or on written notes) there is no productivity loss, and productivity gains can even occur. These gains are due to cognitive stimulation.

(4) Although traditional brainstorming groups are ineffective, most people erroneously believe that they are effective. Several mechanisms underlie this illusion of group productivity, including social comparison processes, overestimations of one's own performance, and fewer failed attempts to generate ideas in a group setting.

(5) After the divergent stage of idea generation, a convergent stage usually follows, in which the most promising ideas are selected for further consideration. However, these selection processes are not always effective, and many people seem to have a bias in favor of feasible rather than original ideas.

(6) A group atmosphere in which individuality rather than conformity is valued seems more conducive to creativity. However, individual-level creativity will lead to creative group products only when groups use effective group processes.

Exercises

(1) Many psychological researchers know that group brainstorming is ineffective, yet they still often have these brainstorms. Why do you think this is the case?

(2) Based on this chapter, what ways can you think of to improve traditional (face-to-face) brainstorming sessions?

(3) Do you think that also on other tasks there may be an illusion of group productivity, and on what kinds of tasks do you think this may be the case?

(4) Idea generation is just one stage in the creative process. Other stages are formulating the problem (i.e., before the brainstorming session), selecting ideas, and implementing ideas. In which of these other stages might it be most useful to use groups?

(5) In the previous chapter it appeared that collectivists less often socially loaf. Here it appears that individualists might be more productive. How can this be explained?

(6) What kind of group processes would be needed to transform individual ideas into a group-level creative product?

Further reading

On motivation and coordination loss in idea generating groups

Stroebe, W., & Diehl, M. (1994). Why groups are less effective than their members: On productivity losses in idea-generating groups. In W. Stroebe & M. Hewstone (Eds.), *European Review of Social Psychology* (Vol. 5, pp. 271–303). London: Wiley.

On cognitive stimulation

Dugosh, K. L., Paulus, P. B., Roland, E. J., & Yang, H. C. (2000). Cognitive stimulation in brainstorming. *Journal of Personality and Social Psychology*, 79, 722–735.

Nijstad, B. A., & Stroebe, W. (2006). How the group affects the mind: A cognitive model of idea generation in groups. *Personality and Social Psychology Review*, 10, 186–213.

On idea selection

Rietzschel, E. F., Nijstad, B. A., & Stroebe, W. (2006). Productivity is not enough: A comparison of interactive and nominal groups on idea generation and selection. *Journal of Experimental Social Psychology*, 42, 244–251.

A multilevel model of group creativity

Taggar, S. (2002). Individual creativity and group ability to utilize individual creative resources: A multilevel model. *Academy of Management Journal, 45,* 315–330.

Group decision-making 7

Group decision-making is, to some extent, the converse of group creativity (Stasser & Birchmeier, 2003): Rather than generating many different options, the group has to converge (reach agreement) on one of them. Decision-making is one of the most important tasks done in groups. Political decisions are made by governments and in committees, decisions regarding the future of a company are made in board meetings, and selection committees decide which prospective employee to hire. Also, more mundane decisions are often made in groups: People decide together what gift to buy for a mutual friend, conference parties decide where to go for dinner, and families decide where to spend their vacation.

There are two reasons why groups rather than individuals make many of these decisions (e.g., Vroom & Yetton, 1973). First, group decisions are made in order to reach consensus and ensure that everyone's opinion is heard, and that (most) group members agree with the decision. This *consensus-building function* of groups is important, because often people are more willing to accept a decision when they had a say in it. The second reason is that groups will usually have more resources to draw on than individuals and might therefore make a better decision. Indeed, some group members might hold information that is unavailable to others. In that case the group has more information than any of its members separately, and is capable of a better-informed choice. This is the *information integration function* of decision-making groups.

Related to these two functions, group members bring two types of resources to the decision table: their preferences and their information. The group's task is to combine preferences into a consensus (even when group members initially disagree) and to combine information into a high-quality decision. In the first part of the chapter we consider combining preferences, and discuss an influential theory of group decision-making: social decision scheme theory (Davis, 1973). In the second part, we consider the role of information during group decision-making. Finally, we consider groupthink and motivational issues related to group decision-making.

Social decision scheme theory

The theory

A fundamental question of group research is how individual contributions are combined into a group response (Chapter 3). Davis' (1973) *social decision scheme theory* addresses this question: How are individual preferences translated into a group decision? The theory is presented schematically in Figure 7.1, and consists of four elements: individual preferences, group composition, social decision schemes, and group response. In the theory, group composition is based on group member preferences. Group composition, in turn, determines the group response, such as the group decision. The way group compositions relate to group decisions is based on the *social decision scheme* (SDS) used by the group.

An SDS is a *decision rule*, which specifies how individual preferences are related to group decisions. It is best explained with a voting analogy (Davis, 1973). One decision rule, for example, is used in politics: Majority wins. In a vote in parliament, the alternative endorsed by a majority of members of parliament is chosen. "Majority wins" here is a formal decision rule, and is accompanied by a formal

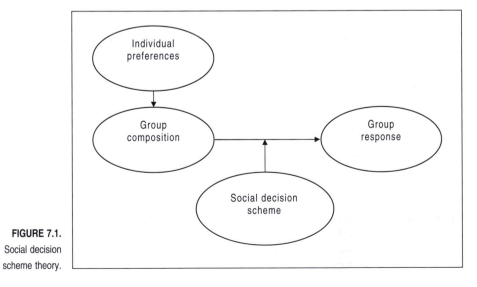

FIGURE 7.1.
Social decision scheme theory.

voting procedure. Groups might also use such a rule in an informal and implicit way: The group chooses the majority's alternative after some discussion, but without a formal vote. However, other types of (informal) decision rules are possible as well, in which minorities sometimes win. SDS theory has been very important for research into group decision-making and problem-solving (Chapter 8). Let's therefore discuss the theory in some detail.

Preference to group composition

SDS theory takes individual preferences as a starting point. A *preference* is an inclination of an individual to select one option from a set of response alternatives. For example, when making a hiring decision among three job candidates, some people in a company may prefer candidate A, others prefer candidate B, and still others prefer candidate C. Suppose that a selection committee is appointed to make the hiring decision, and this committee is composed of four people from the company. Within SDS theory, *group composition* refers to how many people in a group (e.g., the selection committee) prefer each alternative. One possible group composition is that two members prefer candidate A, one prefers B, and one prefers C. A brief way to summarize this group composition is [2, 1, 1], indicating how many group members endorse candidates A, B, and C, respectively.

With four group members and three alternatives, 15 different group compositions are logically possible. These vary from all members unanimously preferring the same candidate (i.e., [4, 0, 0], [0, 4, 0], or [0, 0, 4]) to every possible mixture of preferences (e.g., [2, 2, 0], [2, 1, 1], or [1, 0, 3]). Decisions among more alternatives and decisions made in larger groups have more possible group compositions. With fewer alternatives or smaller groups, the number of possible group compositions is smaller. For example, with a three-person group and two alternatives, only four compositions are possible (i.e., [3, 0], [2, 1], [1, 2], and [0, 3]).

Group composition to group decision

The next step in the theory is from group composition to group decision. This depends on the SDS used by the group, because the SDS is the decision rule that specifies how a group composition is turned into a group decision. Many different SDSs are possible, but three important ones are "majority wins," "proportionality," and "truth wins" (see Table 7.1).

"Majority wins" implies that an alternative is *always* chosen when at least a majority of group members prefer it. In our hiring example,

TABLE 7.1

Three social decision schemes

SDS	Description	Example
Majority wins	The group chooses the alternative that is endorsed by the majority with a probability of 100% (always)	Given a group composition of [1, 3, 0] the group always chooses alternative B
Proportionality	The probability that an alternative is chosen is equal to the proportion of group members endorsing that alternative	Given a group composition of [1, 3, 0], the probability that the group chooses A is 25%, B is 75%, C is 0%
Truth wins	Given that one alternative represents the truth (the "best" alternative), the group always chooses it (with a probability of 100%) when at least one member in the group endorses that alternative	Given that alternative A is correct, and group composition is [1, 3, 0] the group will always choose A (even though only one member favors it)

this would imply that candidate A is always chosen when the group composition is [4, 0, 0], [3, 1, 0], or [3, 0, 1]. Similarly, candidate B would be chosen with [0, 4, 0], [1, 3, 0], or [0, 3, 1], and candidate C with [0, 0, 4], [1, 0, 3], and [0, 1, 3]. Note, however, that a majority-wins SDS gives no solution when no alternative is endorsed by a majority (e.g., [2, 2, 0] or [2, 1, 1]). In a voting system, such as in parliament, often certain procedures are in place for these cases (e.g., the chairperson has a decisive vote). When no formal procedures are present, an additional informal rule has to be applied for cases without a majority (see below).

The proportionality SDS entails that the probability that an alternative is chosen depends on the proportion of group members preferring that alternative. In this SDS, larger factions are more likely to "win" than smaller factions. For example, given a group composition of [2, 1, 1] the probability of this group choosing A is 50 per cent, of choosing B is 25 per cent and of choosing C also is 25 per cent. In a group with composition [3, 1, 0], the probability that the group chooses A is 75 per cent, that it chooses B is 25 per cent, and that it chooses C is 0 per cent. Note that when groups use the proportionality SDS majorities do not *always* win (as with "majority wins"), but are *more likely* to win than minorities.

A third important SDS is "truth wins." Such an SDS might be applicable when one alternative represents "the truth," for example a correct response in a group problem-solving task (Chapter 8), or in a case in which there are decisive arguments in favor of an alternative (e.g., decisive evidence in a criminal case). Truth wins means that the alternative representing the truth is *always* chosen (with a probability of 100 per cent) when *at least one* group member prefers it. Note that this means that a minority will win when this minority has the "correct" preference. Truth wins is associated with *disjunctive tasks* (see Chapter 3): When at least one group member is capable of performing well (in this case: has the "correct" preference), the group is expected to perform well (choose the "correct" alternative). Finally, note that truth wins gives no solution when no member favors the "correct" alternative.

Majority wins gives no solution in case of a draw, and truth wins gives no solution in cases in which no member prefers the correct alternative. It is therefore often necessary to formulate a slightly more complex SDS, which specifies what happens in these cases. An example would be "majority wins, proportionality otherwise." This SDS implies that an alternative is always chosen when a majority favors it, but in the absence of a majority bigger factions are more likely to win. Note that in this SDS numerical support is the *only* factor that determines the group decision. Another example is "truth wins, proportionality otherwise." In that case, numerical support is less important. What is important is whether at least one group member is correct (in which case the correct alternative is chosen). Only when no member is correct does the group rely on numerical support (i.e., proportionality). Many other types of SDS are possible, and all kinds of combinations are possible as well. An example would be two-thirds majority wins (as is sometimes used in parliaments when voting on constitutional changes). What is important is that not every SDS is plausible in each situation. For example, in a problem-solving situation a truth wins SDS is more plausible than when deciding on a gift for a mutual friend (i.e., there is no "truth"). In the latter case, majority wins might be more applicable.

Individuals into groups

Group decisions can be predicted when we know group composition and the SDS used by the group. We can establish group composition directly, for example by asking group members their preference before a group discussion. We can also manipulate group composition, for example by assigning group members to groups based on their preference (e.g., Schulz-Hardt, Brodbeck, Mojzisch, Kerschreiter, & Frey, 2006). One possibility is to measure or manipulate group composition, observe a large number of group decisions, and deduct from these decisions the SDS that was used in these groups.

Another interesting possibility is to compare individual preferences with group decisions. For many decisions, it will be the case that not all alternatives are equally popular. In the hiring decision example, more members of the company may prefer candidate A than candidate B or C, perhaps because candidate A has more relevant experience. What consequences does this have for group decisions? A fundamental prediction from SDS theory is that a majority wins SDS will often augment biases that are present at the individual level. For example, when in our hiring decision example 80 per cent of individual company members would prefer candidate A, a majority wins/proportionality otherwise SDS would predict a 90 per cent probability that groups choose candidate A (e.g., Stasser, 1999). The reason is that with 80 per cent of individuals preferring candidate A it is very likely that a majority of group members prefer candidate A. Using a majority wins SDS would lead all these groups to actually choose candidate A (even when a minority for another candidate is present).

Major findings

Group decisions can often be predicted based on group member initial preferences (group composition), and often using some variant of a majority wins SDS (e.g., Stasser, Kerr, & Davis, 1989). Majorities are powerful, because of informational influence and normative pressure (Deutsch & Gerard, 1955; Chapter 2). The reason why a majority endorses a particular alternative might simply be that it is a good alternative. Thus, the majority might have some very good arguments, and convince the minority. However, when majorities are wrong they often win as well, in particular when it is hard to judge the correctness of a response (Deutsch & Gerard, 1955, Nemeth & Nemeth-Brown, 2003). The reason partly is normative pressure: Deviants are silenced, and sometimes people who have a different opinion dare not express it (i.e., they self-censor). In that case, public compliance rather than private conversion would occur (see Chapter 2).

Nevertheless, majority wins often yields accurate decisions (Hastie & Kameda, 2005). These positive results are observed when group members are motivated to find the best alternative, when they come to their conclusions independently, and also "vote" independently. Indeed, "majority wins" is an adequate way to eliminate biases that occur at the individual level, for example due to lack of information or capabilities. If several group members have independently come to the same conclusion this conclusion is likely to be more valid (less biased) than a conclusion reached by a single individual. One of the problems, however, is that often group members do not independently reach their conclusion or do not vote independently. Recall, for example, the Asch (1955) line-estimation task, in which confederates deliberately gave the wrong response (Chapter 2). An individual confronted with a majority that gave the wrong answer often went along, and such processes might eventually lead to a low-quality group decision. In essence, the reason is that individuals did not vote independently, but rather *after* hearing the opinion of others. This might compromise the eventual quality of a group decision when using a majority wins SDS.

The fact that majorities are powerful does not mean that minorities never have an influence. Indeed, with a "truth wins" SDS, a minority of one group member can in principle convert the entire group, no matter how large the majority is. But also some positions are more easily defended than others. One such case is that of mock jury deliberations. Juries usually are given the instruction that guilt has to be established "beyond reasonable doubt." This implies that it is easier to defend a "not guilty" position, because there often is at least *some* doubt: Eyewitnesses can be wrong, and circumstantial evidence might be counter-argued. Indeed, what has been observed in jury decisions is a *leniency bias*: Pro-acquittal factions are more influential than pro-conviction factions (e.g., MacCoun & Kerr, 1988).

Research has shown that a majority wins/proportionality otherwise SDS cannot accurately predict jury decisions, because of a strong leniency bias. For example, MacCoun and Kerr (1988) report data from 13 studies in which a total number of 345 six-person juries were initially evenly split (three jurors favoring guilty, three favoring not guilty). Of these juries, about 35 per cent failed to reach a verdict (i.e., they were hung and could not reach agreement, making a retrial necessary). In the juries that did reach a verdict, many more juries acquitted (53 per cent of the total number of juries) than convicted (12 per cent), showing that pro-acquittal factions were more influential. Similarly, with an initial [4, 2] majority in favor of conviction (this happened in 371 juries), about 47 per cent of the juries convicted (22 per cent acquitted, and 31 per cent were hung). However, with an initial [2, 4] majority in favor of acquittal (this happened in 344 juries), 76 per cent acquitted (5 per cent convicted, and 17 per cent were hung). Thus, with a similar two-thirds majority, acquittal factions were more influential (they won in 76 per cent of the cases) than conviction factions (they won in only 47 per cent of the cases). These results clearly demonstrate a leniency bias.

Conclusion

SDS theory is a formal theory of group decision-making, and allows one to compute very precise predictions about group decisions (see Stasser, 1999). One of the major advantages is that the theory specifies how individual preferences are turned into a group decision. It can explain why, using a majority wins SDS, individual-level biases are augmented in a group situation. It can further be used to compare individual-level preferences with group-level choices. Data can be used to test which SDS best predicts group decision (e.g., majority/leniency rather than majority/proportionality in jury decision-making). Finally, when we have a good idea about which SDS is used in a particular situation, we can derive predictions about what might happen in different situations, such as with larger groups or with a population in which initial preferences are distributed in another way (Stasser, 1999).

Group decisions and information

Information sharing, hidden profiles, and group decision-making

One reason to use groups when making decisions is that the group as a whole has more information than any group member individually: Group member 1 may know something that member 2 does not, and member 3 may know something altogether different. When group members pool their information, they might arrive at a better (more informed) choice. It is even possible that the group chooses an alternative that is superior to all other alternatives even though no single group member initially preferred it. However, this requires that information is adequately exchanged during the group discussion.

Take a three-member group consisting of Mary, Rick and Chris that has to decide between alternatives A and B (Figure 7.2). Suppose that A_1–A_4 represent four pieces of positive information about alternative A, and B_1–B_3 represent three pieces of positive information about alternative B. If all information is equally important, alternative A is the best choice: It has four pieces of supporting information, whereas B has only three. Now suppose that the information is distributed among group members and that some information is available to all members (*shared information*: A_1, B_1, B_2, and B_3), and some information is only available to one member (*unshared*

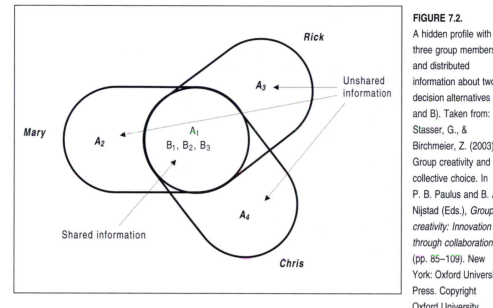

FIGURE 7.2.

A hidden profile with three group members and distributed information about two decision alternatives (A and B). Taken from: Stasser, G., & Birchmeier, Z. (2003). Group creativity and collective choice. In P. B. Paulus and B. A. Nijstad (Eds.), *Group creativity: Innovation through collaboration* (pp. 85–109). New York: Oxford University Press. Copyright Oxford University Press. Reprinted with permission.

information): Only Mary knows A_2, only Rick knows A_3, and only Chris knows A_4. Before the group discussion, all members are expected to prefer alternative B, because they all hold the three pieces of positive information about that alternative (they all know B_1–B_3), whereas each holds only two about alternative A (Mary knows A_1 and A_2; Rick A_1 and A_3; and Chris A_1 and A_4). However, during the group discussion, they may find out that they all were wrong initially, and that alternative A is in fact the better choice. If this would happen, it would represent *process gains*: The group performs better than any member could perform alone.

A situation such as that depicted in Figure 7.2 is known as a *hidden profile*, because the correct solution is initially hidden from group members and can only be detected when group members exchange their unshared information (Stasser, 1988). Stasser and Titus (1985) were the first to study hidden profiles, and investigated whether groups could overcome initial preferences for the wrong alternative and reach the correct conclusion after group discussion. They had four-person groups decide among three candidates for a student body president. Candidate A was the best choice, because more pieces of favorable information about that candidate were available. First, group members individually read information about the candidates, and then discussed the candidates in the group and made a group decision.

Stasser and Titus (1985) created three experimental conditions. In the *all shared condition* group members individually received all information before the group discussion. In the other two conditions, a hidden profile was created. Information was divided among group members, making some information shared (all members were given this information) and other information unshared (it was given to only one group member). Thus, while the group as a whole always had the complete set of information available, each individual group member knew only part of it before the discussion. The correct candidate (A) in these conditions could only be detected after an adequate exchange of unshared information, because the positive information about that candidate was unshared and was divided among the group members. In the *unshared/consensus condition*, all group members were led to favor candidate B instead (the wrong candidate): All positive information about B was given to all members, while the negative information about that candidate was unshared and divided among the four members. In the *unshared/conflict condition*, a different form of information distribution was used. Instead of biasing all group members towards candidate B (creating an initial consensus in favor of that candidate), two group members were led to like B (they were given the positive but not the negative information about candidate B), and two were led to like C (they were given the positive but not the negative information about candidate C).

Stasser and Titus (1985) reasoned that groups would choose candidate A (the correct choice) in the full-information condition, because the correct alternative is not hidden from individual group members. However, groups are not likely to discover the hidden profile in the unshared/consensus condition. Instead, groups would quickly realize that they share the same preference, and using a majority wins type of SDS would agree to choose B (the wrong alternative) without much discussion. However, in the unshared/conflict condition they might discover the hidden profile, and choose the correct candidate although no group member initially preferred it. Because some members preferred B and some C, the groups should more extensively discuss the issue, and during discussion they might find out that in fact A is the better choice. Unfortunately, this is not what happened (see Figure 7.3). In the full-information condition, most groups recognized that candidate A was the best choice. However, groups in which members were led to like B (the unshared/consensus condition) often chose B, and in the unshared/conflict condition most groups chose either B or C, and not the correct

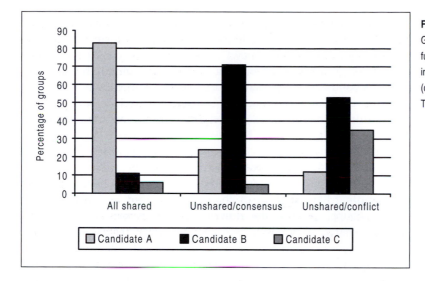

FIGURE 7.3.
Group choice as a function of initial information distribution (data from Stasser & Titus, 1985).

alternative A. The reason, Stasser and Titus (1985) found, was that unshared information favoring candidate A often remained undiscussed, and therefore groups *could* not discover the hidden profile.

Why was unshared information not discussed? There is a simple reason: chance. The probability that a particular piece of information is mentioned during discussion is positively related to the number of group members that hold that piece of information (Stasser & Titus, 1987). Suppose that the probability that a group member recalls a particular piece of information during discussion is $p(R)$, and the probability that this person does *not* recall it is thus $[1 - p(R)]$. If n group members can recall that particular piece of information, the chance that *none* of them recalls it is $[1 - p(R)]^n$, and the chance that *at least one* member recalls it is:

$$p(D) = 1 - [1 - p(R)]^n \quad (1)$$

For example, when $p(R) = .5$, the probability that the piece of information is discussed when it is unshared (i.e., when only one member knows it; $n = 1$) simply is .5. When a piece of information is known to four group members ($n = 4$), the probability that it is discussed becomes $1 - [1 - .5]^4 = .94$.

Formula (1) implies that the more group members can recall a piece of information (i.e., initially knew it), the more likely it is that it is discussed in the group. Think about this for a second. The benefit of group over individual decision-making lies in the possibility that group members can contribute unique (unshared) knowledge; however, they actually are more likely to talk about information that all group members already knew! This severely limits the potential benefits of group decision-making. Indeed, later research has established beyond any doubt that group discussions show a *sampling bias* in favor of shared information: Shared information has a higher probability of being mentioned during discussion than unshared information (e.g., Larson, Foster-Fishman, & Keys, 1994; Stasser, Taylor, & Hanna, 1989). Because groups focus more on shared than on unshared information, they often fail to discover hidden profiles.

Formula (1) has other implications. First, research has shown that the sampling bias in favor of shared information is exacerbated in larger groups, because the number of group members who can mention shared information is higher in larger groups (i.e., with a higher n, $p(D)$ increases; Stasser et al., 1989). Second, the bias depends on information load (i.e., how much decision-relevant information is available). The reason is that with higher information load $p(R)$ is lower (i.e., each piece of information is less likely to be recalled). For example, when $p(R)$ is .8 (rather than .5, reflecting a lower information load), $p(D)$ for unshared information is .8, and for shared information in a four-person group $p(D)$ is $1 - [1 - .8]^4 = .998$. The difference thus is .198, whereas for $p(R) = .5$ it was .44. Thus, the sampling bias is reduced when information load is low (Stasser & Titus, 1987).

Evaluation of shared and unshared information and the common-knowledge effect

Groups tend to talk about things that everyone already knew. But the situation is even worse. Even when unshared information is mentioned during discussion, it is less likely to be picked up by the group. Research has shown that when unshared information is mentioned during group discussion it is *repeated* less often than shared information (e.g., Larson et al., 1994; Stasser et al., 1989). If we take repetition as a sign that information is actually processed and seen as important (Scholten, Van Knippenberg, Nijstad, & De Dreu, 2007), this implies that unshared information does not receive as much weight during group discussion as perhaps it should. There are two reasons why unshared information, even if it is mentioned, does not receive as much weight as shared information.

First, shared information can be *validated* by group members other than the one that mentioned it (e.g., Wittenbaum, Hubbell, &

Zuckerman, 1999). Because other members originally held the same piece of information, they can testify that it is valid. It therefore tends to be seen as more credible than unshared information that cannot be validated by others. This also has the consequence that group members who mention shared as compared to unshared information are rated higher on expertise by other members (Wittenbaum *et al.*, 1999; see also Kameda, Ohtsubo, & Takezawa, 1997). This is somewhat ironical: While groups have more to gain from members who have unique unshared knowledge, they value those members who merely share information that others already had!

Second, people are reluctant to change an initial preference. In a hidden profile situation, group members enter the discussion with a preference for a suboptimal alternative. New unshared information that comes up during discussion implies that this preference was incorrect. However, research has shown that people do not always revise their initial preferences, even when information becomes available during discussion that shows that another alternative is the better choice (e.g., Postmes, Spears, & Cihangir, 2001). Greitemeyer and Schulz-Hardt (2003) have shown that the reason is that people evaluate new information in a biased way. They see information that supports their initial preference as more important than information that supports an initially non-preferred alternative. Furthermore, positive information about the preferred alternative is seen as more positive than positive information about a non-preferred alternative, whereas negative information about the preferred alternative is seen as less negative than negative information about a non-preferred alternative. As a consequence, people do not revise their initial opinion.

These biases contribute to the *common-knowledge effect*: the effect that shared information has a bigger impact on group choice than unshared information (Gigone & Hastie, 1993, 1997). Gigone and Hastie argued that shared information is available to every group member from the start and will affect the initial preferences of each member. It therefore has more impact than unshared information, which can only affect one person (Figure 7.4; arrow 1). Based on SDS theory, simply pooling these preferences, for example using a majority wins SDS, would already lead to many group decisions consistent with shared (rather than unshared) information (arrow 2). This bottom pathway in Figure 7.4 thus refers to a simple preference pooling effect. The top pathway refers to an information exchange and evaluation effect (also see Winquist & Larson, 1998). We have seen that the sampling bias leads groups to focus on shared information (arrow 3). We have further seen that shared information is

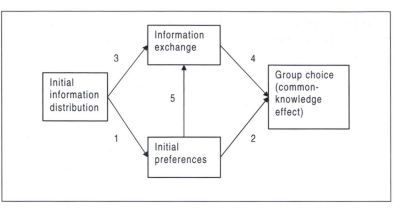

weighed more heavily during group discussion (arrow 4). Again, the implication is that group decisions will mainly reflect shared rather than unshared information. A final arrow in Figure 7.4 is one from member initial preferences to information exchange. This arrow reflects a potential further bias in group discussion, called *advocacy*: group members' tendency to defend their initial preference during group discussion, by mentioning information that is consistent rather than inconsistent with this preference. Advocacy further biases group decisions in the direction of initial preferences.

Overcoming discussion biases

Figure 7.4 paints a rather pessimistic picture of group decision-making. However, there are several ways to counteract biased information-sharing in groups. Let us consider four examples.

Initial preference diversity

In the Stasser and Titus (1985) study an unshared/consensus condition was compared with an unshared/conflict condition. In the consensus condition, group members all initially favored the same suboptimal alternative, while in the conflict condition, members favored different suboptimal alternatives. Stasser and Titus did not find that groups in the conflict condition more often made the correct decision. However, subsequent research has shown that preference diversity (i.e., different members initially having a different preference) does make a difference.

Schulz-Hardt *et al.* (2006) had three-person groups make a decision among four job candidates (A, B, C, and D). Candidate C was the superior candidate, but a hidden profile was created: Each group member individually read biased information in which candidate C was made less attractive than she really was (i.e., positive information was unshared and divided across the group members). After reading the candidate information individually, different participants had different preferences, including some who had a preference for candidate C (even though this candidate was made less attractive). Based on group member initial pre-discussion preferences, members were assigned to groups. In some of these groups, all members preferred the same suboptimal candidate (consensus condition); in other groups, members preferred different suboptimal candidates (diversity condition); and in some groups one member had the correct preference (minority condition). There also was a control condition in which all members received all information from the start (no hidden profile).

Group decisions (percentage choosing the correct candidate C) are shown in Figure 7.5. All groups who had received complete information from the start chose candidate C. Schulz-Hardt *et al.* (2006) further found two effects. One is that preference diversity, even if no member is initially correct, can improve group decisions. Thus, in the condition in which every group member favored the same suboptimal candidate, groups decided in favor of C in only 7 per cent of the cases. In situations in which group members had different incorrect preferences this was around 25 per cent. The reason was that discussions were longer and less biased in these conditions. However, percentage correct was even higher (around 60 per cent) when one group member initially favored the correct candidate. There the main reason was that the information supporting the correct candi-

FIGURE 7.5.

Percentage of correct decisions as a function of group composition. Taken from: Schulz-Hardt, S., Brodbeck, F. C., Mojzisch, A., Kerschreiter, R., & Frey, D. (2006). Group decision making in hidden profile situations: Dissent as a facilitator for decision quality. *Journal of Personality and Social Psychology, 91*, 1080–1093. Copyright American Psychological Association. Reprinted with permission.

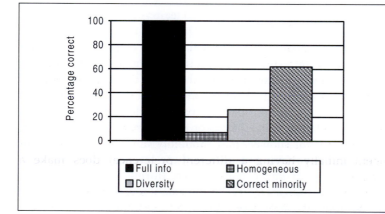

date was discussed more fully. Thus, in these conditions, one correct group member often converted the entire group (cf. truth wins SDS).

Decision framing

Stasser and Stewart (1992) found that another way to reduce discussion bias is to frame the decisional task as a problem to be solved rather than a decision to be made. Groups were given information about a murder case, and had to decide which of three suspects had committed the crime. Either group members individually received full information from the start, or information was divided among group members to create a hidden profile. The murder could be solved through logical reasoning, but this was told to only half of the groups (solve condition). The other half of the groups was told that evidence was inconclusive and that they had to give their best guess which suspect was most likely to have committed the murder (judge condition). Most groups with complete information from the start correctly identified the perpetrator. However, in the hidden profile situation, the correct suspect was identified more often in the solve than in the judge condition. The reason was that the critical information about the murder case was discussed more fully in the solve condition.

Leadership

A third way to stimulate information exchange is through leadership (Larson, Christensen, Abbott, & Franz, 1996; Larson, Foster-Fishman, & Franz, 1998). Larson and colleagues have found that leaders can take the role of *information managers* during group discussion. Larson *et al.* (1996) studied medical decisions in teams made up of a resident, an intern, and a medical student. These groups had to diagnose several patients, and information (diagnostic clues, such as prior medical history and experienced symptoms) was distributed among the group members. Larson *et al.* found that the resident, who was the leader of the group (and of course the person with highest status) asked more questions and repeated both shared and unshared information more often than the interns or the students. In later research, Larson *et al.* (1998) showed that randomly appointed leaders also showed these behaviors, but only if these leaders were trained to encourage group member participation during discussion. Thus, adequate leadership can stimulate information exchange, as well as make sure that information is noticed (by repeating it).

Expert roles

A fourth and perhaps most promising way to counteract biases in group discussions is by assigning expert roles. In a standard hidden profile situation, group members do not know beforehand which information is shared or unshared and they can only find out during group discussion. Suppose, however, that group members have some idea from the start about who knows what (i.e., groups have a *trans-active memory system*; see Chapter 3). This would be the case when group members have mutually recognized areas of expertise (group members know about one another's expertise). This has two beneficial effects (see Stewart & Stasser, 1995; Stasser, Stewart, & Wittenbaum, 1995). First, having a specific area of expertise might increase $p(D)$ for unshared information within this area. If members know *which* unique unshared information they hold, they may offer more of that information either spontaneously or after this is solicited by other members (e.g., "you are an expert on X. What more can you tell us about X?"), both of which would increase the likelihood that unshared information is mentioned during group discussion. Second, if a group member is recognized to be an expert, the unshared information offered by this person might be seen as more credible, despite the fact that other group members cannot validate it. Indeed, it has been found that when expert roles are assigned publicly (i.e., group members know one another's areas of expertise), the exchange of unshared information is enhanced and groups more often solve hidden profiles (Stasser *et al.*, 1995; Stasser, Vaughan, & Stewart, 2000; Stewart & Stasser, 1995).

Conclusion

Groups have the potential to outperform individuals on decision-making tasks when different members have unique unshared information pertaining to the decision. However, we have seen that the role of unshared information during group decision-making is quite uncertain. There is a sampling bias in favor of shared information, and even when unshared information is mentioned, it is not always given the same weight as shared information. However, several conditions counteract these negative effects: pre-discussion preference diversity, task framing, leadership, and expert roles have been shown to enhance group discussion of unshared information and quality of the final group choice.

Groupthink

The groupthink model

We started Chapter 1 with two decisions made by President Kennedy and his group of advisors, and noted that one of them (the Bay of Pigs invasion) is an example of groupthink: "A mode of thinking that people engage in when they are deeply involved in a cohesive in-group, when members' strivings for unanimity override their motivation to realistically appraise alternative courses of action" (Janis, 1972, p. 9). Janis based his groupthink model on six historical cases: the decision to ignore a potential Japanese threat to Pearl Harbor (1941, Admiral Kimmel), the decision to start the Marshall Plan to help European nations recover after the Second World War (1947, President Truman), the decision to invade North Korea (1950, President Truman), the decision to invade Cuba at the Bay of Pigs (1961, President Kennedy), the Cuban missile crisis (1962, President Kennedy), and the decision to escalate the Vietnam War (1964/1965, President Johnson). Two of these decisions were very successful (the Marshall Plan and the Cuban missile crisis), but the others were complete disasters.

Janis (1972) argued that these decision fiascos result from faulty group decision-making. He developed a model that aimed to explain why a group of competent people sometimes make such disastrous decisions. Janis' model argues that certain situations lead to excessive concurrence-seeking, in which groups mainly aim to maintain group harmony and consensus rather than adequately assessing the decision in all its complexity. The model distinguishes among antecedents, symptoms, and consequences of groupthink.

The antecedent conditions can be grouped into three clusters. The first is high group cohesion, often accompanied by a sense of superiority or *esprit de corps*. The second cluster is structural faults, including insulation of the group from outsiders, a lack of leader impartiality, a lack of adequate decision procedures, and high group member homogeneity. The final cluster is high stress due to external stressors, such as external threats to the group, and internal stressors, for example because the group has recently failed. In combination, these three clusters of antecedents lead to excessive concurrence-seeking: The group values consensus because of high group cohesion and high levels of stress. Because of structural faults, this is not corrected during the decision-making process.

Like pathology, groupthink has a number of symptoms. These include an illusion of invulnerability, belief in the inherent morality of the group, collective rationalizations (the group "explains away" counter-evidence), stereotyping of outsiders, self-censorship (not expressing one's true opinions), "mindguards" who "correct" dissenters, pressure on deviants, and the illusion that group members unanimously agree with the decision. This in turn leads to defects during decision-making: Not all alternatives are identified or evaluated, the objectives of the decision are not carefully surveyed, neither the chosen alternative nor rejected alternatives are re-examined, information search and processing is poor and selective, and no contingency plans are developed in case things go wrong. The end result is that it becomes unlikely that the group's decision will be successful.

The groupthink model attracted much attention, and several other decision fiascos have been studied using Janis' model. These include the Watergate scandal (1972–1974, President Nixon), the Iranian hostage crisis (1979–1982, President Carter), and decision-making preceding the 1986 space shuttle *Challenger* disaster (see Esser & Lindoerfer, 1989; Janis, 1982; Smith, 1985). A groupthink analysis of the *Challenger* disaster is presented in Box 7.1.

Empirical evidence

Case Studies

Several case studies more or less support aspects of Janis' model. Tetlock (1979) argued that groupthink would manifest itself in less complex thinking, more stereotyping of outsiders, and a more positive view of the decision-maker's own group. He coded the public statements of people involved in five historical cases originally studied by Janis (1972). He found that public statements were less complex and more positive about the speaker's own group in groupthink situations (Korea, Bay of Pigs, Vietnam) than in non-groupthink situations (Marshall Plan, Cuban missile crisis). However, he did not find differences between groupthink and non-groupthink situations in stereotyping of outside groups (e.g., of the communists).

The groupthink model predicts not only that certain symptoms are present in groupthink situations, but also that variables are linked in specific ways. Tetlock, Peterson, McGuire, Chang, and Feld (1992) carefully coded texts about 10 historic episodes for the presence of

BOX 7.1.
The *Challenger* Disaster

The *Challenger* disaster occurred on January 28, 1986, 73 seconds after launch (Figure 7.6). After the accident, US President Reagan installed a Presidential Committee to investigate its causes. In their report (Report of the Rogers Commission, 1986), the committee concluded that the accident had both a technical and a human component. The technical cause was that gas had escaped from a solid rocket booster (a rocket to help the Space Shuttle develop enough speed). Gas could escape because the rubber O-rings that were in place to prevent this did not function adequately. The reason was low temperature at launch, which was approximately 0° C (−31° Fahrenheit). Under low temperatures the O-rings did not completely seal off the gas in the solid rocket boosters. Gas escaped and caught fire, which triggered a chain reaction that eventually destroyed the *Challenger*, and killed its crew of seven.

FIGURE 7.6.
The Space Shuttle *Challenger* explodes on January 28, 1986, after faulty decision-making at NASA.

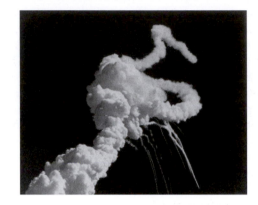

This committee also looked at decision-making at NASA prior to launch. The most remarkable finding was that the problem with the O-rings was known and was even discussed in the days preceding launch. Several engineers raised concerns about launch temperature and what this might do to the O-rings, and argued that launch should be delayed. However, NASA management did not consider the evidence carefully, because they strongly preferred to go ahead with the launch. The *Challenger* flight had already been delayed a few times, and because NASA had an ambitious Space Shuttle program planned, it would have been hard to complete that program after more delays. This decision to ignore the evidence and take the risk eventually led to disaster.

Applying Janis' groupthink model (also see Esser & Lindoerfer, 1989), several elements of the groupthink model are apparent. NASA was (and still is) an organization with high status and *esprit de corps*. Furthermore, it was under pressure: If NASA delayed launch, it could not accomplish its objectives for that year. Indeed, managers made it very clear that they strongly favored launching the *Challenger*. Thus, several antecedents of groupthink were present. When we look at the symptoms, we see that dissenters were silenced (e.g., engineers who argued that launch had to be delayed). Also, some rationalization occurred: Rather than seeing temperature as a possible problem, it was rationalized away and managers strongly preferred the conclusion that no clear evidence was present that launch temperature was a problem. The assessment of the evidence thus was poor and selective, which eventually led to a poor decision, costing the lives of seven people.

antecedents, symptoms, and consequences of groupthink, and then established quantitative relations among these variables. They found relatively strong relations between structural faults and concurrence-seeking, between concurrence-seeking and symptoms of groupthink, and between these symptoms and defective decision-making. However, they did not find that either high cohesion or internal/external stressors affected concurrence-seeking. Tetlock *et al.* therefore proposed that these factors may not be highly important.

Experimental evidence

Besides case-studies, some experimental work has been done testing the groupthink model (for overviews, see Aldag & Fuller, 1993; Baron, 2005; Esser, 1998). Most studies have considered group cohesion, and these studies generally failed to find support for the prediction that high group cohesion would lead to groupthink (e.g., Flowers, 1977; Fodor & Smith, 1982). On the other hand, laboratory experiments support the prediction that lack of leader impartiality produces groupthink phenomena. For example, Flowers (1977) found that groups with directive leaders used less available information and suggested fewer solutions than groups without directive leaders. Mullen, Anthony, Salas, and Driskell (1994) found that directive leadership was associated with more self-censorship and more mind-guarding, and Moorhead and Montanari (1986) found that directive leaders tended to discourage dissent. These last authors also found that insulated groups considered fewer alternatives and made poorer decision than non-insulated groups.

It thus appears that experimental evidence for groupthink theory is mixed: Some predictions are supported, but others are not. What is perhaps most disappointing is the lack of effects of group cohesion: It would have been counterintuitive and important when cohesion had *negative* rather than positive effects on group performance (also see Chapter 1). One possibility is that it is not cohesion *per se* that produces groupthink, but rather the combination of high cohesion, external threats, and structural faults. For example, Turner, Pratkanis, Probasco, and Leve (1992) manipulated threats to the group (participants were told that their discussion would be videotaped and shown to others) and cohesion, and found that the *combination* of high threat and high cohesion led to groupthink phenomena. Unfortunately, not many studies have tested the combined effects of several factors at the same time (but see Park, 2000).

Taking stock

Janis' (1972, 1982) groupthink model has attracted a lot of attention, but has not always received unequivocal support in empirical tests. The groupthink model might best be seen as a heuristic model rather than a validated theory. It provides insight into the mechanisms that might underlie defective group decision-making in high-stake situations. However, the presence of certain antecedents will not always lead to defective decision-making, and defective decisions can also occur when these antecedents are not present (Kerr & Tindale, 2004).

Integration

We started this chapter with two functions of group decision-making: consensus-building and information integration. Sometimes, groups might primarily focus on reaching and maintaining consensus, and these groups might be characterized as "preference driven." At other times, groups might primarily focus on reaching high-quality decisions and on the exchange of information and arguments ("information driven"). Finally, groups may use a mixture of both these strategies (Hastie, Penrod, & Pennington, 1983; Stasser & Birchmeier, 2003).

When group interaction is mainly preference driven, there will be frequent exchanges of preferences but not much discussion and elaboration of information. These groups will usually adopt the majority's position without much discussion and minorities might be disregarded or silenced. Information-processing will be biased and directed at confirmation of initial preferences. Such a preference-driven strategy is usually quick, and may lead to excellent decisions when the majority endorses a good alternative. However, sometimes it will lead the group astray. In extreme cases, when groups have a strong preference for a certain alternative (e.g., the group leader is strongly in favor of that alternative and other alternatives seem unacceptable), groups might only focus on convincing themselves that a certain alternative should be adopted, which may eventually lead to groupthink.

When group interaction is primarily "information driven," groups will use more time to arrive at a decision, and the discussion will be less biased. This strategy is slower (and less appropriate in high-emergency situations) but may be more accurate, especially when good (or the best) alternatives might only be discovered after extensive discussions (e.g., in hidden-profile situations). In these situations, minorities may win when they are successful in convincing the others.

De Dreu *et al.* (2008) argued that an information-driven strategy is more effortful and will only be used if group members are *motivated* to process decision-relevant information. This will happen when group members are uncertain about the accuracy of their preferences, while they do perceive that the decision is important. Indeed, when group members are convinced that their preferred alternative is the best choice, there is no reason to engage in elaborate information-processing. However, when group members are less convinced and when they believe that the decision is important, they will be more motivated to exert effort and really consider the available evidence.

Several conditions may lead groups to use an information- rather than a preference-driven decision strategy. One of these is preference diversity. When different group members have different preferences, it is not really possible to arrive at a group decision by merely exchanging preferences (i.e., there is no *a priori* consensus). Further, group members' certainty will be lower, because other group members have come to a different conclusion. Thus, groups are more likely to switch to information-driven strategies, and try to find an alternative that is supported by the evidence (cf. Schulz-Hardt *et al.*, 2006). Also, framing a decision as a problem to be solved (rather than a judgment to be made) may lead groups to focus on information more than on preferences (cf. Stasser & Stewart, 1992). Finally, having mutually recognized areas of expertise suggests that group members have unique unshared information, which may lead groups to adopt an information-driven strategy (cf. Stewart & Stasser, 1995).

Chapter summary

(1) There are two reasons why groups are used to make decisions: consensus-building and information integration.
(2) Social decision scheme (SDS) theory specifies how individual preferences are transformed to a group decision, and consists of four elements: individual preferences, group composition, social decision schemes, and group response. An SDS is a decision rule that links group composition to group response.
(3) One type of SDS that is often used is "majority wins." One property of a majority wins SDS is that initial majorities at the

individual level can be augmented at the group level. Occasionally minorities will be influential, when groups use a "truth wins" SDS or when a certain position is more easily defended than another position. An example is the leniency bias in jury decision-making, when pro-acquittal factions are more influential than pro-conviction factions.

(4) Often, group discussions focus more on shared information (information that was available to all group members) at the expense of unshared information (information available to just one member). As a consequence, groups often fail to discover hidden profiles.

(5) Shared information has more impact on group choice than unshared information (the common-knowledge effect), and even when unshared information is discussed it does not receive the same weight as shared information.

(6) Biases in group discussion are weaker when groups have diverse preferences, when the decision is framed as a problem to be solved, when group leaders function as information managers, and when group members have mutually recognized areas of expertise.

(7) Janis' groupthink model argued that decision fiascos may occur when excessive concurrence-seeking interferes with a careful evaluation of the decision. The model distinguishes among antecedents (high cohesion, structural faults, high stress), symptoms, and consequences of groupthink, and has attracted much attention. However, experimental research has not yielded unequivocal support for the model, although case-studies have been more supportive.

(8) Groups may use a preference- or information-driven strategy, and will consider more information and will be less biased when they are uncertain about the accuracy of their choice.

Exercises

(1) In which way does information exchange and integration play a role in SDS theory?

(2) Preferences sometimes are based on information (cf. Figure 7.4) but can also be based on personal interests (e.g., when group members benefit personally from a choice for a certain alternative). In which way do you think that group interaction changes when personal interests play a role?

(3) What might happen when there is no clear majority in favor of a particular alternative and the different factions within a group refuse to give in?

(4) What might be conditions in which it is unwise to have groups decide, but one should rather leave the decision to an individual decision-maker?

(5) Do you think that Janis' groupthink model can be studied in laboratory experiments, and why do you think so?

Further reading

Social decision scheme theory

Davis, J. H. (1973). Group decision and social interaction: A theory of social decision schemes. *Psychological Review, 80*, 97–125.

Stasser, G. (1999). A primer of social decision scheme theory: Models of group influence, competitive model-testing, and prospective modeling. *Organizational Behavior and Human Decision Processes, 80*, 3–20.

Information sharing and the common-knowledge effect

Gigone, D., & Hastie, R. (1997). The impact of information on small group choice. *Journal of Personality and Social Psychology, 72*, 132–140.

Stasser, G. (1999). The uncertain role of unshared information in collective choice. In L. Thompson, J. M. Levine, & D. M. Messick (Eds.), *Shared cognition in organizations: The management of knowledge* (pp. 49–69). Mahwah, NJ: Lawrence Erlbaum Associates.

Groupthink

Esser, J. K. (1998). Alive and well after 25 years: A review of groupthink research. *Organizational Behavior and Human Decision Processes, 73*, 116–141.

Janis, I. L. (1982). *Victims of groupthink* (2nd ed.). Boston: Houghton-Mifflin.

Motivation and group decision-making

De Dreu, C. K. W., Nijstad, B. A., & Van Knippenberg, D. (2008). Motivated information processing in group judgment and decision making. *Personality and Social Psychology Review, 12*, 22–49.

Group problem-solving and group judgment 8

Group decision-making is about reaching consensus on a particular decision alternative. Decision alternatives may vary in quality, but often one cannot say that one alternative is "correct" while another alternative is "incorrect." In group problem-solving situations this is different. Here, groups can reach a correct or incorrect conclusion, and one topic that has received considerable attention is how well groups do when solving problems with correct answers. Much of this research has applied social decision scheme theory, which we discussed in the previous chapter. In particular, researchers have investigated whether in a problem-solving task one correct group member is enough for the group to get the correct answer (i.e., do groups use a *truth wins* social decision scheme?).

Group problem-solving is about getting the correct answer. Some other research has looked into a perhaps equally important issue: avoiding mistakes. We know that individuals often make systematic errors in some types of judgments (see, e.g., Tversky & Kahneman, 1974). One question that has received attention is whether we can expect groups to do better, for example because group members correct each other's errors. Let's start with group problem-solving.

Group problem-solving

One of the first studies of group problem-solving was performed by Shaw (1932). She asked both individuals and four-person groups to solve several problems that had a correct solution. Consider the following example.

> Three married couples want to cross a river, but they only
> have one rowing boat, and it can only carry three people.
> Further, only husbands are allowed to row, and these

husbands are very jealous: They will not allow that their wives are in the presence of another man if they are not present as well. How can this problem be solved?[1]

Shaw (1932) found that groups were more successful than individuals in solving these tasks. For example, the husbands-and-wives problem was solved by only three of 21 individuals (14 per cent), but by three out of five groups (60 per cent). She argued that groups were superior because group members can correct each other's errors and reject incorrect solutions.

Lorge, Fox, Davitz, and Brenner (1958), however, argued that Shaw's problem has a particular property: When someone finds a solution, this would immediately be recognized as correct by the others. Lorge *et al.* called these types of problem *Eureka tasks*, and argued that a group could in principle solve the problem when the group has *at least one* smart member who could solve it. When we know the proportion of individuals $p(i)$ that can solve the problem ($p(i) = .14$, in this example), and we know group size ($n = 4$ in the example), we can compute how many groups are expected to solve it, $p(G)$. The formula is in fact identical to formula (1) in Chapter 7:

$$p(G) = 1 - [1 - p(i)]^n \quad (1)$$

In this example, with $p(i) = .14$ and $n = 4$, $p(G) = .45$ and about 45 per cent of groups are expected to have at least one member who can solve the problem. This is not very different from what Shaw found (60 per cent).

Problem-solving, social decision schemes, and demonstrability

Equation (1) is applicable when groups use a "truth wins" social decision scheme: The group chooses the correct solution when at least one member prefers it (see Chapter 7). When can groups be expected to use a truth wins SDS? Laughlin (1980; Laughlin & Ellis, 1986)

1   The solution is as follows. First husband 1 crosses with his wife, and leaves her on the other side. Then he goes back, and the three husbands next cross together. Husband 1 gets off on the other side to join his wife, and husband 2 and 3 row back. There, husband 2 picks up his wife, and they cross together with husband 3. Husband 2 and his wife stay behind, and husband 3 rows back to pick up his wife.

proposed that this depends on the degree of *demonstrability* of a task. He argued that demonstrability is a continuum along which tasks can be ordered, varying from judgmental to intellective tasks.

Judgmental tasks are "evaluative, behavioral, or aesthetic judgments for which there does not exist a demonstrably correct answer" (Laughlin & Ellis, 1986, p. 177). According to Laughlin and Ellis (1986), the criterion for success in this case is the achievement of consensus. An example would be to determine a group's favorite color. *Intellective tasks* are "problems or decisions for which there exists a demonstrably correct answer within a verbal or mathematical conceptual system" (p. 177). The criterion for success, evidently, is the achievement of this correct answer. The prime example would be a math problem. However, many problems will be somewhere in the middle of the continuum: Some responses are more "correct" than others, but there is no single correct response. This would be true for most decisions, including President Kennedy's response to the Cuba crisis (see Chapters 1 and 7): The response certainly was adequate, but cannot really be seen as *the only* correct solution to that problem. At the same time, worse decisions were possible.

When working on a problem with high demonstrability, groups might thus use a truth wins social decision scheme, and one correct group member should be enough for the group to get the right answer. According to Laughlin and Ellis (1986), this will happen when:

(1) the group agrees on a verbal or mathematical system that can be used to solve the problem
(2) there is enough information to solve the problem
(3) group members who cannot solve the problem have sufficient knowledge to recognize a correct solution when it is proposed
(4) the correct group member is able and willing to share the solution with the other group members in a way that they understand.

Laughlin and Ellis (1986) argued that some tasks may have a correct answer that is not demonstrable: Asking a group how many traffic accidents took place in the USA last year is an example. Another example would be an English vocabulary task (e.g., "What is the word used in English for a mixture of metals, one of quality with a poorer one?"): Although correct answers exist ("alloy"), this correct answer is not demonstrable when group members are unfamiliar with the word (i.e., condition 3 above is not satisfied). Basically, *the more demonstrable the solution, the fewer correct members are necessary for groups to choose it.*

An important finding is that for some tasks, such as Eureka tasks, only one correct group member seems necessary (truth wins), but for some other tasks the correct member needs at least one supporter (i.e., at least *two* correct members are necessary). The SDS associated with the latter case is often referred to as "truth-supported wins." With truth wins, more groups are expected to get the correct solution than with truth-supported wins, simply because it is more likely that the group contains at least one solver than it is that the group contains at least two solvers.

For example, when the task is difficult and only 20 per cent of individuals get the correct answer, a truth wins SDS when group size is four would predict that 59 per cent of groups get the correct answer (i.e., 59 per cent of the groups are expected to contain at least one solver; note that equation (1) above would also give that answer). However, with a truth-supported wins SDS this drops to only 18 per cent, because it is fairly unlikely that the group contains *at least two* solvers. With a moderately difficult task, where 50 per cent of individuals are able to find the correct solution, we expect about 94 per cent of the groups to be correct under truth wins and about 69 per cent under truth-supported wins – both numbers are higher than the 50 per cent at the individual level. According to this analysis, the likelihood that a group solves a particular problem correctly thus depends on a number of parameters. First, the combination of the likelihood that individuals get the correct answer (the difficulty of the task) and group size determines the number of solvers we expect per group. Second, group success depends on the SDS used by the group, and this in turn depends on demonstrability.

Laughlin and Ellis (1986) argued that with basic mathematics problems, of which most group members would have some knowledge, groups should adopt a truth wins SDS. They performed an experiment, in which participants were asked to solve ten different problems, such as (see Laughlin & Ellis, 1986, p. 181):

If $X + 3Y = 6$ and $X/Y = 3$, then X is equal to?[2]

A. 0 B. 1 C. 3/2 D. 2 E. 3

[2] The solution is as follows. If $X/Y = 3$, then $X = 3Y$ and $Y = X/3$. Substituting $X/3$ for Y in $X + 3Y = 6$ gives $X + (3X/3) = 6$ or $2X = 6$. Thus $X = 3$ and answer E is correct.

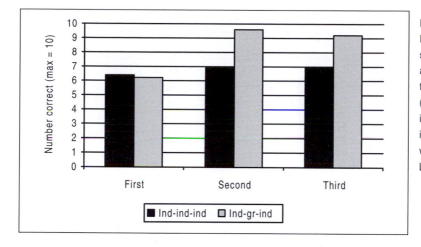

FIGURE 8.1.

Number of correctly solved math problems across three trials in two conditions (individual–individual–individual vs. individual–group–individual) (data from Laughlin & Ellis, 1986).

There were two experimental conditions. In the first condition, individuals were asked to solve these problems three times (individual–individual–individual), while in the second condition, participants first solved the problems individually, then in a five-person group, then again individually (individual–group–individual). Figure 8.1 shows the results (number of problems correctly solved). As can be seen, there were no differences between the two conditions in the first trial, where everybody worked individually. However, in the second trial, groups clearly outperformed the individuals. Further, in the last individual trial, those who had been in a group before had learned, and outperformed those who had not been in a group. Finally, and most importantly, Laughlin and Ellis found that groups were generally able to solve a problem with only one correct member, and on these types of intellective problems groups use a truth wins SDS.

As noted before, however, other types of problems seem to need at least two correct members (i.e., truth-supported wins). Examples are English vocabulary, general world knowledge, and analogies (e.g., Laughlin & Adamopoulos, 1980; Laughlin, Kerr, Davis, Halff, & Marciniak, 1975; Laughlin, Kerr, Munch, & Haggarty, 1976). Consider, for example, the following two analogies, in the form of A:B as C:D (taken from Laughlin & Adamopoulos, 1980, p. 942):

(1) rectangle : cube as oval : square, circle, oblong, round, sphere?
(2) dressmaker : silk as cabinetmaker : wood, screws, glue, mahogany, hemlock?[3]

3 Correct answers are *sphere* and *mahogany*.

FIGURE 8.2.

Number of correctly
solved analogies
across three trials in
two conditions
(individual–individual–
individual vs.
individual–group–indi-
vidual) (data from
Laughlin &
Adamopoulos, 1980).

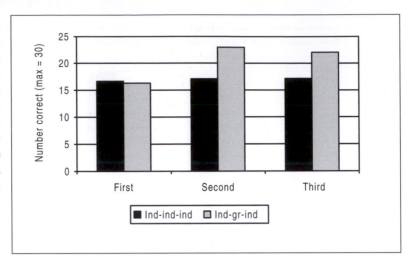

Laughlin and Adamopoulos (1980) used a design similar to Laughlin and Ellis (1986) with two conditions: one condition with consecutive individual–individual–individual trials, and one with individual–group–individual trials. Participants were asked to solve 30 analogies, and results are shown in Figure 8.2. They are similar to those presented in Figure 8.1: Groups do better than individuals in the second trial, and individuals do better after a group trial. However, Laughlin and Adamopoulos found that not truth wins, but truth-supported wins was the SDS that fitted the data best. The reason seems that analogies are less demonstrable than math problems, perhaps because a verbal-logical system is less formalized than a mathematical-formal system. Indeed, it seems easier to present the answer to a math problem (e.g., as in Footnote 2) than to explain why the answer to the second analogy is mahogany.

To demonstrate the difference between a truth wins and a truth supported wins SDS, Table 8.1 shows the relation between group composition (in terms of number of group members initially correct) and group response (proportion of groups giving the correct response), for both the Laughlin and Ellis (1986) study and the Laughlin and Adamopoulos (1980) study. As can be seen, in both studies a large majority of groups gave the correct response when groups contained at least two solvers. However, with only one solver, 83 per cent of groups were correct while working on a math task, but only 28 per cent when working on verbal analogies. This clearly demonstrates the different SDS used in the two different tasks.

TABLE 8.1

Relation between group composition and proportion of groups correct in two different studies

Laughlin & Ellis, 1986 (math problems: truth wins)		Laughlin & Adamopoulos, 1980 (analogies: truth-supported wins)	
Group composition	Proportion of groups correct	Group composition	Proportion of groups correct
[5, 0]	1.00	[6, 0]	1.00
[4, 1]	.99	[5, 1]	.99
[3, 2]	.97	[4, 2]	.96
[2, 3]	.97	[3, 3]	.90
[1, 4]	.83	[2, 4]	.67
[0, 5]	.50	[1, 5]	.28
		[0, 6]	.05

Collective induction and process gains

Some tasks have both intellective and judgmental aspects, and one of these is *collective induction*. Collective induction has been extensively studied by Laughlin and his colleagues (Laughlin, 1999, for an overview). During collective induction, groups must induce a general rule from available evidence. Induction is important in science, because scientists are interested in finding general rules that predict and explain certain phenomena (e.g., the behavior of particles in physics or the behavior of humans in psychology). However, also mechanics or physicians have to induce a "rule" from the available evidence: Mechanics have to find out why a car will not start, and physicians have to diagnose a disease from the patient's symptoms. In all these cases, induction involves the generation of a hypothesis (e.g., the patient may have a bacteriological infection), followed by a test of that hypothesis (e.g., run blood tests).

Laughlin and colleagues have studied collective induction using playing cards. In this task, groups or individuals have to induce rules such as "only hearts," "any card below 9," or "two hearts and two spades alternate." A trial starts with one card that is consistent with the rule (see Figure 8.3). For example, when the rule is "two hearts and two spades alternate," the trial might start out with the 7 of hearts. Next, each group member generates a hypothesis, after which the group as a whole decides on a hypothesis (not necessarily one that a group member has generated). The group then plays a card to

FIGURE 8.3.

Example of a rule
induction task with
eight trials. The rule is
"two hearts and two
spades alternate." The
trial starts with one
card that confirms to
the rule (7♥); next the
group proposes a
hypothesis (numbers
below 8) and plays a
card (6♦). Because the
card is inconsistent
with the rule, it is
placed under the
original card. Then the
group proposes a new
hypothesis (hearts and
clubs) and plays a new
card to test it (K♣).
This goes on for a fixed
number of trials.

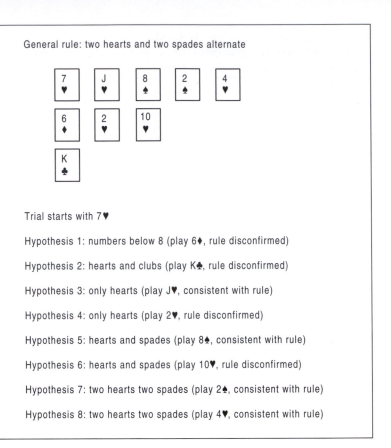

General rule: two hearts and two spades alternate

Trial starts with 7♥

Hypothesis 1: numbers below 8 (play 6♦, rule disconfirmed)

Hypothesis 2: hearts and clubs (play K♣, rule disconfirmed)

Hypothesis 3: only hearts (play J♥, consistent with rule)

Hypothesis 4: only hearts (play 2♥, rule disconfirmed)

Hypothesis 5: hearts and spades (play 8♠, consistent with rule)

Hypothesis 6: hearts and spades (play 10♥, rule disconfirmed)

Hypothesis 7: two hearts two spades (play 2♠, consistent with rule)

Hypothesis 8: two hearts two spades (play 4♥, consistent with rule)

test its hypothesis. For example, the group may propose the hypothesis "any number below 8" and play the 6 of diamonds to test it. When a card is inconsistent with the rule, it is placed under the previous card (that would be the case here). When it is consistent with the rule, it is placed to the right of the last card that was consistent with the rule. Participants are next asked to generate a new hypothesis, and play a new card to test this. This goes on for a fixed number of trials (e.g., 10 or 15 trials), and it is noted whether the final hypothesis is correct.

In this task, there are three types of hypotheses (e.g., Laughlin, VanderStoep, & Hollingshead, 1991): the correct hypothesis, plausible hypotheses, and non-plausible hypotheses. Non-plausible hypotheses are hypotheses that cannot be correct given previous trials, whereas plausible hypotheses could be correct in principle. If groups more often than individuals find the correct rule, this would be evidence that groups are better at recognizing a correct answer. Further, if groups less often than individuals propose a non-plausible hypothesis, this would imply that groups are better than individuals at recognizing and correcting errors. In fact, non-plausible hypotheses can be demonstrated to be wrong (i.e., this aspect of the task has a high degree of demonstrability), and we would – considering the previous section – expect groups to be better than the average individual. Indeed, groups are better than individuals in these rule induction tasks: They more often find the correct rule and they less often propose non-plausible hypotheses (e.g., Laughlin, 1999; Laughlin *et al.*, 1991; Laughlin & McGlynn, 1986; Laughlin & Shippy, 1983).

However, like other problem-solving tasks, rule induction might be seen as a disjunctive task (see Chapter 3): The potential performance of the group is determined by the group's *best* member (and not the average member). Indeed, with one high-ability group member, groups can in principle perform well. It therefore is interesting to compare group performance with the potential performance of the group given the abilities of the best member. One way to approach this is to use *nominal groups* (see also Chapter 6). One could compare the performance of, for example, four-person groups with the performance of nominal groups consisting of four people working separately. Of these nominal groups, one can establish who performs best, and see whether groups are able to perform at the level of this best individual. When groups perform below that level, there would be process losses; when they perform above that level, there would be process gains.

Laughlin *et al.* (1991) have made this comparison. In a first experiment, they found that groups performed at the level of the *second* best individual when correct hypotheses were considered. However, groups proposed as few non-plausible hypotheses as the *best* individual. In a second experiment, Laughlin *et al.* showed that groups could also perform at the level of the best individual when groups were allowed to play more cards (i.e., gather more evidence) and when groups were given sufficient time to induce the correct rule from the evidence. Thus, under these conditions, groups performed at their potential level. Laughlin *et al.* argued that this provides evidence that groups can deal with large quantities of information better than (most) individuals (see also Laughlin, Bonner, & Altermatt, 1998).

More recently, Laughlin and his colleagues (Laughlin, Bonner, & Miner, 2002; Laughlin, Hatch, Silver, & Boh, 2006; Laughlin, Zander,

Knievel, & Tan, 2003) have obtained evidence for *process gains* in another collective induction task: the letters-to-numbers task. In this task, each of the letters A through J represents a number from 0 through 9. The task is to find the correct number for each letter. Participants first propose an equation in letters (e.g., A + B = ?) and get an answer in letters (e.g., A + B = D). Next participants propose one mapping (e.g., A = 3) and receive feedback (i.e., true or false). Finally, they propose a full mapping of all letters and receive feedback (true or false). Then the next trial starts, with a new equation, feedback, etc. The problem is solved when the complete mapping is correct.

There are several strategies possible to solve the letters-to-numbers task, but some strategies are more efficient than others. In general, using just two letters per equation is inefficient, because using more letters per equation gives more information (Laughlin *et al.*, 2002). Laughlin *et al.* (2002) compared four-person groups with four-person nominal groups (i.e., four participants working individually). Within the nominal groups, they distinguished between the best, second best, third best and worst member, based on the average number of trials required to get the complete coding. Laughlin *et al.* found that the groups needed fewer trials to get all letters right than the *best* of the four individuals. Further, the reason appeared to be that the groups used more letters per equation on average. Laughlin *et al.* (2003) replicated this finding for three-person groups, and Laughlin *et al.* (2006) found that groups of size three and over outperformed the best individual but that dyads did not. Thus, on the letters-to-numbers problem groups show evidence of process gains, because they use more complex strategies.

Conclusion

In problem-solving tasks the performance of groups depends strongly on the demonstrability of the task. On highly demonstrable tasks, such as math problems and Eureka tasks, groups often perform as well as their best member. When tasks are less demonstrable, such as verbal analogies or vocabulary tasks, often two correct members are needed to get the correct answer. In more complex tasks, such as rule induction tasks, groups seem to be able to profit more from large quantities of information, and sometimes even outperform their best member. So far, these process gains have not been found very often, and future research needs to establish when exactly they might be found.

Errors and biases in judgment

One of the reasons why groups might be better than individuals in problem-solving or decision-making tasks is that group members can correct one another's errors. Much research at the individual level has shown that people are susceptible to all kinds of cognitive biases and errors: systematic departures from some normatively defined standard of judgment. Table 8.2 contains descriptions of some of these biases and errors. Consider the following two examples.

(1) A given city has two cab companies that use blue and green cars, respectively. Assume that 85 per cent of the cabs are blue, and 15 per cent are green. One of the cabs is involved in a hit-and-run accident at night-time and a witness reports that the cab was green. The witness is tested for his ability to distinguish between blue and green cabs at night, and he is 80 per cent accurate and makes equal numbers of errors for each type of cab. What is the

TABLE 8.2
Some judgmental biases and errors

Bias or error	Description	Findings*
Base-rate fallacy	Tendency to ignore base-rate information when giving probability judgments	Mixed
Conjunction error	Estimating the probability of a joint event as being greater than the smaller probability of the two events separately	Mixed
Hindsight bias	Estimating the probability of an unlikely event as greater after knowing it has occurred ("I knew it all along")	Groups less susceptible
Fundamental attribution error	Under-use of situational information when making behavioral attributions (e.g., attribute behavior to personality rather than to situational constraints)	Groups less susceptible
Framing bias	Responding differently when the same choice is framed in terms of losses versus in terms of gains	Mixed
Sunk cost effect	Oversensitivity to irreversible costs made previously (e.g., holding on to an investment despite substantial losses)	Groups more susceptible
Availability heuristic	Over-reliance on highly salient information (e.g., judging someone's performance based on one big and salient error, ignoring other information)	Groups less susceptible

* Based on Kerr et al. (1996).

probability that the cab involved in the accident was in fact green? (taken from Kahneman & Tversky, 1972)

(2) Linda is a young woman, who is single, outspoken, and concerned with issues of discrimination and social justice. Is Linda more likely to be (a) a bank teller or (b) a feminist bank teller? (taken from Tversky & Kahneman, 1983)

Kahneman and Tversky (1972) found that most people respond to the first problem with a probability judgment of around 80 per cent that the car is green. This answer is entirely based on the eyewitness accuracy, and ignores the fact that most cabs in that city are blue. This base-rate information (i.e., how many blue and green cabs there are) implies that the chance that the cab was blue (rather than green) should be higher. The correct solution, according to Bayesian probability logic, would be only 41 per cent that the car in fact was green.[4] That people ignore base-rate information when making probability estimates is known as the "base-rate fallacy" (Table 8.2).

The second problem illustrates the "conjunction error" (Table 8.2). A conjunction error in this case would occur when the estimated probability of answer (b) would be greater than the estimated probability of answer (a). Formal logic dictates that the probability of a single event (Linda being a bank teller) should always be greater or equal to the probability of a conjunction of this event *and* another event (Linda being a bank teller *and* a feminist). People often are led astray in these cases (Tversky and Kahneman, 1983, report that about 85 per cent of people made these conjunction errors): They estimate it likely that Linda is a feminist given her description, and can more easily envision her as a feminist bank teller than as a bank teller (for which they have other stereotypes), and consequently overestimate the chance that she is a feminist bank teller.

It is important to note that people do not make random errors when working on these tasks – the errors they make are quite

---

4   To understand this, suppose that the witness observes 100 cars, of which in reality 85 are blue and 15 are green, and he is correct in 80 per cent of the cases. He would then identify .8 × 15 cars (= 12) correctly as green (and three erroneously as blue) and .8 × 85 cars (= 68 cars) correctly as blue (and 17 incorrectly as green). Of the 100 cars, our witness would thus call 29 (12 + 17) cars green – many more than the 15 that really are green. According to the Bayesian rule, one should divide the proportion of cars expected to be correctly called "green" (.12) by the total number of cars expected to be called green (.29) to get the correct probability judgment (.12/.29 = .41).

systematic. Furthermore, these errors, fallacies, and biases can potentially lead to serious consequences when making judgments or
decisions. An important question therefore is whether groups are less
susceptible to these errors and biases than individuals. Recall that
Shaw (1932) argued that groups are better problem-solvers than
individuals because group members can correct one another's errors.
Will this also lead groups to do better on tasks such as those
described above? As so often, this question has no simple answer.

For example, Tindale (1993) reports some studies that compared
individuals and groups on the prevalence of several biases, including
the base-rate fallacy and the conjunction error. In one study, he used
the "cab problem" described above, and manipulated eyewitness
accuracy (80 per cent, 60 per cent, 50 per cent, 40 per cent, and 20 per
cent) and whether participants worked alone or in four-person
groups. Using this design, Tindale could see whether groups or
individuals were more susceptible to the base-rate fallacy. Figure 8.4
shows the result. As you can see, at the lower levels of witness
accuracy (20–50 per cent), the groups were closer to the Bayesian
normative solution than the individuals. However, at the higher
levels (with 80 per cent witness accuracy), groups showed a stronger
base-rate fallacy than individuals. The pattern of results seems to
suggest that individual-level tendencies to give high or low probability estimates are exacerbated in groups. This resembles group
polarization (see Chapter 2) or majority wins type processes (see
Chapter 7).

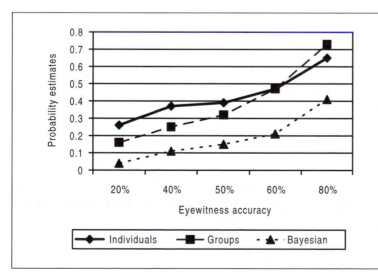

FIGURE 8.4.
The base-rate fallacy
for individuals and four-
person groups. Taken
from: Tindale, R. S.
(1993). Decision errors
made by individuals
and groups. In
N. Castellan Jr. (Ed.),
*Individual and group
decision making:
Current issues* (pp.
109–124). Hillsdale,
NJ: Lawrence Erlbaum
Associates. Copyright
Lawrence Erlbaum
Associates. Reprinted
with permission.

Now consider the conjunction fallacy data from Tindale (1993). He had individuals and four-person groups read short stories depicting a person, and then give probability estimates for category membership of the persons (e.g., "what is the likelihood that Linda is a bank teller?"). For each target person, a number of probability estimates had to be given, including estimates of likely (e.g., Linda is a feminist) and unlikely categories (e.g., Linda is a bank teller), and of combinations of these categories (e.g., Linda is a feminist bank teller). Each time a combination of categories was judged to be more likely than any of the categories separately, a conjunction error was made. What Tindale (1993) found, quite surprisingly, was that groups made *more* errors (73 per cent) than individuals (65 per cent). Tindale argued that the high prevalence of conjunction errors at the individual level (about two-thirds making the error) was exacerbated at the group level. He also presented some data that in many cases only one *incorrect* group member was enough to have the whole group fall prey to the conjunction error. In other words, the social decision scheme (SDS) that was used in these groups was "error wins" rather than "truth wins"!

Kerr, MacCoun, and Kramer (1996) give an overview of studies that compared various judgmental errors and biases committed by groups and individuals, and some of their conclusions are summarized in Table 8.2 (column 3). As you can see, no clear pattern emerges: sometimes groups are less susceptible to a certain bias or error, sometimes they seem to be more susceptible, and sometimes the evidence is mixed. Using SDS theory, Kerr *et al.* show that bias in group as compared to individual judgment (i.e., the *relative bias* of groups as compared to individuals) depends on a number of factors. Not surprisingly, given our previous discussion, three of these factors are group size, the proportion of individuals that make a certain error or show a certain bias, and the SDS used by the group. Thus, group size in combination with the proportion of individuals that make an error determines group composition (how many group members do and do not make the error), and the SDS (e.g., truth wins versus majority wins versus error wins) used will determine the relation between group composition and relative bias.

Kerr *et al.* (1996) further argued that some of these biases imply that people use information that they should not use while making these judgments (e.g., hindsight bias and framing bias), and others imply that people do not use certain information that they should use (e.g., base-rate fallacy). Interestingly, sometimes the availability of information affects group judgments because it changes the SDS used by the group. One example can be found in jury decision-making (see Kerr *et al.*, 1996; MacCoun, 1990). In Chapter 7, we have seen that jury decision-making usually does not follow a pure majority wins SDS, but rather that juries have a leniency bias (i.e., pro-acquittal factions have more influence than pro-conviction factions). MacCoun, however, did observe such a leniency bias for attractive defendants, but not for unattractive defendants (i.e., pro-conviction factions more often won). Thus, (1) groups took irrelevant information into account (the defendants' attractiveness) and (2) attractiveness information influenced the SDS used in groups.

To conclude, although error checking does occur sometimes, the relative bias of groups compared to individuals depends on a number of factors, including group size, proportion of individuals who make an error, the type of error, and group processes (i.e., the SDS used in the group). As such, the question "who is more biased, individuals or groups?" can only be answered with "well, it depends . . ." (Kerr *et al.*, 1996, p. 713).

Chapter summary

(1) There might be two reasons why groups outperform individuals when solving problems, which are correction of errors or recognition (or generation) of the correct response.

(2) Tasks can be ordered along a continuum of demonstrability. Demonstrability requires that group members agree on a formal system to solve the problem, that enough information is present to solve it, that incorrect members recognize the correct solution when it is proposed, and that correct members are willing and able to share their answer with the others. The more demonstrable a task is, the fewer correct group members are needed to solve it as a group.

(3) Consequently, groups use a truth wins SDS when problems are highly demonstrable (e.g., Eureka tasks), and a truth-supported wins SDS when problems are slightly less demonstrable.

(4) Work on collective induction suggests that groups may be better able to deal with large quantities of information than individuals, and on some tasks, groups have been shown to even outperform their best member.

(5) When making judgments, a number of systematic biases and errors have been observed for individuals. Sometimes groups

are more susceptible to these biases and errors, and sometimes less susceptible. Relative bias of groups depends on the type of bias, group size, the proportion of individuals who show the bias, and the SDS used by the group.

Exercises

(1) Groups might outperform individuals because of error checking or because groups are better at generating or recognizing correct solutions. Do you think that there is a difference in demonstrability in showing that an answer is wrong versus showing that it is correct?

(2) Look at the errors and biases displayed in Table 8.2. Could you order these according to the level of demonstrability?

(3) How would group member expertise influence group problem-solving? Use the concept of indispensability (Chapter 5) and the literature on information-sharing in groups (Chapter 7) in your answer.

Further reading

Demonstrability and group problem-solving

Laughlin, P. R., & Ellis, A. L. (1986). Demonstrability and social combination processes on mathematical intellective tasks. *Journal of Experimental Social Psychology, 22*, 177–189.

Collective induction, process gains

Laughlin, P. R. (1999). Collective induction: Twelve postulates. *Organizational Behavior and Human Decision Processes, 80*, 50–69.

Bias in individuals and groups

Kerr, N. L., MacCoun, R. J., & Kramer, G. P. (1996). Bias in judgment: Comparing individuals and groups. *Psychological Review, 103*, 687–719.

Teamwork and leadership 9

Consider the following description of a work group. What, do you think, is the task this group has to perform?

> [X] are particularly intense work groups. Members are reciprocally interdependent . . . using each other's outputs as their own inputs, and vice versa. Their interdependence is also complete and immediate: their work is done as a unit; they cannot perform [their task] without all of the members working together simultaneously.
>
> (Murnighan & Conlon, 1991, p. 165)

In this chapter we will look at teamwork and leadership. Teams are a special kind of group. One characteristic that is associated with teams (and not necessarily with all groups) is interdependence, which is very prominent in the above quote. Cohen and Bailey (1997, p. 241) define *teams* as follows:

> A team is a collection of individuals who are inter-dependent in their tasks, who share responsibility for outcomes, who see themselves and are seen by others as an intact social entity embedded in one or more social systems (for example, business unit or the corporation), and who manage their relationships across organizational boundaries.

Examples of teams that would fit this definition are readily available: Cohen and Bailey review work about police teams, mining crews, retail sales groups, hospital health care teams, quality circles, research and development (R&D) project teams, and top management teams. Other examples would be military tank crews, rock bands, airplane crews (see Figure 9.1), film crews, football teams, and string quartets.

Indeed, the first quote above is taken from Murnighan and Conlon's (1991) study of British string quartets.

Most research we have discussed in the previous chapters was carried out in the psychological laboratory, and used *ad hoc* groups of mostly student participants, who had to perform one specific task (e.g., make a decision, solve a series of problems, or pull a rope). While these studies have yielded important insights into group functioning and performance, some issues have not received much attention. In this chapter we will therefore consider issues around teamwork, and look at ongoing teams (instead of *ad hoc* groups) that have to perform several tasks (instead of just one) with sometimes very diverse team members (instead of homogeneous groups of students) who are highly interdependent. As teams often have to report to a manager or team leader, we also consider leadership. We start out with some basic issues.

FIGURE 9.1. The Moncur Crew, Molesworth, England, who flew the B17 *Thunderbird* on 28 combat missions to the European continent in late 1943 and 1944 during the Second World War. The crew consisted of a pilot and co-pilot, navigator, bombardier, engineer, radio operator, and four gunners. They had to work closely together when airborne. Reprinted by kind permission from the Vern L. Moncur Family.

Basic issues in teamwork

Types of teams

In recent decades, the use of teams in organizations has grown dramatically. For example, Lawler, Mohrman, and Ledford (1995) reported that 68 per cent of Fortune 1000 companies (the 1000 largest companies in the USA) use work teams, and Gordon (1992) reported that 82 per cent of the companies with more than 100 employees use teams. Evidently, organizational teams are "big business," and much of the current research that addresses group performance focuses on organizational teams (Moreland, Hogg, & Hains, 1994; Sanna & Parks, 1997).

Cohen and Bailey (1997) distinguish among work, parallel, project, and management teams. *Work teams* are continuing work units responsible for producing goods or providing services. Usually work teams have a supervisor, although sometimes these teams are given some autonomy (they can decide how to carry out their work; autonomous or semi-autonomous work teams). *Parallel teams* exist parallel to an organization, and perform functions that the regular organization is not equipped to perform well. Examples are quality circles, which are meant to monitor and improve the functioning of (parts of) an organization. *Project teams* are time-limited teams that work at one-time outputs, typically a new product or service. Project teams often draw their members from different parts of an organization or from different disciplines. After the output is provided, team members move on to a new project team, or return to their normal unit. *Management teams*, finally, coordinate and provide direction to sub-units under their jurisdiction and are responsible for the overall performance of those sub-units.

Inputs, mediators, and outputs

The dominant approach taken in team research is the *input–process–output (IPO) model* of performance (Ilgen, Hollenbeck, Johnson, & Jundt, 2005). According to this basic model, input variables (such as team size and composition, organizational climate, or leadership) affect group processes (e.g., information-sharing, conflict) and these in turn determine group output (e.g., team performance, team member satisfaction). Ilgen *et al.* (2005), however, argued that this basic IPO model is too static. They see teams as dynamic systems that evolve over time, and argue that outputs at time t might be the inputs at a later time $t + 1$. For example, performance at time t might affect cohesion at time $t + 1$ and cohesion might subsequently influence certain group processes and outcomes at time $t + 2$ (see Chapter 1).

Marks, Mathieu, and Zaccaro (2001) have made the distinction between team processes and team emergent states. *Team processes* are defined as "members' interdependent acts that convert inputs to outcomes through cognitive, verbal, and behavioral activities directed toward organizing taskwork to achieve collective goals" (p. 357). Team processes involve members who are interacting with other members or with their environment, and these processes are used to direct, align, and monitor taskwork (i.e., activities aimed at task completion). Examples of team processes are information-sharing (Chapter 7), problem-solving (Chapter 8), and conflict management. *Emergent states* are "properties of the team that are typically dynamic in nature and vary as a function of team context, inputs, processes, and outcomes" (p. 357). Emergent states do not represent team actions or interactions, but are products of team experience. Examples are cohesion, trust, and team climate. These emergent states are at the same time outputs (they are affected by previous team interaction) and inputs (they in turn affect future interactions and outcomes).

FIGURE 9.2.
An input–mediator–
output–input (IMOI)
model of team
performance (after
Cohen & Bailey, 1997;
Ilgen *et al.*, 2005).

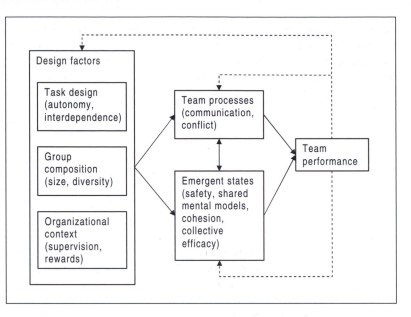

Incorporating these ideas, Ilgen *et al.* (2005) proposed an input–mediator–output–input (IMOI) model of team performance (see Figure 9.2). In this model, not only team processes but also emergent states determine how inputs are transformed into outputs. Both team processes and emergent states are so-called *mediators*: they are "in-between-variables" that explain why a certain input variable (e.g., team diversity) has an effect on certain outcome variables (e.g., group performance). For example, team diversity may lead to miscommunication (a team process variable) and therefore to poor performance. Alternatively, team diversity might associate with lack of trust (an emergent state), which in turn might lead to poor performance. In the remainder of this chapter, we will use the IMOI model to consider three issues in more detail: effects of diversity, effects of inter-dependence, and leadership.

Team diversity

Diversity implies differences among team members, and can be defined as "a characteristic of a social grouping that reflects the degree to which objective or subjective differences exist between group members" (Van Knippenberg & Schippers, 2007, p. 516). Due to factors such as globalization, immigration, and the increasing participation of women in the workforce, many teams consist of people who differ on demographic characteristics such as age, gender, and ethnicity. Further, many teams consist of people who differ in functional or educational background. An important question – from both an applied and a theoretical perspective – is how diversity affects team performance.

Unfortunately, the effects of team diversity on team processes and outcomes are highly inconsistent: Some research has shown that diverse teams are more innovative or productive, whereas other research has shown that diversity associates with dissatisfaction, conflict, lack of cohesion, and lower productivity (Milliken & Martins, 1996; Van Knippenberg & Schippers, 2007; Williams & O'Reilly, 1998). How can these contrasting effects be understood?

Team diversity research has largely been guided by two broad research traditions: the information processing perspective and the social categorization perspective (Williams & O'Reilly, 1998). The information-processing perspective argues that diversity associates with an increase in available resources. Because team members differ in, for example, educational background, previous experiences, or functional background, each team member brings unique knowledge, insights, and abilities to the team. Given that the team task requires these different inputs (Chapter 3), a diverse team has a higher potential performance than a homogeneous team. When individual members' contributions are combined in the appropriate way (there are no process losses or there are process gains), one might expect diverse teams to be superior to homogeneous teams (see also Hinsz, Tindale, & Vollrath, 1997; Nijstad & Paulus, 2003).

The social categorization perspective is derived from social identity and self-categorization theory (Chapter 1). People tend to use diversity as a basis for social categorization: People who are similar to the self are categorized as ingroup; people who are different from the self are categorized as outgroup. This might lead to the emergence of subgroups within a team (e.g., "us, psychologists vs. them, economists"). In general, people tend to favor ingroup members over outgroup members, trust ingroup members more, and are more willing to cooperate with them (Brewer, 1979; Tajfel & Turner, 1986). Further, people like similar others more than dissimilar others (Berscheid & Reis, 1998; Byrne, 1971). As a consequence, members of diverse teams trust each other less, are less willing to cooperate closely, have more conflicts, and so on. This leads to ineffective group processes (i.e., productivity losses) and diverse teams therefore perform worse than homogeneous teams.

Evidently, these perspectives lead to divergent predictions. Researchers have suggested several solutions for this paradox. First, the effects of diversity might depend on the type of diversity, or on combinations of diversity within the same team. Second, the effects of diversity might depend on other variables.

Types of diversity

Some researchers have suggested that there are different types of diversity, and that some types have positive effects whereas other types have negative effects (e.g., Jehn, Northcraft, & Neale, 1999; Pelled, Eisenhardt, & Xin, 1999). A logical distinction would be between *informational diversity*, referring to differences in educational or functional background, and *social category diversity*, referring to differences in demographic characteristics such as gender, age, and ethnicity. The prediction would be that informational diversity has positive effects and social category diversity has negative effects on team performance. Although plausible, this prediction has not received support. Webber and Donahue (2001) discuss 24 studies of team diversity, and find no evidence that informational diversity has positive effects and social category diversity negative effects. Box 9.1 is about a related discussion on types of conflict.

Harrison and Klein (2007) have recently argued that the term "diversity" itself is too unspecific, and that diversity can be conceptualized in different ways. This becomes clear when considering the question: When is diversity maximal? For example, is a four-person team with two psychologists and two economists more diverse than a team with one psychologist, one economist, one physician, and one engineer? Or is a team with two young and two old members more diverse than a team with three young and one old member? Harrison and Klein argued that the answer to this question depends on the type of diversity one is interested in.

Harrison and Klein distinguished among three types of diversity: separation, variety, and disparity (Figure 9.3). *Separation* implies differences among members in position or opinion (a horizontal continuum), and these differences reflect disagreement or opposition on values, beliefs, or attitudes. Separation is assumed to be maximal when there are two opposing factions at either end of the continuum (i.e., when groups are polarized). *Variety* is concerned with differences in kind or category, primarily in terms of information, knowledge, or expertise. Variety is maximal when all members differ from one another (there is *no overlap* among members in expertise and

One important group process often assumed to mediate the effects of diversity is conflict. *Conflict* can be defined as "the process resulting from tensions between team members because of real or perceived differences" (De Dreu & Weingart, 2003, p. 741). The literature on conflict suggests that there are at least two different types of conflict. *Task conflicts* are "conflicts about the distribution of resources, procedures and policies, and judgments and interpretation of facts," whereas *relationship conflicts* are "conflicts about personal taste, political preferences, values, and interpersonal style" (De Dreu & Weingart, 2003, p. 741). Task conflict is measured with items such as "to what extent are there differences of opinions regarding the task within your team?" whereas relationship conflict (sometimes labeled "emotional conflict") is measured with items such as "how much friction is present in your team?" (based on Jehn, 1994).

Jehn (1994, 1995) argued that relationship conflict tends to become emotional and will generally undermine satisfaction and performance. However, task conflict might have beneficial effects, because it stimulates debate which in turn might associate with superior performance. Jehn argued that this positive effect of task conflict will be found when task performance profits from more debate, which should be the case when tasks are relatively non-routine (on routine tasks no debate is necessary). This interesting perspective suggests that stimulating conflicts might in fact have beneficial effects, at least when the team performs non-routine tasks and when conflict does not become personal and emotional.

Unfortunately, subsequent research has yielded little support for this idea. De Dreu and Weingart (2003) summarized the results from 30 studies and found: (1) these were consistent with Jehn's ideas that relationship conflict is negatively related to team performance and team member satisfaction; (2) these were inconsistent with Jehn's ideas that also task conflict negatively relates to team performance and member satisfaction; and (3) task conflict and relationship conflict were strongly correlated. From these results it seems that conflict is bad – no matter what the conflict is about. This is partly due to the strong relation between task conflict and relationship conflict: When task conflict escalates, it may become emotional and when that happens it is bound to have negative effects.

every member can contribute unique resources). *Disparity* represents differences among members along a vertical continuum of valued social assets, such as power, pay, and status. Here diversity is maximal when one member has everything and all other members have nothing.

Often diversity on the same attribute can be conceptualized as different types of diversity. Take age diversity. First, age might be associated with a certain opinion, attitude, or belief (e.g., older members are more conservative than younger members). In this case, age diversity might be conceptualized as separation. In a four-person team, diversity would consequently be maximal with two old and two young members. Second, one might distinguish certain age cohorts, which are qualitatively different (e.g., pre-internet vs. post-internet cohorts) and therefore hold different information or

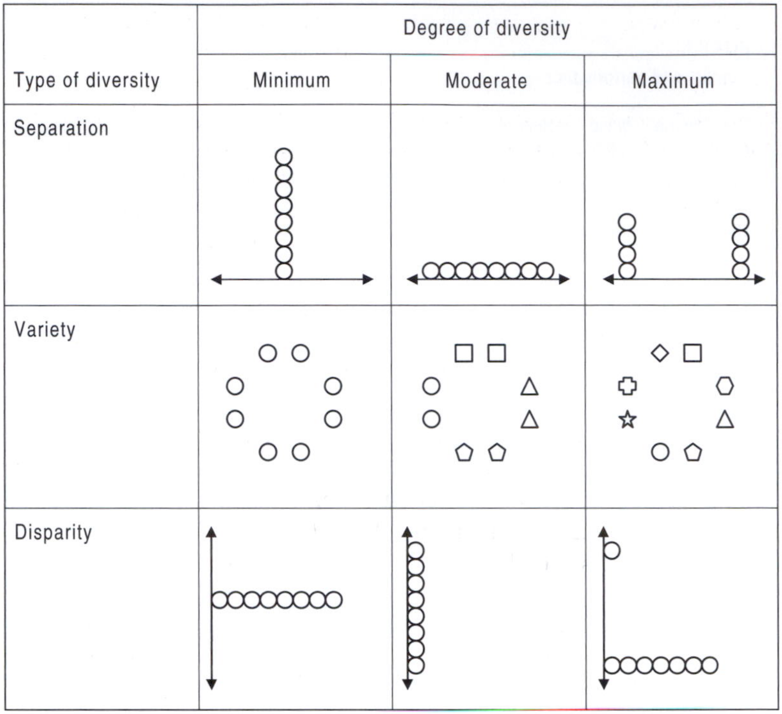

FIGURE 9.3.
Types and degrees of diversity. Reprinted from: D. A. Harrison & K. J. Klein (2007). What's the difference? Diversity constructs as separation, variety, or disparity in organizations. *Academy of Management Review, 32*, 1199–1228. Copyright Academy of Management. Reprinted with permission.

Type of diversity	Degree of diversity		
	Minimum	Moderate	Maximum
Separation			
Variety			
Disparity			

expertise. In that case, age diversity might better be conceptualized as variety, and diversity would be maximal when every team member comes from a different age cohort. Finally, age often is associated with status: Older people have more status than younger people (also Chapter 2). Seen this way, age diversity might best be conceptualized as disparity. Diversity in a four-person group would be maximal with one old and three young members.

Theoretically, diversity as separation fits with the social categorization perspective. Harrison and Klein therefore argue that minimum separation on attributes such as opinions, values, and beliefs will be psychologically comforting and will lead to mutual liking among team members, low levels of conflict, and positive interactions. Maximum separation might, on the other hand, lead to conflicts among opposing factions, decreases in liking, and so on. Note that it does not matter whether separation stems from social category diversity (e.g., people have different opinions because they have different ethnical backgrounds) or from informational diversity (e.g., because they have different functional backgrounds).

Diversity as variety fits with the information-processing approach. With minimum levels of variety (every group member has identical resources), team members are *redundant* and no benefits of working as a team can be expected (each group member could complete the task individually). However, with maximum variety, every team member can contribute unique knowledge or insights, and (provided that these unique contributions are needed) the team has a higher potential. In other words, every contribution might be useful.

Diversity as disparity, finally, is associated with inequality in an economic or sociological sense (some people have it all, others have nothing). This might have different effects, depending on the level of disparity, and factors such as legitimacy of the inequality. On the one hand, it may lead to competition for scarce resources and power struggles (perhaps especially when inequality is perceived to be illegitimate or unfair). On the other hand, it may lead to conformity, silence, suppression of deviance, and withdrawal. This might happen, for example, when a low-status team member interacts with a few high-status members (i.e., the low-status member is afraid to speak up).

Harrison and Klein's (2007) analysis suggests that we need to be very careful about what exactly we mean when we use the word "diversity." The way diversity is conceptualized has implications for the consequences it is likely to have.

Combinations of diversity: Faultlines

A second solution that has been suggested to resolve the inconsistencies in the literature is to look at combinations of diversity. Consider two four-person teams. Team 1 consists of two women and two men; both women have a degree in sociology and both men have a degree in economics. Team 2 also consists of two women and two men: One woman has a degree in sociology and the other woman in economics; similarly, one man has a degree in sociology and the other man in economics. Which team, do you think, will have more constructive group processes and better performance?

The teams in the example are equally diverse on two attributes (gender and educational background). However, they differ in the extent to which these attributes are correlated: Being a woman in team 1 correlates with being a sociologist and being a man with being an economist, but in team 2 this is not true. According to Lau and Murnighan (1998), team 1 has a stronger *faultline*, with faultlines defined as "hypothetical dividing lines that may split a group into subgroups based on one or more attributes" (p. 328). The strength of a faultline depends on the alignment of attributes: Faultline strength increases when more attributes are correlated within the team.

This analysis thus suggests that it is not the *degree* of diversity that has certain consequences, but rather the *alignment* of diversity on different attributes. It fits with the self-categorization perspective on team diversity: When dimensions of diversity converge (and lead to strong faultlines), group members are more likely to categorize team members as ingroup or outgroup because the differences between subgroups become more salient (see also Van Knippenberg, De Dreu, & Homan, 2004). The consequence would be less cohesion, more conflict, and poorer performance. Indeed, these effects have been observed. For example, Li and Hambrick (2005) found that stronger faultlines were associated with more conflict, lower cohesion, and poorer performance. Sawyer, Houlette, and Yeagley (2006) also found that faultlines were associated with poorer performance: When ethnic background converged with informational diversity, groups made poorer decisions than when ethnic background and information were not related. However, other results were not as predicted. For example, Lau and Murnighan (2005) report that faultlines were actually associated with lower relational conflict (also Box 9.1) and higher satisfaction, a result that runs counter to the faultline idea.

Moderators of the diversity–performance relation

The inconsistent findings in the diversity literature might partly be solved with better conceptualizations of (combinations of) diversity, but this is not the complete story. The effects of diversity often depend on the conditions under which teams work. In technical terms this implies that the effect of diversity on team performance is *moderated* by other variables, and these variables are referred to as moderators (not to be confused with mediators). For example, the effect of diversity on team performance might depend on the team task: A certain type of diversity (e.g., variety in educational background) has positive effects only when the team works on a non-routine task, and no (or perhaps even negative) effects when the team task is routine (cf. Jehn, 1994, 1995). Another possibility is that effects of disparity in status depend on team climate: The presence of a high-status group member leads to conformity only in a team climate in which members are afraid to speak their mind, and not when they feel "safe" within the team (cf. Edmondson, 1999). Or the effects of diversity depend on leadership, or on how long the groups has already been together (e.g., Milliken, Bartel, & Kurtzberg, 2003).

As a promising example of this approach, consider a recent study by Homan, van Knippenberg, van Kleef, and De Dreu (2007). They had four-person groups, consisting of two men and two women, work at a desert survival problem (they had to generate items that would be useful when one has to survive in a desert). Before the group discussion, group members individually received information about the task. In half the groups, all group members received all information. In the other half, group members received incomplete information: Some information was given only to the men, and some only to the women. In order to perform well in these latter groups, men and women had to exchange and process their unique information adequately. Homan *et al.* reasoned that the extent to which elaboration of information would take place would depend on diversity beliefs: When information was distributed among the men and women, adequate information elaboration should lead to high performance *only* when group members perceived diversity to be valuable. To manipulate these diversity beliefs, half of the groups were told that gender-diverse groups typically perform better at this task (pro-diversity beliefs), while the other half were told that gender-homogeneous groups typically perform better (pro-similarity beliefs). Figure 9.4 shows the findings with regard to group performance (the quality of the list of items they had generated, as judged by experts): indeed, for groups with heterogeneous information, pro-diversity beliefs led to better performance than pro-similarity beliefs.

FIGURE 9.4.

Performance of mixed-gender groups with homogeneous (complete) and heterogeneous information and with different diversity beliefs. Taken from: A. C. Homan, D. van Knippenberg, G. A. van Kleef, & C. K. De Dreu (2007). Bridging faultlines by valuing diversity: Diversity beliefs, information elaboration, and performance in diverse work groups. *Journal of Applied Psychology*, *92*, 1189–1199. Copyright American Psychological Association. Reprinted with permission.

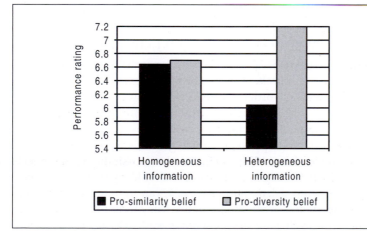

It seems that the effects of diversity often depend on other factors (on moderators). The problem is that the number of potential moderators of the diversity–performance relation is unlimited. What therefore is sorely needed is a theory from which important moderators can be identified, or which can be used to organize moderators into meaningful categories. Unfortunately, not many of these theories really exist (but see, e.g., Van Knippenberg *et al.*, 2004). However, a useful concept in this regard might be indispensability (see Chapter 5, also De Dreu *et al.*, 2008). Diversity can be expected to potentially have beneficial effects when group members can contribute non-redundant resources (such as unique knowledge; cf. Harrison & Klein, 2007), and when the task requires these different resources (cf. Jehn, 1994, 1995). That is, diversity has the potential to lead to better performance when team members' inputs are indispensable given the team task. However, equally important is that group members recognize this: Group members need to be aware that their own and others' resources are needed to perform well (and they also need to value high team performance). They need to be aware that their own inputs are indispensable; otherwise group members may have a tendency to free-ride on the efforts of others, or may think that their contribution is not relevant (see Chapter 5). They must further believe that the contributions of others are indispensable (even when these others are very different from oneself; cf. diversity beliefs); otherwise these contributions might be ignored or not taken seriously.

Interdependence and team mental models

Types of interdependence and team performance

A defining characteristic of teams is interdependence: Team members usually need one another to perform the team task (*task interdependence*), but also in order to obtain certain outcomes (e.g., a group reward; *outcome interdependence*; Chapter 1). It therefore is important to understand the effects of interdependence.

Task and outcome interdependence do not necessarily co-occur. For example, a team might have to work closely together, but individual team members rather than the team as a whole are evaluated and rewarded. Similarly, a room full of telemarketers may have very low task interdependence (they individually try to sell a product), but still may get collective feedback (e.g., about how many products were sold by the collective; Van der Vegt & Van de Vliert, 2002). Research has shown that such a mismatch between task and outcome interdependence has detrimental effects on team functioning, and that congruence between task and outcome interdependence (rather than incongruence) leads to higher levels of job satisfaction and commitment (Van der Vegt, Emans, & Van de Vliert, 2000), and to better performance (Saavedra, Earley, & Van Dyne, 1993; Wageman, 1995).

These findings point to the importance of team design. Many organizations implement team-based work structures, often because they expect teams to deal more flexibly with (changing) work conditions. However, when introducing team-based work, one should keep in mind that other organizational structures, such as evaluation and reward structures, need to change in parallel. If organizations fail to do so, they might not reap the potential benefits of team-based work, but rather experience negative effects, including low levels of satisfaction and commitment and poor team performance (Van der Vegt & Van de Vliert, 2002).

Interdependence and team mental models

Task interdependence implies that team members must coordinate their activities. How can teams achieve coordination and function effectively and smoothly, especially if their task is complex and there is no time to talk explicitly about coordination? To address this question, Cannon-Bowers, Salas, and Converse (1990) suggested the construct of *team mental models* (often also called *shared* mental models). In general, mental models refer to organized knowledge structures that allow people to interact with their environment. For example, we all have a mental model of the concept "car," which includes organized knowledge about a car's function, form, and the way it works. Having mental models enables us to describe, predict, and explain events in our environment (e.g., we know that a car will not run without petrol, why this is the case, and what to do if it runs out of petrol). Similarly, team mental models refer to organized knowledge structures that allow team members to interact with each other and perform the team's task.

Cannon-Bowers *et al.* (1990) reasoned that to coordinate activities, team members must be able to predict what teammates are going to do and what they need to do it. Especially when explicit communication about these issues is difficult, for example because of excessive workload or time pressure, team members must rely on previous

knowledge, stored and organized in a team mental model (Cannon-Bowers, Salas, & Converse, 1993). Thus, especially when interacting within a dynamic and demanding setting, team mental models may help teams to coordinate their activities. For example, team members might provide one another with the information they need (without even having to ask for it), they may assist other members when their workload is getting too high, or assign tasks to members who are in the best position to perform them (see Figure 9.5).

Team mental models can include organized knowledge about the team itself as well as about the team task (e.g., Mathieu, Heffner, Goodwin, Salas, & Cannon-Bowers, 2000). Task knowledge includes knowledge about equipment, technology, task procedures, and strategies. Team knowledge includes knowledge about team interaction (e.g., roles and responsibilities) and the team itself (e.g., other members' knowledge, skills, and preferences; cf. transactive memory, Chapter 3). Of course, these knowledge structures can be accurate, but they can also be inaccurate. Further, all team members might have identical team mental models (that is why they are sometimes called shared mental models), but team members may also vary in the mental models they have. Both mental model accuracy and "sharedness" (or similarity) have been linked to team performance (Edwards, Day, Arthur, & Bell, 2006; Lim & Klein, 2006; Marks, Sabella, Burke, & Zaccaro, 2002; Mathieu et al., 2000).

For example, Lim and Klein (2006) studied 71 military combat teams of the Singapore Armed Forces. These teams had to complete a combat circuit in a jungle environment as part of their training, consisting of six military tasks (e.g., securing a bridge, reacting to an ambush, evacuating injured comrades). Military assessors scored the team's performance on efficiency and quality for each of the six tasks. A few weeks before the exercise, team members completed an assessment of their team mental models. They were presented with a list of statements (e.g., "team members understand the team's task" and "team members are proficient with their weapons"), and had to indicate to which degree these statements were related, thus measuring the *organization* of knowledge. The resulting mental models were compared to those provided by experts (military captains) to assess accuracy, and within a team it was established to which degree different team members gave the same answers, to assess similarity.

Lim and Klein found that both accuracy and similarity of team mental models were positively related to team performance.

Edwards *et al.* (2006) found similar results for dyads playing a videogame: Team mental model accuracy and similarity were positively associated with performance. They also considered the question of how team mental models develop, and what determines their accuracy and the degree to which they are shared within a team. Team mental models are assumed to develop when the team works together, and one would expect team mental models to become both more accurate and more shared over time. These mental models can therefore be seen as an emergent state (rather than a team process): They are the consequence of previous interaction and can also influence subsequent interaction and performance. Edwards *et al.* found that team members' general mental ability (i.e., IQ) predicted the degree to which they formed accurate team mental models, and the superior performance of teams high in general mental ability was due to their better mental models.

One interesting way to build team mental models is through *cross-training*: "an instructional strategy in which each team member is trained in the duties of his or her teammates" (Volpe, Cannon-Bowers, Salas, & Spector, 1996, p. 87). The goal of cross-training is to enhance the knowledge of other team members' roles and responsibilities, and thus enhance coordination among team members. There are several types of cross-training. Blickensderfer, Cannon-Bowers, and Salas (1998) distinguished positional *clarification* (verbally presenting team members with information about teammates' jobs), positional *modeling* (observing the behaviors of other team members performing their jobs) and positional *rotation* (performing the teammate's job oneself).

Marks *et al.* (2002) investigated the effects of different kinds of cross-training on the development of team mental models and team performance. Their teams worked on highly interdependent action tasks, requiring rapid, complex, and coordinated team activity. Marks *et al.* found that cross-training increased the degree to which teams developed shared mental models. Because of the shared mental models, teams that had received cross-training performed better than teams that had not received cross-training. Thus, indeed, cross-training can be an effective instrument to improve team coordination and aid the development of a shared mental model. In addition, Marks *et al.* found some evidence that more in-depth types of cross-training (positional modeling and rotation) were more effective than positional clarification, but the differences were not very large.

Leadership and team performance

Teams usually have to report to a supervisor, such as a manager or team leader, and the characteristics of leaders and their behaviors will affect team functioning and team performance. *Leadership* might be defined as "a process of social influence in which one person is able to enlist the aid and support of others in the accomplishment of a common task" (Chemers, 2000, p. 27). Often, teams in an organization have a formal leader, who is given the authority by the organization to influence other team members. Sometimes there are informal leaders, who have no formal authority, but who nevertheless exert an influence on other team members, for example because of special skills or talents (Chapter 2).

In the IMOI model of Figure 9.2, leadership is usually considered an input variable that affects group processes as well as emergent states, sometimes in combination with other variables (such as team diversity and interdependence). Thus, a leader might stimulate information exchange (a team process, see Chapter 7), or impact team climate or trust (emergent states). However, especially when informal leadership is considered, leadership may itself develop as a consequence of team interaction. In that case, leadership is an emergent state rather than an input variable. At the end of this section we will consider this, as we discuss emergent and shared leadership. But let's first discuss leadership as an input variable.

Leadership as input: Initiating structure and consideration

We defined leadership as a process of social influence, but what behaviors might leaders use to influence their followers to assure the accomplishment of common tasks? In Chapter 2 we discussed Bales' interaction process analysis (IPA), and the distinction between task behaviors and socio-emotional behaviors (e.g., Bales & Slater, 1955). This corresponds with a distinction made in leadership research, between initiating structure (task-related) and consideration (socio-emotional or person-related) (Halpin & Winer, 1957; Judge, Piccolo, & Ilies, 2004). *Initiating structure* consists of leader behaviors that ensure that followers perform their jobs, such as to assign tasks, set goals, plan ahead, and make decisions about how work should be done. It emphasizes the minimization of role ambiguity and conflict, and involves giving directions and making autocratic decisions (rather than consulting followers or making democratic decisions). *Considera-tion* refers to behaviors that indicate respect and trust, and communicates that leaders value good relationships with followers. Examples are being friendly and respectful, giving followers a say in decisions, or explaining these decisions. These types of behaviors reflect two-way open communication, rather than one-way, directional, or autocratic communication.

How do initiating structure and consideration relate to team performance? Fiedler (1964, 1967) suggested in his *contingency theory of leadership* that the behavioral style of the leader should match the situation. He argued that it is not the case that one style (initiating structure or consideration) is better than the other, but rather that the effectiveness of a certain leadership style is *contingent* on the situation (hence contingency theory). In particular, it depends on how favorable the situation is to the leader. The favorability of the situation is a function of leader–member relations, task structure, and the leader's level of position power. First, leaders with good leader–member relations will more easily influence their members. Second, leaders can more easily direct their followers in tasks that are structured (have clear goals and procedures to achieve these goals) than in unstructured tasks (that lack clear goals or procedures). Finally, when leaders have more position power, because they have official authority and can reward or punish their members, they can more easily influence them. These three dimensions together form eight combinations (or octants) that can be ordered according to the favorability of the situation to the leader (Figure 9.6).

Fiedler argued that nondirective behavior and permissive attitudes (consideration) are neither appropriate nor beneficial when a leader is well liked and the task is highly structured (under favorable conditions), and in those cases leaders should use a more directive style (initiating structure). For example, leaders should not ask the group how to proceed during a very structured task such as a missile countdown. Also when the situation is very *un*favorable (when leader–member relations are poor, the task is unstructured, and the leader's position power is weak) consideration is less appropriate, because permissive behavior will merely result in inactivity on part of the group. However, under conditions of moderate favorability, consideration would work better. Thus, when the task is structured but the leader is disliked, the leader should be diplomatic. Further, when tasks are ambiguous, leaders must draw on the input, creativity, and contributions of their members, and consideration is important. Fiedler's predictions on the relation between consideration (as the

FIGURE 9.6. Fiedler's contingency theory of leadership (after Fiedler, 1967). The light-shaded area indicates a favorable situation; the dark-shaded area indicates a very unfavorable situation; and the white area indicates a moderately favorable situation. Consideration (as measured with the Least Preferred Co-worker (LPC) scale) is predicted to be negatively related to team performance in favorable and very unfavorable situations, but positively in moderately favorable situations. "Pre-theory data" refers to data on which Fiedler originally based his theory; "validation data" refers to studies that were performed to test the theory after it was formulated (data from Peters et al., 1985).

	Situation (octant)							
	I	II	III	IV	V	VI	VII	VIII
Leader–member relations	Good	Good	Good	Good	Poor	Poor	Poor	Poor
Task structure	High	High	Low	Low	High	High	Low	Low
Position power	High	Low	High	Low	High	Low	High	Low
Expected and obtained relation between LPC and task performance								
Expected	–	–	–	+	+	+	+	–
Pre-Theory Data	–.49	–.58	–.19	.41	.40		.21	–.38
Validation Data	–.38	–.06	–.20	.27	.33	.25	.19	–.42

opposite of initiating structure) and performance are also shown in Figure 9.6.

To test these predictions, Fiedler and others have measured the leader's behavioral style using the Least Preferred Coworker (LPC) scale. This questionnaire asks leaders to think about their least preferred coworker and rate this person on a number of dimensions (e.g., how friendly, enthusiastic, and pleasant this person is). High scores on this scale (the LPC is rated positively) are assumed to reflect consideration rather than initiating structure. This measure is then correlated with group performance under different conditions. The last two rows in Figure 9.6 show the results of a total of 35 studies that tested (parts of) Fiedler's contingency theory (data from Peters, Hartke, & Pohlmann, 1985). The row labeled "pre-theory data" shows data that were collected before Fiedler formulated his theory, and formed the input for his theory (Fiedler tried to explain these data with his theory) – not surprisingly, these data generally are consistent with Fiedler's predictions. Importantly, the data collected after the theory was formulated (labeled "validation data" in Figure 9.6) also generally support the theory. Although the correlations are not always high, they are consistently in the right direction (positive or negative).

Yet Fiedler's theory can be criticized because it assumes that initiating structure and consideration form two ends of a single continuum of leadership style (as measured by the LPC). It assumes that leadership style is fixed: Some leaders are high on consideration, while others are high on initiating structure. However, at least in principle, leaders can adapt to the situation, and might sometimes use consideration and sometimes initiate structure. Thus, these two types of behaviors are complementary rather than mutually exclusive, and leaders can use both (see also Judge *et al.*, 2004). More recent research summaries have further found that both initiating structure and consideration show positive effects on team performance, although the effects are relatively small (correlations around .25; Burke *et al.*, 2006; Judge *et al.*, 2004).

Nevertheless, researchers largely agree that under some conditions consideration works better (e.g., participative leadership), while under other conditions initiating structure (e.g., directive leadership) might be best. However, researchers nowadays would assess these dimensions with separate questionnaires, rather than with Fiedler's LPC scale. For example, Somech (2006) studied primary health care teams, and measured participative and directive leadership with two different questionnaires (these styles were uncorrelated). Somech found that the effects of leadership style varied depending on the functional heterogeneity of the team (diversity in roles, distinguishing e.g., among physicians, nurses, and social workers) and the type of outcome that was assessed. In terms of *team innovation* (the introduction and application within a team of new and useful ideas, processes, products, or procedures; West, 1990), participative leadership was better, especially for heterogeneous teams. In terms of *regular job performance*, however, directive leadership was better, again especially for heterogeneous teams. Note that this seems compatible with Fiedler's ideas: For structured tasks (normal job performance) directive leadership was better, while for unstructured tasks (innovation) participative leadership was better. However, over time both may be applied by the same leader.

Leadership as input: Transactional and transformational leadership

Much of the more recent research on leadership focuses on transactional and transformational leadership. These terms were originally

introduced by Burns (1978), and were further developed by Bass (1985) and Bass and Avolio (1990a, 1990b). *Transactional leadership* focuses on reward contingencies and exchange relations: Leaders influence their followers by rewarding high performance and reprimanding mistakes and substandard performance. *Transformational leadership* refers to leader behaviors that aim to stimulate followers to move beyond immediate self-interest (such as rewards and punishments), and strive towards a higher collective purpose, mission, or vision. Leaders accomplish this by developing, intellectually stimulating, and inspiring their followers. Transformational leadership is often associated with *charisma* (Figure 9.7).

FIGURE 9.7. Barack Obama, 44th President of the USA, is considered a charismatic leader by many.

To measure transactional and transformational leadership, Bass and Avolio (1990b) have constructed the widely used *Multi-Factor Leadership Questionnaire* (MLQ). The MLQ measures three dimensions of transactional leadership (contingent rewards, active management by exception, and passive management by exception) and four dimensions of transformational leadership (idealized influence, inspirational motivation, intellectual stimulation, and individualized consideration). Besides these dimensions, the MLQ also measures non-leadership, or *laissez-faire* leadership. Table 9.1 explains these dimensions. Usually followers rate their leaders on these different dimensions, and by now a huge body of research exists using the MLQ to predict leadership outcomes (see Judge & Piccolo, 2004).

Before discussing how transactional and transformational leadership relate to team performance, it is important to discuss how they relate to each other. Burns (1978) originally thought they represented two ends of a single continuum (leaders are either transactional or transformational, but not both). However, more recent conceptualizations suggest that successful leaders use both styles, and that transformational leadership works best when it builds upon the foundations of transactional leadership (Bass, 1998, 1999). Transactional leadership should ensure that followers do their work (and are rewarded accordingly), and transformational leadership would motivate them to move beyond expectations and work towards collective goals (Bass, 1998). Empirically, research shows a strong and

TABLE 9.1

Dimensions of transactional, transformational, and non-leadership (based on Bass & Avolio's, 1990, Multi-Factor Leadership Questionnaire)

Leadership dimension	Description	Sample item
Transactional leadership		
Contingent rewards	Providing tangible (e.g., money) and intangible resources (e.g., praise) in exchange for effort and performance	"My leader works out agreements with me on what I will receive when I do what needs to be done"
Active management by exception	Monitoring performance and taking corrective action when necessary	"My leader focuses attention on irregularities, mistakes, exceptions, and deviations from what is expected of me"
Passive management by exception	Intervening only when problems become serious	"Problems have to be chronic before my leader will take action"
Transformational leadership		
Idealized influence	Showing extreme levels of competency and trustworthiness	"I am ready to trust my leader to overcome any obstacle"
Inspirational motivation	Articulating the group's goals in emotional, moral, and visionary terms	"My leader talks enthusiastically about what needs to be accomplished"
Intellectual stimulation	Encouraging followers to think independently and creatively and move away from past ideas or limitations	"My leader introduces new projects and new challenges"
Individualized consideration	Understanding each follower's personal needs and goals	"My leader listens to my concerns"
Non-leadership		
Laissez-faire	Avoiding leadership responsibilities	"My leader avoids getting involved when important issues arise"

positive correlation (around .75) between transformational leadership and the contingent rewards dimension of transactional leadership, but the correlations with the two other dimensions of transactional leadership are weak. Transformational leadership correlates negatively with *laissez-faire* leadership (around −.50) (Judge & Piccolo, 2004). Thus, some leaders engage in both transactional and transformational leadership, while others engage in neither and take a *laissez-faire* approach.

Now, how do these leadership styles influence important outcomes? In summarizing much of the work, Judge and Piccolo (2004) concluded that both contingent rewards and transformational leadership are *positively* related to all kinds of outcomes, including follower job satisfaction, follower motivation, and leader effectiveness ratings. *Laissez-faire* behavior, in contrast, leads to *lower* levels of satisfaction, motivation, and leader effectiveness ratings. Active and passive management by exception do not relate strongly to these outcomes. Unfortunately, much of the work summarized by Judge and Piccolo (2004) did not look at measures of team performance. However, more recently Burke *et al.* (2006) summarized the literature specifically looking at team performance. They concluded that also team performance is positively related to transformational leadership and contingent rewards, although the relations are weaker (around .25) than for the subjective measures (such as satisfaction and self-rated motivation).

One reason why the effects of transactional and transformational leadership on team performance were not very strong overall might be that these types of leadership only work (or work better) under specific circumstances (i.e., the effects are contingent on the situation; cf. Fiedler's work). For example, Lim and Ployhart (2004) studied the effects of transformational leadership. There are several reasons to expect positive effects of transformational leadership on team performance: Transformational leaders should inspire their team members to work hard for the team, should create a sense of collective identity and high levels of cohesion, and should create high levels of collective efficacy (i.e., the belief that the team is able to perform well). However, the willingness to work hard for the team and high levels of collective efficacy might be more important when the team is under stress to perform well. Lim and Ployhart expected that the relation between transformational leadership and team performance would be stronger in stressful situations than in day-to-day performance contexts.

Their study was done with teams of the Singapore Armed Forces who were undergoing military training. Approximately 10 weeks into training, team members completed the MLQ about their supervisors. At the end of the training period, supervisors rated the performance in day-to-day situations of each of the teams. Performance in stressful situations was assessed during a (highly stressful) one-day military exercise (see the earlier description of Lim & Klein, 2006, for details). Lim and Ployhart (2004) found that transformational leadership was positively related to team performance in day-to-day performance contexts (correlation of .32); however, this correlation was much stronger in stressful performance contexts (correlation of .60). Thus, transformational leadership may indeed pay off, especially under stressful situations (also see Bass, Avolio, Jung, & Berson, 2003).

Schaubroeck, Lam, and Cha (2007) suggested that some teams might more readily accept the influence of transformational leaders than other teams. They argued that this depends on team *cultural values*: shared beliefs about ideal modes of behavior and ideal end-states. Schaubroeck *et al.* focused on two types of cultural values: power distance and collectivism. They argued that in teams with high power distance (the degree to which team members regard status differences as legitimate), the influence of a leader is more readily accepted. Consequently, the influence of transformational leadership should be stronger for these teams. Also teams with higher levels of collectivism (the degree to which group members believe that the group's needs and obligations are superordinate to individual needs and desires) should be more susceptible to transformational leadership. Transformational leaders try to motivate and inspire followers to move beyond self-interest and work towards collective goals, and teams high in collectivism should more readily accept this. These predictions were supported in a study among 218 financial service teams in the US and Hong Kong. Transformational leadership had especially strong effects on team performance when teams were high in power distance and collectivism.

These results seem compatible with a social identity approach to leadership (Hogg *et al.*, 2005). These authors argued that for teams in which collective outcomes are important, for example because team members identify strongly with their team (when they have a strong *social identity* as a team member; see Chapters 1 and 10) or because of collectivistic values, team leaders are more effective when they take a group-oriented approach (e.g., emphasize collective goals, as in transformational leadership). For teams in which team members do not identify strongly with the team or hold individualistic values, a personalized approach (e.g., rewarding or punishing individuals, as in transactional leadership) should work better. Indeed, Hogg *et al.* found support for this line of reasoning: Group-oriented leadership was more effective when team members had a stronger social identity as a team member, while individualized approaches worked better in the absence of a strong social identity.

Leadership as emergent state: Emergent leaders and shared leadership

So far, we have considered leadership as an input variable in the IMOI model of Figure 9.2. However, sometimes leadership is not a given (there are no formal leaders), but informal leaders emerge during group interaction. In that case, leadership is an emergent state rather than an input variable. Because many organizations now use teams without formal leaders, such as autonomous and semi-autonomous teams (e.g., Lawler, Mohrman, & Benson, 2001), questions around emergent leadership become increasingly important. At least two questions arise. First, what determines who will emerge as the leader (if anybody does)? Second, what consequences does this have for team performance?

The first question was partly addressed in Chapter 2, where we discussed expectation states theory (Berger et al., 1980). According to that theory, certain characteristics, such as age, gender (diffuse status characteristics), skills and abilities (specific status characteristics) associate with performance expectations. In a self-fulfilling way, these performance expectations of other group members in turn determine whether a person is influential (e.g., becomes the emergent leader).

Further, quite some research has considered whether leadership can be predicted using personality traits and intelligence. Summarizing this work, Lord, De Vader, and Alliger (1986) found that intelligence was the best predictor of emergent leadership: Intelligent people were more often rated high in leadership and were more often appointed the leader of a group. Personality traits that predicted leader emergence were masculinity (being aggressive, decisive, and non-emotional) and dominance (being determined and directive). A more recent review of the link between personality and leadership (Judge, Bono, Ilies, & Gerhardt, 2002) looked at the *Big Five* personality traits. Many researchers believe that the most salient aspects of personality can be described using five broad personality traits: neuroticism, extraversion, openness to experience, agreeableness, and conscientiousness (Costa & McCrae, 1988; McCrae & Costa, 1997). These dimensions are explained in Table 9.2, and that table also contains the estimated correlation between these personality factors and emergent leadership. As can be seen, neuroticism was found to be negatively related to leader emergence, while extraversion, openness to experience, and conscientiousness were positively related to leader emergence. Agreeableness showed no consistent relation with leadership emergence. Thus, personality does predict leader emergence.

Another important question is the effect of gender on leadership emergence. As discussed in Chapter 2, gender is often taken to be a diffuse status characteristic, and in mixed-gender groups women emerge as leaders less often than men (e.g., Dobbins, Long, Dedrick, & Clemons, 1990; Kent & Moss, 1994). However, this also depends on

TABLE 9.2

The Big Five personality traits and their association with leadership emergence (data from Judge et al., 2002)

Big Five dimension	Description	Correlation with leadership emergence
Neuroticism	The tendency to show poor emotional adjustment and experience negative affect, such as anxiety and depression	−.24
Extraversion	The tendency to be sociable, assertive, active, and experience positive affect	.33
Openness to experience	The tendency to be imaginative, nonconforming, unconventional, and autonomous	.24
Agreeableness	The tendency to be trusting, compliant, caring, and gentle	.05
Conscientiousness	The tendency to be dependable and achievement-oriented	.33

other factors, such as the group task and the numerical proportion of men and women in the group. For example, Karakowsky and Siegel (1999) found that group members exhibited less leadership when their gender was incongruent with the gender orientation of the task: Men less often emerged as leader in the female-oriented task and women less often in the male-oriented task. Further, this incongruence effect was especially strong when in a numerical minority position: A man in a minority position (a group with five women and one man) was extremely unlikely to emerge as a leader when working at the female-oriented task; a woman in a minority (five men and one woman) was extremely unlikely to emerge as a leader in a male-oriented task.

The results of Karakowsky and Siegel (1999) fit with a social identity theory of leadership (Hogg, 2001). The theory argues that group membership contributes to our identity (i.e., social identity). Like people, groups are perceived to have certain characteristics (e.g., the group is "tough"; see also Chapter 1) and if people value the group they are part of, they will value these characteristics. Some group members may share more characteristics with the group than others, and these members are therefore more *prototypical* group members. The theory predicts that more prototypical group members are more likely to become the group leader than less prototypical members, because the attributes of the prototypical member are valued in the context of the group. Applied to the Karakowsky and

Siegel results, a woman in a female-dominated team working on a feminine task is more prototypical than a man; therefore a woman is more likely to emerge as a leader. However, also prototypicality of group members on other attributes such as attitudes makes it more likely that they emerge as a leader (e.g., Hains, Hogg, & Duck, 1997).

In sum, there are a number of factors that determine who will emerge as a leader, including intelligence; personality traits such as dominance, extraversion, and conscientiousness; diffuse (e.g., gender) and specific status characteristics; and prototypicality. However, do groups in which a leader emerges eventually perform better than groups in which nobody takes the lead? Further, is it better when one group member takes the lead or when several members share leadership?

There are reasons to assume that it will generally be helpful that a team member does take a leadership role. The reason is that leaders perform certain functions that in turn allow a team to perform well: "The leadership role in a team largely involves facilitating team processes – initiating or formulating goals, encouraging interaction between all team members, finding the necessary resources to get the job done, encouraging diverse points of view, acting as coach, clarifying team member responses, and organizing the group's thinking" (Taggar, Hackett, & Saha, 1999, p. 900; see also Zaccaro, Rittman, & Marks, 2001). Emergent leaders would therefore be expected to facilitate team processes, and thus stimulate higher levels of performance.

Although there have not been many studies on the effects of emergent leadership on team performance, the studies that are there suggest that emergent leadership has positive effect. Taggar *et al.* (1999), for example, studied 94 teams of students (five or six members per team) during a 13-week course. Each week, these teams had to complete an exercise, such as a case analysis or an evaluation of a newspaper article, and had to write a report. Performance was assessed by a course instructor as the quality of these weekly reports. Emergent leadership was measured using peer ratings: each team member rated the other members on leadership. The person who, on average, received the highest peer ratings was considered the emergent leader. Of course, some of these emergent leaders received higher ratings than others, and Taggar *et al.* predicted team performance with these leadership ratings of the emergent leaders. However, they also looked at the average ratings of the other team members. What Taggar *et al.* found was that both mattered: Teams in which both the emergent leader *and* the other team members scored high on leadership performed better than other teams (see Figure 9.8).

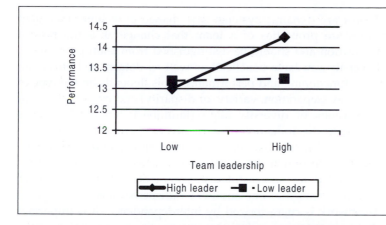

FIGURE 9.8.

Team performance as a function of emergent leadership (the score of the highest scoring group member on leadership ratings) and team leadership (the average score of the other group members) (data from Taggar et al., 1999).

The results of Taggar *et al.* (1999) suggest that it might be beneficial if no one person takes the lead, but all group members exemplify leadership behaviors. This possibility has been further explored by Carson, Tesluk, and Marrone (2007), who studied *shared leadership*, which they defined as "an emergent team property that results from the distribution of leadership influence across multiple team members" (p. 1218). Shared leadership is higher when more team members have a high degree of influence in the team. Carson *et al.* studied the effects of shared leadership in a sample of 59 consulting teams. Team members rated one another on leadership, and the measure of shared leadership was the average of these ratings. Performance was assessed with satisfaction ratings of the teams' clients. Carson *et al.* found that shared leadership indeed had a positive effect on team performance.

In all, it appears that emergent leadership as well as shared leadership contributes to task performance. However, as with the other types of leadership we discussed, it seems quite possible that emergent and shared leadership work better under some than under other conditions. Future studies will have to look into that.

Chapter summary

(1) Teams are social units characterized by a common task and high interdependence, and are part of a larger system (i.e., an organization). Several types of team can be distinguished, such as work, parallel, project, and management teams.

(2) Teams are dynamic systems that change over time. Emergent states are properties of a team that change as a function of interaction and should be distinguished from team processes.

(3) Diversity can have beneficial as well as detrimental effects on team functioning and performance. This depends on the type of diversity (separation, variety, or disparity) and on how different dimensions of diversity align (faultlines). Situational factors moderate the influence of diversity on performance. Positive effects of diversity may be expected when group members have unique, non-redundant contributions; when these contributions are needed for successful task completion; and when group members recognize one another's indispensability.

(4) Teamwork is characterized by interdependence. It is important that task and outcome interdependence be congruent. Especially in complex and dynamic task environments, shared and accurate team mental models help effective coordination. These mental models will develop over time, and can be learned through cross-training.

(5) Initiating structure and consideration are two leadership styles that contribute positively to group performance, but according to Fiedler's contingency theory the effectiveness of each depends on the situation.

(6) Transformational leadership and transactional leadership (especially contingent rewards) are positively associated with team performance. However, this association is stronger when the team is under pressure to perform well, when teams accept this kind of leadership, and for teams with a strong social identity.

(7) Without formal leadership, informal leaders may emerge. Who is likely to be the leader depends on intelligence, personality traits, status characteristics, and prototypicality. Both emergent and shared leadership seem to be positively related to team performance.

Exercises

(1) Teams in organizations differ from groups studied in the psychological laboratory. Do you think that the results from laboratory groups will usually generalize to teams in organizations?

(2) Emergent states change over time. Think of different emergent states (e.g., cohesion, team climate, shared mental models): What will cause these different emergent states to change?

(3) From the study by Homan *et al.* (2007) it appears that diversity beliefs moderate the relationship between diversity and team performance. What other variables might moderate this relationship?

(4) To what degree are the concepts of team mental models and transactive memory systems identical and different? Do they have similar antecedents and consequences?

(5) Do you see any overlap in the concepts of initiating structure/consideration on one hand and transactional/transformational leadership on the other?

(6) What would be the conditions under which formal leadership is better than emergent or shared leadership? Under which conditions will this be reversed?

Further reading

Group processes versus emergent states

Marks, M. A., Mathieu, J. E., & Zaccaro, S. J. (2001). A temporally based framework and taxonomy of team processes. *Academy of Management Review, 26*, 356–376.

Team diversity

Harrison, D. A., & Klein, K. J. (2007). What's the difference? Diversity constructs as separation, variety, or disparity in organizations. *Academy of Management Review, 32*, 1199–1228.

Van Knippenberg, D., De Dreu, C. K. W., & Homan, A. C. (2004). Work group diversity and group performance: An integrative model and research agenda. *Journal of Applied Psychology, 89*, 1008–1022.

Shared mental models

Lim, B. C., & Klein, K. J. (2006). Team mental models and team performance: A field study of the effects of team mental model similarity and accuracy. *Journal of Organizational Behavior, 27*, 403–418.

Leadership

Chemers, M. M. (2000). Leadership research and theory: A functional integration. *Group Dynamics: Theory, Research, and Practice, 4*, 27–43.

Fiedler, F. E. (1964). A contingency model of leadership effectiveness. In L. Berkowitz (Ed.), *Advances in experimental social psychology* (Vol. 1, pp. 149–190). New York: Academic Press.

Taggar, S., Hackett, R., & Saha, S. (1999). Leadership emergence in autonomous work teams: Antecedents and outcomes. *Personnel Psychology*, 52, 899–926.

Groups in context 10

Groups do not exist in a vacuum, but function within a particular (social) context, such as a company or a school. In Chapter 3, groups were therefore conceptualized as multilevel and open systems, in which the group's context influences group processes and performance. How the context might influence groups and groups might influence the context will be considered in this chapter.

In the first section, we consider the connection between groups and their environment. One way in which groups connect with their environment is through interactions with people outside the group. For example, a member of an organizational team may interact with members from other teams, higher management, and clients. These interactions often involve the exchange of certain resources such as money and information (cf. social exchange; Chapter 1). This topic will be discussed under the label of boundary-spanning activities. Besides the exchange of resources with people outside the team, groups are open systems in another way. Not only can resources (such as information) flow to and from groups, but sometimes old members leave and new members enter groups. We also consider some consequences of membership change.

A second theme is that groups often function in a context in which other groups are present. This inevitably creates certain intergroup processes, and these processes have received substantial research attention especially within the framework of social identity theory (see Chapter 1). Using this theoretical framework, we discuss the influence of the *inter*group context on *intra*group behavior and we discuss intergroup competition and cooperation. Finally, the social identity framework will be used to discuss situations in which two or more groups are combined to form a new and bigger group, as happens during reorganizations and mergers.

Groups as open systems

Boundary-spanning

How do groups manage their relation with the environment in which they operate? Ancona and Caldwell (1988) studied this question in a qualitative study, aiming to describe and classify a set of activities that link a group to its environment. They called these activities *boundary-spanning*.

Ancona and Caldwell interviewed 38 managers of project teams within the technological industry. These managers described the activities that they and other team members carried out with people outside the group boundaries (e.g., with management, manufacturing, marketing). Ancona and Caldwell also asked 15 team members to record all interactions with people outside the team for one week (e.g., in meetings, one-on-one discussions, and telephone calls). After identifying the boundary activities that were mentioned, Ancona and Caldwell clustered them in categories of related sets of activities. The resulting categories are displayed in Table 10.1. The main clusters were scout activities (importing information and resources), ambassador activities (exporting information and resources), sentry activities (controlling the information and resources others want to send to the group), and guard activities (controlling the information and resources others want from the group). Ancona and Caldwell (1988) further found that team leaders engaged in boundary activities more than team members, and this was especially true for ambassadorial activities. Further, more boundary activities were performed by teams that worked on important or innovative products, and when the team was competing with other teams over scarce resources (e.g., the use of specific equipment). In terms of consequences for team performance, Ancona and Caldwell suggested that more boundary activities are required when teams are dependent on other teams, under conditions of uncertainty, or when teams work on innovative tasks.

Later research showed that boundary spanning activities can have positive effects on team performance. Ancona and Caldwell (1992) studied 45 project teams. Team members reported on their boundary-spanning activities, and managers reported on project completion and quality of the final team product. Ancona and Caldwell found that especially ambassadorial activities (exporting resources and information; mainly directed towards higher management), were positively related to team performance (e.g., to product innovativeness). Ancona and Caldwell (1992) also found that more external

TABLE 10.1

Boundary activities of organizational teams (after Ancona & Caldwell, 1988)

Main category	Sub-category
Scout activities "Bringing in information and resources needed by the group"	*Modeling* Gaining general knowledge about the external environment (e.g., Who supports us and who doesn't?) *Gathering information and resources* Acquiring specific resources that the group needs (e.g., use of equipment) *Scanning* Collecting information that is not immediately relevant (e.g., early signs of trouble) *Feedback-seeking* Collecting outsiders' perceptions of the group (e.g., present a new idea to management)
Ambassador activities "Exporting information and resources to outsiders"	*Opening up communication channels* Establishing relationships with outsiders (e.g., have coffee with someone from a different department) *Informing* Informing outsiders of the team's progress (e.g., sending copies of minutes to management) *Coordinating and negotiating* Resolving issues of interdependence with outsiders (e.g., coordinate the use of equipment) *Molding* Influencing the external environment (e.g., boast about the team)
Sentry activities "Controlling the information and resources that others want to send to the group"	*Allowing entry* Providing outsiders with access to the team (e.g., to give input about the product) *Translating* Interpreting information to make it useful for the group (e.g., translate into own jargon) *Filtering* Not giving all information to the group (e.g., buffer the group from outside pressure)
Guard activities "Controlling the resources that others request from the group"	*Classifying* Delaying the response to a request (e.g., not providing details about a product) *Delivering* Giving the requested information or resources *Protecting* Preventing the release of information or resources

communication was associated with *less* internal communication and *lower* levels of cohesion within the team. It seems that boundary activities (of the right kind) can lead to higher levels of performance, but that these activities might be at the expense of within-team communication and cohesion.

Another study complements this picture. Keller (2001) studied 93 project teams, and considered both antecedents and consequences of boundary-spanning. He was interested in the role of functional diversity (see Chapter 9). Team members with different functional backgrounds (e.g., in engineering, chemistry, or manufacturing) often differ in the outside contacts they have (their social network). Therefore, Keller predicted that higher levels of functional diversity would be associated with *more* external communication. However, diversity is often associated with lower levels of mutual liking and cohesion (see Chapter 9). Keller thus predicted that functional diversity would be associated with *less* internal communication and *lower* team cohesion. Because both external and internal communication is necessary for high team performance, it is unclear what to expect for performance: on the one hand functional diversity increases external communication which is good for performance; on the other hand it decreases internal communication which is bad for performance. Keller (2001) indeed found that functional diversity was associated with more external communication (boundary-spanning) and less internal communication. Furthermore, external communication was beneficial for most measures of performance, such as the quality of the final team product. However, external communication was negatively related to team cohesion while internal communication had positive effects.

These studies suggest that teams have to strike a balance between internal and external communication. While boundary-spanning can enhance performance, too much of it may distract from internal communication, which in the end may undermine cohesion and performance. However, a word of caution is in order. There is not much research on boundary spanning yet, and the work that has been done has mainly looked at project teams. It is therefore unclear whether these results generalize to other types of teams, such as regular work teams (see Chapter 9).

Membership change

Boundary-spanning involves moving resources, such as information, into the group or from the group to other parts of an organization. Many groups are also open systems in the sense that group members can leave or enter the group (Ziller, 1965). In Chapter 2, we have discussed how new group members are socialized, and why members may eventually (voluntarily or not) leave a group. We now consider how membership change affects group performance.

Membership change can take three forms: members who leave (making the group smaller), members who enter (making it bigger), and members who are replaced (one person leaves and another enters). Membership change can affect group performance in two different ways. First, because the main resources of groups reside with their members, membership change affects the resources available to groups and therefore their *potential* performance (see Chapter 3). Thus, a person leaving a group may imply loss of resources (e.g., knowledge or skills) while a person entering a group may imply a gain in resources. The extent to which this impacts performance depends on the degree to which these resources are necessary for task performance. Second, membership change affects group processes, which will influence the group's *actual* performance. For example, while new members are learning their new role, a group temporarily functions less well (Moreland & Levine, 1982). Further, a newcomer might force the group to reconsider its way of working, which might lead members to abandon ineffective processes and implement more effective ones. Thus, both positive (e.g., gains in resources, better ways of working) and negative effects (e.g., loss of resources, inefficiency) of membership change are possible.

In recent years, a number of studies have investigated the effects of member replacement. Choi and Thompson (2005) studied the effects of member replacement on group creativity (Chapter 6). They argued that newcomers may bring a fresh perspective to the group, and this may stimulate creativity. Three-person groups did an initial brainstorming task, after which in half the groups one member was replaced, whereas the other half stayed intact. Next, all groups generated ideas on another topic. In two studies, Choi and Thompson found that groups that had experienced membership change generated more ideas than groups that had stayed intact. Furthermore, newcomers who were particularly productive during the first task (before they were moved to another group) were more stimulating than newcomers who were relatively unproductive, attesting to the importance of the "quality" of newcomers. Hence, the resources (e.g., a fresh perspective) brought in by a new member enhanced group performance.

Newcomers may also disrupt the functioning of groups. Lewis, Belliveau, Herndon, and Keller (2007) argued that groups build up a transactive memory system, in which members know who knows what, which positively affects group performance because it improves coordination among group members (see Chapters 3 and 9). After member replacement, however, this transactive memory system is no longer accurate: An old member who was responsible for specific knowledge has left the group, and there is a gap in the transactive memory system that a newcomer might not be able to fill. When groups continue to rely on their (no longer accurate) transactive memory after member replacement, performance will suffer.

Lewis *et al.* (2007) had three-person groups first learn how to assemble a telephone kit in a practice session. During this practice session, a transactive memory system was formed: Group members learned who was good at which part of the task. One week later, groups were asked to assemble the telephone kit again. Some groups stayed intact (intact groups), for some groups one member was

FIGURE 10.1. replaced by a member from another group (partially intact groups), and some groups were newly created and consisted of three members from three different groups (reconstituted groups). Lewis *et al.* found that intact groups outperformed the other groups. The partially intact groups performed as poorly as the completely reconstituted groups because the old group members continued to rely on the transactive memory system that was formed during training, even though it was no longer adequate. Furthermore, Lewis *et al.* found that the negative effect of member replacement in the partially intact groups disappeared when these groups were explicitly asked to reflect on the task. This procedure prevented a "mindless" application of the inadequate transactive memory system and prevented productivity loss (see Figure 10.1).

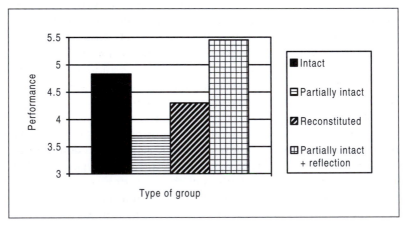

FIGURE 10.1. Performance of different types of groups on a telephone assembly task (maximum performance was 7). Due to their transactive memory system, intact groups outperformed partially intact groups (with member replacement) and reconstituted groups (i.e., with members who had not worked together yet). However, partially intact groups that were asked to reflect on the task before performing it performed as well as intact groups, because they were better able to use their members' knowledge (data from Lewis *et al.*, 2007).

Newcomers can bring new resources and ideas to a group (Choi & Thompson, 2005), but oldtimers might not always accept newcomers' ideas (Choi & Levine, 2004). When might newcomers effectively influence groups to adopt their ideas? Based on social identity theory (Tajfel & Turner, 1979, 1986), Kane, Argote, and Levine (2005) argued that groups are more likely to pay attention to newcomers who are part of the ingroup, because ingroup members are perceived to be more trustworthy and valuable than outgroup members (also Chapters 1 and 9). However, newcomers do *not* come from the ingroup, but from another group. The solution Kane *et al.* proposed is based on the *Common Ingroup Identity Model* (Gaertner & Dovidio, 2000; see also below). This model argues that *ingroup bias* (perceiving ingroup members as more valuable than outgroup members) will be reduced when different groups have a common superordinate identity: when members of two groups perceive that both groups belong to a larger overarching group. For example, a team in the R&D department might perceive that it shares a superordinate identity with a team in the sales department: Both are part of the same organization. Kane *et al.* reasoned that a suggestion coming from a newcomer from the outgroup would normally be disregarded. However, when the outgroup member shares a superordinate identity with the other group members, the suggestion would be closely scrutinized. When the suggestion is of high quality, it will be adopted, and will also improve group performance (because it is a good suggestion); when it is of low quality it will not be adopted, and group performance should be unaffected.

Participants came to the laboratory in groups of six. They were told that they would be making origami (i.e., folded paper) sailboats in two different three-person assembly lines, and that their performance was equal to the number of correctly folded sailboats. In the superordinate identity condition, the two three-person groups shared a common name, had the same color nametags, and were told that the best performing *six*-person group would receive a $60 bonus. In the no superordinate identity condition, the two three-person groups were given different names, different color nametags, and were told that the best performing *three*-person group would receive a $30 bonus. The two three-person groups were next taken to separate rooms, where they learned how to fold the sailboats. In both groups, the procedure consisted of several steps that had to be performed by the three members sequentially, but the two groups were given a different procedure. One procedure was more difficult to learn, but required fewer folds to complete, and therefore was superior. After training, each group performed two trials, in which they had to fold as many sailboats as possible. Then the middle member of the assembly line was rotated, in such a way that the groups that had learned the superior routine received a member who was trained in the inferior routine and vice versa. Next followed two more trials, in which performance was assessed after membership change.

Kane *et al.* (2005) found that groups were unlikely to adopt the routine of the newcomer when it was inferior. However, when the newcomer's routine was superior, only the groups with a superordinate identity often adopted it (75 per cent), and not the groups without a superordinate identity (only 25 per cent). Thus, lack of a superordinate identity led to rejection of the newcomer's suggestion, regardless of its quality, while sharing a superordinate identity led to adoption of high-quality suggestions only. In terms of performance, the groups that had learned the superior routine in the first place in general performed well, irrespective of superordinate identity, because they continued to use their superior routine. The groups that had originally learned the inferior routine had something to gain from the newcomer, but this only happened with a shared superordinate identity (see Figure 10.2). Groups without a superordinate identity continued to use the inferior routine and their performance did not improve as a result of the newcomer's suggestions.

In sum, membership change might positively and negatively affect group performance. When newcomers bring new ideas and resources

FIGURE 10.2. Performance (number of folded origami sailboats) as a function of the quality of the newcomer's alternative routine (inferior, superior) and the presence of a superordinate identity. Groups in which the newcomer's routine was inferior had nothing to gain, continued to use their superior routine, and performed well. However, groups in which a newcomer suggested a better routine improved only when the group shared a superordinate identity with the newcomer (data from Kane *et al.*, 2005).

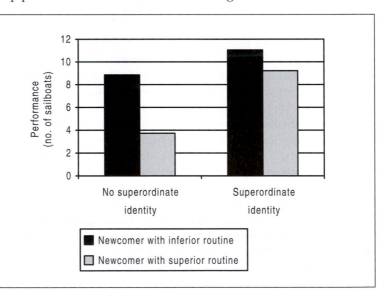

to the group, group performance might benefit. However, groups are not always likely to adopt a newcomer's suggestions. They are more likely to do so when they are motivated to pay attention to newcomers, for example because they share a superordinate identity with the other members, but also when the group has previously failed on its task (Choi & Levine, 2004).

Groups in the social context: Intergroup relations

Creating a positive social identity

Groups often function in the presence of other groups. For example, multiple groups exist alongside each other in organizations (e.g., different departments, different teams), when students are divided into groups during a course, or in sports competitions. Sometimes groups have to cooperate (e.g., within an organization) or compete with each other (e.g., sports teams). The presence of other groups creates certain *inter*group processes which in turn have consequences for *intra*group dynamics.

Intergroup relations are usually studied from the theoretical perspective of social identity and self-categorization theory. According to these theories (Tajfel & Turner, 1979, 1986; Turner, 1982; Turner *et al.*, 1987), people's self-concept consists of both a personal identity (what makes an individual unique) and a social identity (see also Chapters 1 and 9). Social identity is that part of the self-concept that derives from group membership combined with the value and significance of that membership. Social identity theory assumes that people strive for a positive self-view, and because social identity is part of the self-concept they also strive for a positive social identity. This can be achieved when one's own group is perceived to be superior to other groups on some relevant dimension (e.g., performance, intelligence, morality). People are assumed to *identify* with a group when group membership provides them with a positive social identity.

That people strive for a positive social identity motivates group members to compare their group with other groups (intergroup social comparisons) and to positively distinguish their groups from other groups. This may lead to ingroup bias, the tendency to treat and evaluate members of one's own group more favorably than members of other groups (see, e.g., Hewstone, Rubin, & Willis, 2002). In fact, merely categorizing people into meaningless groups (e.g., a blue group versus a green group) can lead to ingroup bias (Rabbie & Horowitz, 1969; Tajfel, Billig, Bundy, & Flament, 1971). Further, this striving for a positive social identity can lead to intergroup *competition*: One can show that one's group is superior to other groups by "beating" them in a competition. A consequence is that group members are prepared to work hard for their group when their group is being compared with other groups.

These processes are illustrated in a study by James and Greenberg (1989). These authors predicted that group members would work hard for their group when they thought that their group's performance would be compared to that of another group. However, this would only happen when their group membership was made *salient*. Indeed, we are not always aware of all the groups of which we are a member, but increasing this awareness should increase people's tendency to distinguish their group positively from other groups. James and Greenberg (1989) asked University of Arizona (UA) students to solve anagrams. They manipulated intergroup competition, and told half the participants that their performance would be compared to the performance of University of Washington (UW) students, whereas instructions to the other half made no reference to another group. Participants were then given a practice anagram, meant to manipulate the salience of group membership. For half the students the practice anagram solved as *wildcats*, which is the UA mascot. For the other half it solved as *beavers*, which was unrelated to group membership. Next participants solved as many anagrams as they could. Performance in the different conditions is shown in Figure 10.3: When group membership was made salient *and* there was intergroup competition performance was high. When there was no intergroup competition, group salience decreased performance, possibly reflecting a social loafing effect (see Chapter 5). Thus, the combination of group salience and intergroup competition can motivate group members to work harder to distinguish their group positively from other groups. This is especially true for people who identify strongly with their group (e.g., James & Cropanzano, 1994; Ouwerkerk, de Gilder, & de Vries, 2000; see also Lount & Phillips, 2007, for an illustration in the context of the Köhler motivation gain effect).

Self-categorization, conformity, and polarization

The salience of group membership and people's identification with their group influence how hard members are prepared to work for

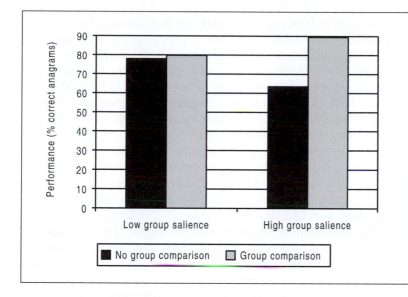

FIGURE 10.3.
Percentage of correctly
solved anagrams as a
function of group
salience and the
presence of intergroup
comparisons (data
from James &
Greenberg, 1989).

their group. These factors also affect how people see themselves and others, and this can have implications for group processes and per-formance. According to self-categorization theory (Turner *et al.*, 1987), we have a tendency to categorize people into meaningful social categories. There are multiple ways in which people can be categor-ized (e.g., in terms of ethnicity, profession, department, or even hair color), but not all of these are equally likely to be used. In which way (if at all) people are categorized depends on the salience of these categories. This salience depends firstly on how well a certain categ-orization makes clear distinctions between groups. Categorizations that can distinguish among groups based on several different attri-butes at the same time (also see the discussion of faultlines in Chapter 9) or on highly visible attributes (e.g., gender or ethnicity) are applied more easily. Secondly, it depends on the degree to which this categorization makes sense in a specific context. Thus, categorizing people by hair color usually does not happen, but it might make sense for a hairdresser.

When these social categorization processes occur, they tend to lead to *depersonalization*: a shift from seeing people as individuals to seeing them as group members. A consequence is that similarities *within* groups and differences *between* groups are accentuated (e.g., Tajfel & Wilkes, 1963). Thus people *within* one group are perceived to be more similar than they really are (e.g., "*all* people in the sales department are only interested in their bonus"), while differences *between* groups are perceived to be bigger than they are (e.g., seeing unrealistically large differences between attitudes of people in the sales and production departments). Social categorization is not restricted to others, but people also *self-categorize* as group members. A consequence of seeing oneself as a group member rather than an individual is that people behave in ways that are consistent with their group membership, especially when they identify strongly with their group. For example, people will follow the norms of their group more and respond more strongly to group members who deviate from these norms when their group membership is made salient and when people identify with their group (e.g., Abrams, Wetherell, Cochrane, Hogg, & Turner, 1990; Marques, Yzerbyt, & Leyens, 1988). The result is conformity (see Chapter 2).

Social categorization processes also contribute to group polarization. Recall that group polarization occurs when opinions and attitudes of group members become more extreme after group discussion (Chapter 2). Mackie (1986) argued that *inter*group competition would increase people's awareness of their group membership and lead to social categorization. This, in turn, would lead people to see their group as more homogeneous and more extreme than it really is. Conforming to these more extreme views would lead to polarization of their attitudes. Mackie further argued that *intra*group competition would make people focus on themselves as individuals (instead of group members), which would lead them to see their group as less homogeneous and extreme, and would reduce attitude polarization.

Individual participants listened to a taped group discussion, in which a three-person group discussed an immediate freeze on the production of nuclear weapons (the group was mildly in favor), and were told that they would later join the group on the tape. To manipulate *inter*group competition Mackie told some participants that the *group* with the best discussion would win a $12 bonus, whereas no reference to other groups was made in the other condition. Participants in the *intra*group competition condition were told that the best *individual* member of each group could win a $4 bonus, whereas no such bonus could be won in the other condition. After listening to the tape, participants rated the group's position on the issue and were also asked to rate their own position. Results were that the presence of intergroup competition led to the perception that the group was more extreme, while the presence of intragroup competition led to the perception that the group was less extreme. Participants' own attitude polarization is shown in Figure 10.4. As compared to a pretest (before listening to the tape), attitudes polarized (became more

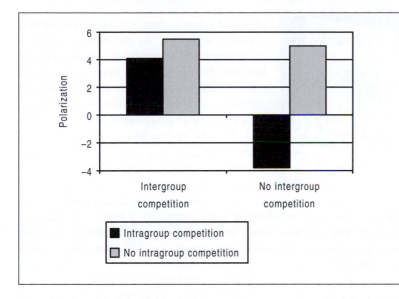

FIGURE 10.4.
Attitude polarization in the presence or absence of intergroup and intragroup competition. Attitudes polarized in all conditions (positive values), except in the no intergroup/intragroup competition condition. In that condition attitudes even de-polarized (negative values) (data from Mackie, 1986).

positive) in all conditions except when intergroup competition was absent and intragroup competition was present. There attitudes even de-polarized, because people focused on individuality rather than group membership. Social categorization processes can thus lead to polarization, because they lead members to see their group as more homogeneous and more extreme, and conforming to the group produces polarization.

Interdependence, intergroup competition and cooperation

The studies discussed so far involved situations in which other groups were referred to, but no real interaction between groups took place. However, often groups do interact with (people from) other groups. For example, different teams within an organization may have to collaborate to create a product or deliver a service. At other times, these teams have to compete for scarce resources within the organization (e.g., the use of equipment or a budget to finish a project). What do we know about intergroup cooperation and competition?

A classic field study was performed by Sherif, Harvey, White, Hood, and Sherif (1961). They organized a summer camp for 12-year-old boys at Robbers Cave, Oklahoma. The study consisted of three stages. In the group formation stage, two different groups of boys were formed ("The Eagles" and "The Rattlers") that were unaware

FIGURE 10.5.
A picture of a banner
produced by the
Eagles during the
second stage
(intergroup conflict).
Taken from: M. Sherif,
O. J. Harvey, B. J.
White, W. R. Hood, &
C. W. Sherif (1961).
Intergroup conflict and
cooperation: The
Robbers Cave
experiment. Copyright
1988 by Muzafer Sherif
and reprinted by
permission of
Wesleyan University
Press.

of each other's existence and performed separate activities. In the second stage – of intergroup competition – the groups became aware of each other, and direct competitive encounters (e.g., a tug-of-war competition) were organized between them. This led to intergroup hostility (Figure 10.5), and these hostilities became so severe (e.g., name-calling, destruction of property, fist-fights) that the researchers ended this stage sooner than planned. In a third stage, inter-group cooperation was introduced. Suppo-sedly, a truck that had to bring both groups their lunch was stuck in the mud, and all boys were needed to pull it out. After a series of such cooperative activities, the hostilities between the groups gradually disappeared.

Sherif *et al.* (1961) conducted the Robbers Cave experiment to test realistic conflict theory (Sherif, 1966). That theory ascribes an important role to intergroup interdependence: the degree to which groups are dependent on each other to achieve valued outcomes (see also Chapters 1 and 9). Under *positive* or cooperative interdependence groups need each other to accomplish their goals, and their interests are aligned. Under *negative* or competitive interdependence groups can only reach their goals at the expense of other groups. Realistic conflict theory assumes that hostilities and negative attitudes between groups develop under conditions of negative interdepen-dence, while positive intergroup relations develop under positive interdependence. The Robbers Cave experiment confirmed these expectations, and showed that intergroup relations depend on the type of intergroup interdependence (positive or negative).

Often, however, interdependence between groups is neither uniformly positive nor uniformly negative. *Mixed-motive situations* are characterized by the presence of both incentives to cooperate and incentives to compete. For example, different teams within an organ-ization have to cooperate to achieve success for the entire organiza-tion. However, sometimes these teams also compete, for example to obtain scarce resources (e.g., money to hire new people). The best solution for the collective (the entire organization) would be to allocate resources to the team that might best use them to enhance organizational success. However, the different teams also have their own interests, and therefore might try to obtain the resources even though they would be more useful to another team. Thus, the interests of the teams are partly aligned (both have an interest in the welfare of the entire organization) and partly opposed (both want the resource for themselves). The question is whether in these situations groups are inclined to cooperate (e.g., try to find the division of resources that is best for the entire organization) or compete (e.g., try to get the resources for their own team).

A robust finding in social psychology is that groups tend to be more competitive than individuals in these mixed-motive situations. Individuals often choose to cooperate with other individuals to get the best collective outcomes, but groups often choose to compete. Thus, in our example groups would often claim the resources for themselves, and would pursue their self-interest rather than the interest of the whole organization. This in turn would lead to competition between groups, and often to lower outcomes for the collective (i.e., the organizational resources are not used in an optimal way). The difference between individuals and groups in competitive behavior is so big that this finding has been called the *discontinuity effect* (see Wildschut, Pinter, Vevea, Insko, & Schopler, 2003, for a review).

There are two reasons why intergroup relations in mixed-motive situations are more competitive than interpersonal relations. First, pursuing self-interest (rather than collective interest) has anti-normative qualities, and individuals are reluctant to do so. However, when in a group, members can convince one another that it is justifiable to pursue self-interest instead of joint interests (Wildschut, Insko, & Gaertner, 2002). Furthermore, group members are less likely to feel personally responsible for their amoral behavior, because they can "hide in the crowd" (see also Chapter 5). This makes groups more likely to focus on self-interest rather than joint interests. Second, group members often expect that other groups will be competitive, and they fear that they will be exploited when they act cooperatively. Indeed, evidence indicates that people have learned expectations that intergroup interactions are aggressive and competitive (e.g., Pemberton, Insko, & Schopler, 1996). This would lead groups to choose competition to protect themselves against the expected bad intentions of the other group. There is good evidence that both these factors contribute to the discontinuity effect (Wildschut et al., 2003).

Intergroup contact, de-categorization, and re-categorization

Ingroup bias and the discontinuity effect lead to pessimistic views about intergroup cooperation. How can one achieve intergroup cooperation despite the fact that people like ingroup members more and distrust outgroups, and that intergroup situations easily lead to competition? How ingroup bias can be prevented has been extensively studied in the context of prejudice and discrimination (the groups in these situations often being ethnic groups). An important idea, put forward by Allport (1954) in his classic book *The Nature of Prejudice*, is the *contact hypothesis*, which argues that direct positive contact between people from different groups will reduce prejudice and ingroup bias. This reduction in bias is expected especially under certain optimal *contact conditions*: when the groups have equal status, when they have common goals, when intergroup cooperation is present, and with support from authorities, law or custom. The contact hypothesis is not without problems (e.g., Pettigrew, 1998), but evidence on the whole indicates that contact between members of different groups does reduce prejudice and ingroup bias, and that this reduction is stronger under more favorable contact conditions (see Pettigrew & Tropp, 2006, for a review).

One reason why these contact conditions reduce ingroup bias is that they influence social categorization processes. Take the example of two three-person teams working within one department. There are at least four different ways in which these six people may be categorized (Figure 10.6). First, one might perceive two distinct three-person groups. Such a two-group categorization is likely to lead to ingroup bias and intergroup competition. Second, one may not categorize them at all, but rather see them as six separate individuals (de-categorization). Third, one may see them as six members of one group (i.e., the department) and emphasize their common ingroup identity (see also Kane *et al.*, 2005, discussed above). Finally, one may perceive two groups embedded in a larger group (a dual identity, as

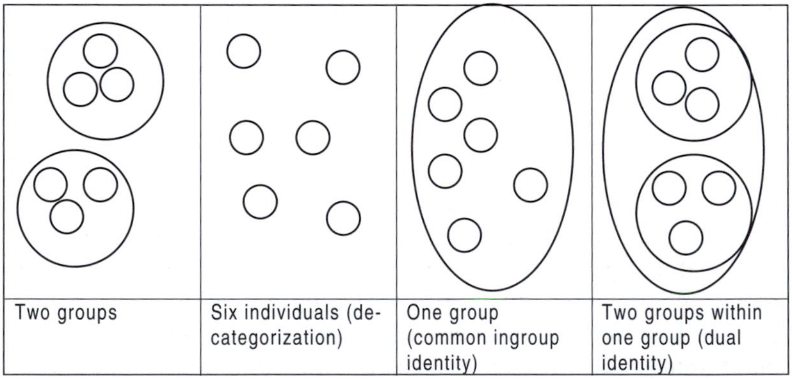

| Two groups | Six individuals (de-categorization) | One group (common ingroup identity) | Two groups within one group (dual identity) |

FIGURE 10.6.
Four different ways in which to represent six members of two subgroups within one larger group.

both a team member and a member of the overarching department). Contact between the teams might cause de-categorization or re-categorization, which in turn may reduce ingroup bias and stimulate cooperation between the teams.

A first way of reducing ingroup bias might thus be to emphasize individuality rather than group membership (de-categorization). As you will recall, Mackie (1986) introduced intragroup competition, which made participants focus on their individual identity, which in turn reduced polarization effects (see above). Bettencourt, Brewer, Croak, and Miller (1992) found that de-categorization also reduces ingroup bias. Members of two groups were brought into contact. Ingroup bias (i.e., less favorable impressions of outgroup members as compared to ingroup members) was reduced especially when people were instructed to form an accurate impression of the *individual* members of the other group. The reason was that the focus on individuals led to de-categorization, which in turn reduced ingroup bias.

A second way to reduce ingroup bias is to focus group members on an overarching social category that encompasses both groups (on a common ingroup identity). Research has shown that introducing cooperation between groups or emphasizing similarity between groups leads to more inclusive representations of the groups (i.e., seeing the aggregate of several groups as one group), which in turn reduces ingroup bias (see Dovidio, Gaertner, & Saguy, 2007, for an overview). For example, Dovidio et al. (1997) divided six participants into two three-person groups, allegedly based on their score on a personality test. These two groups generated a name for their group and separately performed a task. After this, the two groups were brought together and jointly worked on another task, under two different conditions. In the two-group condition, members of one subgroup sat at one side of the table and members of the other subgroup at the other (the seating pattern was AAABBB). Further, each subgroup wore a different-color T-shirt, and subgroups retained their separate names. In the one-group condition, the members sat in an integrated seating pattern (ABABAB), all six participants wore same-color T-shirts, and they were given a new name for the entire six-person group. After the task, participants were asked their perceptions of group membership and of ingroup and outgroup members. Dovodio et al. found that participants in the two-group condition perceived the aggregate group more as two groups while participants in the one-group condition perceived the aggregate more as one group. In turn, the perception of the aggregate as two groups led to ingroup bias. However, in the one-group condition the evaluation of (former) outgroup members was as positive as the evaluation of (former) ingroup members. Thus, perceptually blurring the distinction between groups can lead group members to re-categorize in terms of the overarching group (create a common ingroup identity) and reduce ingroup bias.

A disadvantage of creating a common ingroup identity is that people may resist this form of re-categorization. Indeed, people often value their group membership and identify strongly with their group. Introducing a common ingroup identity implies giving up your "old" social identity and embracing a "new" superordinate identity (also see the discussion of mergers below). Another way to reduce ingroup bias would be by creating a *dual* identity: emphasizing membership of the subordinate and the superordinate category simultaneously.

For example, in a study by Gaertner *et al.* (1999), six participants were divided into two three-person groups based on their endorsement of the Republican or Democratic Party (which had been assessed before). These two groups separately performed a task, and created a name for their group. The two groups were next brought together in one room and performed another task: They had to prioritize a list of measures to reduce the government's budget deficit. They were told that groups performing well on this task could earn a $10 per person bonus. Two variables were manipulated: intergroup interaction and common fate. Subgroups were either allowed to interact while working on this task or not; the bonus was dependent on either the performance of one's own subgroup or the combined performance of the two subgroups. After this task, participants were questioned about their perceptions of the two groups and of the members of both groups. Gaertner *et al.* found that interaction and common fate both reduced ingroup bias. More importantly, the reason was that these factors led to participants' perception of group membership as two subgroups within one group.

There is some debate as to which strategy (de-categorization, common ingroup identity, dual identity) is more effective in reducing ingroup bias (e.g., Hewstone *et al.*, 2002). However, it is clear that contact conditions such as direct cooperative interaction and common fate influence social categorization processes, which in turn reduce ingroup bias. It is interesting to note that we have encountered many of the contact conditions before, including face-to-face interaction, similarity between the members of different groups, introducing common fate or positive interdependence. In Chapter 1 these conditions were linked to perceptions of group entitativity. It appears that this holds at the level of (sub)groups, but also at the level of superordinate groups. In other words, if the overarching group is made more entitative, ingroup bias is reduced.

Mergers, ingroup bias, status, and identification

One situation in which re-categorization becomes an issue is the case that two or more groups not merely have to work together but merge to form one bigger group. During mergers social identity is at stake: Old groups cease to exist and are combined into a new group. Mergers have been studied both in laboratory and in field research. The field studies have addressed what happens to employees of merging organizations, while the laboratory studies have looked at the effects of merging of smaller groups (as might happen after reorganizations *within* a company). Two questions that have been addressed in these studies are what happens with ingroup bias after a merger and what determines people's identification with the new (post-merger) group or organization. It is assumed that members of the different pre-merger groups will work together more effectively in the post-merger group when ingroup bias between members of the pre-merger groups is minimized and when they identify with their new group.

Based on the previous discussion of re-categorization, it is to be expected that ingroup bias can be reduced when people perceive both groups to be part of a larger group (i.e., adopt either a common ingroup identity or a dual identity). Giessner and Mummendey (2008) have argued that ingroup bias in addition to categorization also depends on merger success. They created two three-person groups in the laboratory that had to perform separate tasks, and next merged them into one six-person group. In this post-merger group they manipulated social categorization. Either pre-merger group membership was made salient (two-group categorization), or post-merger group membership (common ingroup identity), or both (dual identity), by using colored coats, seating arrangements, and so on. The post-merger group had to perform two tasks, and received performance feedback after the first, saying that the group had been either very successful or very unsuccessful. Giessner and Mummendey argued that ingroup bias would be low regardless of social categorization after success feedback, because the group members would identify with their new and successful group. However, after failure feedback ingroup bias was expected to be higher, especially in the two-group categorization condition. This is exactly what was found (Figure 10.7).

FIGURE 10.7.

Ingroup bias
(evaluation of ingroup
members minus
evaluation of outgroup
members) after a
merger as a function of
merger success and
categorization (data
from Giessner &
Mummendey, 2008).

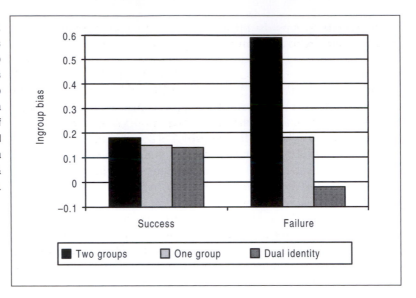

It thus seems clear that social re-categorization processes are important during mergers. So far we have discussed these issues in cases where the two groups were equal in status (this also was one of Allport's (1954) contact conditions). However, in many merger situations the two groups are not equal in status; one group has a higher status or is more dominant than the other (e.g., in a company takeover). In these situations, an important psychological aspect of mergers is the degree to which the new (post-merger) group feels like a continuation of the old (pre-merger) group. For example, when two companies merge but one company is much bigger in terms of number of employees or profit and takes over the smaller company, the bigger company will probably dominate the post-merger organization. Research has shown that in these cases the members of the dominant group (or organization) experience continuity of their social identity. For members of the dominant group there consequently is a strong relation between identification with their pre-merger group and identification with the post-merger group: The more they identified with their old group, the more they identify with the new group. Employees of the dominated group do not experience this continuity, and for them there is a much weaker relation between their pre- and post-merger identification (Van Knippenberg, van Knippenberg, Monden, & de Lima, 2002; also Boen, Vanbeselaere, Brebels, Huybens, & Millet, 2007; Van Leeuwen, van Knippenberg, & Ellemers, 2003).

The reason why pre-merger dominance affects experienced continuity is that it relates to "merger integration patterns," or the way in which the pre-merger groups are represented in the post-merger group (Mottola, Bachman, Gaertner, & Dovidio, 1997). Mottola *et al.* distinguished among three integration patterns: absorb, blend, and combine. The absorb pattern often applies to takeovers: The post-merger group closely resembles the acquiring group but does not include features of the acquired group (A + B = A). The blend pattern refers to a situation in which features of both groups are maintained in the new group (A + B = AB). The combine pattern refers to a situation in which the post-merger group resembles neither pre-merger group, but has distinct new features (A + B = C). Members of dominant pre-merger groups tend to favor the absorb pattern, whereas members of non-dominant pre-merger groups favor the blend or combine pattern (Giessner, Viki, Otten, Terry, & Täuber, 2006). This is not strange, because members of dominant groups expect to experience continuity after the merger in the case of the absorb pattern, which means that they can maintain their social identity and dominance. Members of the dominated groups dislike the absorb pattern because it implies a loss of their (pre-merger) social identity and complete adaptation to the dominant group.

Pre-merger dominance is related to status, and being a member of a high-status group provides people with a positive social identity. When a low-status and a high-status group merge, this can be threatening to members of both groups. Members of the low-status group will compare unfavorably to members of the high-status group, which may lead them to resist the merger. Members of the high-status group, on the other hand, may fear that when the groups are combined they will lose their status through the association with the lower status group. In a longitudinal study of two merging air carriers that differed in status, it was indeed found that both employees of the high- and those of the low-status air carrier initially felt threatened by the merger (Amiot, Terry, & Callan, 2007). The merger followed the absorb pattern, and after a few years the members of the high-status organization no longer felt threatened and increased their identification with the post-merger organization. However, those initially in the low-status organization continued to feel threatened, identified less with the post-merger organization and were less satisfied with their job, even after several years.

It therefore seems that mergers might be especially problematic when pre-merger groups differ in dominance and/or status. Usually, the dominant, high-status group will also dominate in the post-merger group, and this might easily lead to dissatisfaction and lack of identification by members of the dominated low-status group. These problems might be one reason why organizational mergers often fail to bring the benefits that were initially expected (Marks & Mirvis, 1985; McCann & Gilkey, 1988). Emphasizing dual identities and valuing both the high- and the low-status pre-merger groups might be one way to reduce these problems (e.g., Dovidio *et al.*, 2007). However, this is not an easy task.

Chapter summary

(1) Boundary-spanning activities link a group to its environment. Boundary-spanning can be good for performance, but may distract from internal communication.

(2) Membership change can have both negative and positive effects. Negative effects occur when membership change implies a loss of resources or less efficient group processes (e.g., an inaccurate transactive memory). Positive effects occur when newcomers bring in valuable resources or more efficient procedures. However, oldtimers need to be motivated to scrutinize newcomers' ideas carefully before they will adopt them.

(3) Group members are motivated to distinguish their group positively from other groups. This may lead them to work hard for their group when their group membership is salient, when they identify with their group, and when they believe that their group is being compared with other groups. It may also lead to ingroup bias (evaluating and treating ingroup members more positively than outgroup members).

(4) Social categorization processes lead to depersonalization and the tendency to see people (including oneself) as group members rather than as individuals. Self-categorization leads to greater conformity and contributes to group polarization.

(5) Intergroup interactions can be competitive under negative interdependence, but also in mixed-motive situations. Here it has been found that groups are more competitive than individuals (the discontinuity effect).

(6) Cooperative intergroup interaction and a reduction in ingroup bias can be achieved through de-categorization (a focus on individuality rather than group membership) or re-categorization (a common ingroup identity or a dual identity). Contact

conditions such as common fate, direct interaction, and similarity produce re-categorization and in turn reduce ingroup bias.

(7) Mergers often take place between groups that are unequal in dominance and status. Members of dominant groups experience continuity and after time will often identify with the post-merger group. However, members of dominated groups may experience a loss of identity and lower identification and satisfaction.

Exercises

(1) Boundary-spanning often involves contact between members of different groups (e.g., between members of different departments). Based on the discussion of intergroup situations, when is boundary-spanning likely to be successful?

(2) What would be the relations among staffing level (see Chapter 2), membership change, and group performance? When is membership change especially likely to lead to problems?

(3) How might you use social identity theory to explain football hooliganism?

(4) Consider a group of which you are a member. How would you feel when this group merged with another group? Can you explain your feelings with the concepts used in this chapter?

Further reading

Boundary-spanning and membership change

Ancona, D. G., & Caldwell, D. F. (1992). Bridging the boundary: External activity and performance in organizational teams. *Administrative Science Quarterly, 37,* 634–665.

Kane, A. A., Argote, L., & Levine, J. M. (2005). Knowledge transfer between groups via personnel rotation: Effects of social identity and knowledge quality. *Organizational Behavior and Human Decision Processes, 96,* 46–71.

Intergroup processes

James, K., & Greenberg, J. (1989). In-group salience, intergroup comparison, and individual performance and self-esteem. *Personality and Social Psychology Bulletin, 15,* 604–616.

Terry, D. J. (2003). A social identity perspective on organizational mergers: The role of group status, permeability, and similarity. In M. J. Platow, N. Ellemers, A. S. Haslam, & D. van Knippenberg (Eds.), *Social identity at work: Developing theory for organizational practice* (pp. 223–240). New York: Psychology Press.

Wildschut, T., Pinter, B., Vevea, J. L., Insko, C. A., & Schopler, J. (2003). Beyond the group mind: A quantitative review of the interindividual–intergroup discontinuity effect. *Psychological Bulletin, 129,* 698–722.

Groups and technology 11

Recent years have seen enormous developments in information and communication technology (ICT). It is hard to imagine that only a couple of decades ago employees often did not have a personal computer, mobile phones were extremely uncommon, and email or the internet did not exist for individual use. These developments in ICT have also had consequences for groups and teamwork. Groups nowadays do not have to meet face to face but can use a variety of communication media, including teleconferencing, videoconferencing and computer networks. How do these alternative means of communication affect group functioning and performance? How well do groups perform when group members work in different parts of the world? These kinds of issue have received substantial research attention.

In this chapter, two issues will be addressed. First, a main area of study has been the comparison between face-to-face groups and groups using other media (e.g., computer-mediated communication, videoconferencing) on important outcomes, such as group performance and team member satisfaction. The studies we discuss in this section mainly look at groups that had to perform one task (e.g., decision-making) using different kinds of media. The second topic is the topic of "virtual teams," in which collaboration takes place over a more extended period of time and usually involves different tasks. Virtual teams are characterized by geographical dispersion and therefore are usually highly dependent on electronic media (e.g., Gibson & Gibbs, 2006). When different team members are in different parts of the world, the group dynamics obviously are quite different from teams that regularly meet face to face. These differences are discussed in the second session.

Effectiveness of groups using synchronous media

Communication is the exchange of information through messages, and this exchange can be synchronous and asynchronous (Table 11.1). In synchronous communication transmitted messages are immediately available to the receiver, and the receiver can respond immediately to the message. Several communication media are synchronous, including face-to-face meetings, videoconferencing, teleconferencing; and certain types of computer-mediated communication are almost synchronous (e.g., chat). Messages can also be exchanged asynchronously, as in video messaging, voicemail, email, and written text (e.g., letters). Face-to-face meetings require that participants are collocated (at the same place at the same time), but for most other media this is not the case, which is a major advantage.

One important aspect on which different communication media differ is "media richness" (Daft & Lengel, 1986). *Media richness* refers to the degree to which a medium contains cues regarding the meaning of messages and provides immediate feedback so that the interpretation of a message can be checked. Face-to-face communication is very "rich," because it not only conveys meaning through the use of language, but also conveys paralinguistic (e.g., tone and loudness of voice) and nonverbal cues (e.g., gestures, facial expressions). For example, saying "that's great" with a smile versus a frown on one's face conveys a completely different message. Furthermore, face-to-face meetings allow for immediate feedback (i.e., receivers can immediately respond to messages). Videoconferencing is relatively rich as well, although certain cues may be lost (e.g., direction of gaze; gestures when the whole body is not visible). Teleconferences obviously lose all visual cues, but paralinguistic cues are still present (albeit, perhaps, of lower quality). Finally, text-based communication,

TABLE 11.1
Types of communication according to levels of dispersion and synchronicity

	Synchronous	Asynchronous
Collocated	Some forms of CMC Face-to-face meetings	Bulletin boards, notes, reports
Dispersed	Chat, some forms of CMC Telephone Videoconferencing	Email, regular mail, SMS Voicemail Video-mail

such as email, chat, or SMS, is less rich (or "leaner") still (e.g., Driskell, Radtke, & Salas, 2003). For example, it is hard (harder than most people think) to communicate subtle things such as sarcasm, humor, or emotions through email (Kruger, Epley, Parker, & Ng, 2005). Thus, an important downside of using ICT to communicate is the loss of nonverbal and/or paralinguistic cues (although for some purposes losing these cues may actually be beneficial, see below), which may lead to problems with the interpretation of messages.

One area of research has been comparing the performance of groups using different types of media. Many of these studies have compared computer-mediated communication (CMC) with face-to-face (FTF) communication. Fewer studies have looked at other types of media, such as teleconferencing and videoconferencing.

Face-to-face versus computer-mediated communication

In the 1980s and thereafter, several computer systems have been developed that were aimed at making group meetings more effective (e.g., Dennis, George, Jessup, Nunamaker, & Vogel, 1988). Figure 11.1 shows a photograph of an electronic meeting system. These systems often complement rather than replace FTF meetings, and participants can communicate verbally as well as through a computer network. The messages that participants enter into their computers are made available to the other participants through the computer network (and sometimes on a screen in the front). Of course these systems might also be used when participants are not collocated, in which case they may (but do not need to be) complemented by video and/or audio connections.

The idea behind these systems is that meetings can be made more efficient and effective through the use of computer technology. There are several reasons why CMC might be more effective than communicating FTF. First, different software tools can be incorporated in these systems, for example a tool for voting during group decision-making, or a tool that makes it easy to exchange and store ideas or information for later use. Second, participants can often enter their messages anonymously, which may have certain advantages such as

FIGURE 11.1.
A photo of an electronic meeting system. Participants can use their computers to communicate, and results can be projected on the screens. However, participants can also talk to each other. Reprinted with kind permission of Jay F. Nunamaker.

reduced evaluation apprehension (Chapter 6) or reduced conformity (Chapter 2). Third, people can type their messages simultaneously. Thus, while in FTF discussions only one person can speak at any given time, CMC has the advantage of parallel access. Finally, partly as a result of parallel access and anonymity, unequal participation may be less of a problem: While in face-to-face meetings a few group members often dominate a discussion (see the discussion of speaking hierarchies in Chapter 2), this will generally be less true in CMC.

The use of CMC also has some downsides. First, an obvious downside is that for most people typing is much slower than speaking, which makes CMC less efficient. Second, reduced media richness might cause certain problems, such as misinterpretations. Also cues regarding status or expertise may be lost, which may imply that everyone's opinion is weighed equally even though some people have more expertise than others. Third, anonymity might also have certain downsides; for example, it may lead to social loafing (Chapter 5) and people have argued that it may also lead to disinhibited or antisocial behavior (e.g., name-calling or "flaming"; Kiesler, Zubrow, Moses, & Geller, 1985). Finally, parallel access might also mean that many people are typing but nobody is actually reading what other people type, or it may result in information overload when the number of messages exceed people's information processing capacity (see Table 11.2 for an overview).

Several authors have argued that the type of task that a group has to perform will determine whether the advantages of CMC will outweigh the disadvantages. For example, Straus and McGrath (1994) argued that tasks in which task interdependence among group members is high require more nonverbal and paralinguistic cues, because these cues are needed to regulate the discussion, recognize

TABLE 11.2

An overview of the potential advantages and disadvantages of CMC as compared to face-to-face meetings

Characteristic	(Potential) advantage	(Potential) disadvantage
General	Use of certain tools (e.g., for voting) and external storage of messages	Typing is slower than speaking
Anonymity	Less evaluation apprehension, less conformity	Social loafing, loss of useful status cues, disinhibited behavior
Parallel access	Less production blocking, more equal participation (also in combination with anonymity)	Less attention to other's contributions, information overload, less coordination

expertise (e.g., make sure that important messages receive more attention), and reconcile differences of opinion. Straus and McGrath compared three-person FTF and CMC groups on three tasks: an idea-generation task (Chapter 6), a problem-solving task with a correct answer (Chapter 8), and a judgmental task (Chapter 7). They argued that in idea-generation tasks not much coordination is needed, because participants can contribute their ideas independently of each other, and consequently CMC groups would do as well as (or better than) FTF groups. Problem-solving tasks require more coordination, but when a problem solution is clearly demonstrable (see Chapter 8) people will recognize the solution irrespective of the medium. Straus and McGrath therefore predicted that CMC groups would encounter most problems when working at a judgmental task, because participants need to reach a consensus for which an adequate coordination of group members' opinions is needed.

Straus and McGrath (1994) found that CMC groups performed about equally well as FTF groups in the idea-generation task and the problem-solving task. However, FTF groups outperformed CMC groups in the judgmental task. One reason was that task progress was slower in the CMC groups, and Straus and McGrath suggest that CMC groups would perhaps have been able to perform better had they been given more time. Further, group member satisfaction did not differ in the idea-generation task, but members of FTF groups were more satisfied than those of CMC groups after the problem-solving and judgmental tasks.

The results of Straus and McGrath seem to hold generally. As we have seen in Chapter 6, parallel access eliminates production blocking (i.e., turn-taking among group members), which is a major problem in FTF idea-generating groups. Furthermore, little coordination is required during idea generation and CMC groups seem to generally outperform FTF groups (DeRosa, Smith, & Hantula, 2006), especially when group size is large (Dennis & Williams, 2003). Perhaps Straus and McGrath (1994) did not find superior performance of CMC groups as compared to FTF groups because they used relatively small groups (group size was three). When groups are larger, production blocking makes FTF groups less and less effective, while this is not true for CMC groups. However, small CMC groups may not always outperform small FTF groups because typing is slower than speaking.

In tasks requiring more coordination among members, such as decision-making tasks (Chapter 7), FTF groups generally outperform CMC groups. Indeed, in a quantitative summary of decision-making research, Baltes, Dickson, Sherman, Bauer, and LaGanke (2002) concluded that "computer-mediated communication leads to decreases in group effectiveness, increases in time required to complete tasks, and decreases in member satisfaction compared to face-to-face groups" (p. 156). This pessimistic overall conclusion needs some refinement, however. Anonymity in CMC groups was associated with a smaller difference between CMC and FTF groups in decision quality but also with a larger difference in discussion time and member satisfaction. The reason might be that allowing anonymous communication makes people more willing to disagree with others, which may in the end lead to better (but slower) decisions (see also Chapter 7). Further, giving CMC groups unlimited time for discussion also reduces the advantage of FTF groups over CMC groups in terms of decision effectiveness. This seems to confirm Straus and McGrath's suggestion that CMC groups might sometimes overcome their problems when given enough time. Of course, CMC would still be less efficient in terms of time required.

Another topic that has received much attention in the comparison between CMC and FTF groups is the effects that anonymity might have on group processes. While FTF interactions (or even teleconferencing or videoconferencing) cannot be anonymous, interactions using CMC can. This might have a number of effects (see Table 11.2), some of which might be detrimental but others might enhance group performance. In the context of idea generation, for example, it has been suggested (and sometimes found) that anonymity reduces evaluation apprehension (i.e., fear of being negatively evaluated), which in turn may stimulate the generation of especially original and unusual ideas (e.g., Cooper, Gallupe, Pollard, & Cadsby, 1998). However, anonymity has also been found to increase the number of critical remarks during brainstorming, which might in fact increase evaluation apprehension (Valacich, Dennis, & Nunamaker, 1992). Further, it has been argued that anonymity will also reduce (normative) social influence and may even lead to anti-normative behaviors (Kiesler et al., 1985; McLeod, Baron, Marti, & Yoon, 1997). Indeed, while being anonymous it is less possible to exert (or experience) normative pressure, and people may conform less to group norms.

Counterintuitively, the opposite prediction has been made by Spears, Lea, and Lee (1990; also Postmes, Spears, & Lea, 1998). Based on social identity and self-categorization theory they have developed the *Social Identity Model of Deindividuation Effects (SIDE)*, arguing that under certain conditions anonymity may even *increase* social influence and conformity to group norms. In particular, when group members' social identity is salient (i.e., they are aware of their membership of a valued group), anonymity will reduce clues to people's individual identity (see also Chapter 10). As a consequence they may self-categorize more as group members (rather than seeing themselves as individuals), which in turn leads them to follow group norms more. This compliance with group norms, however, does not arise because of normative pressure from other group member, but rather from within. According to Postmes, Spears, Sakhel, and De Groot (2001, p. 1253): "Paradoxically, reducing the presence of individuals within the group may actually serve to accentuate the presence of the group within the individual."

For example, Postmes *et al.* (2001) first had groups do an exercise to make their group membership salient. Then the groups discussed a dilemma of a small hospital that had problems due to an increase in number of patients. All groups used CMC, but half the groups were anonymous and half were not (pictures of group members were or were not displayed on the computer screens). Before the group discussion, Postmes *et al.* subtly manipulated group norms that emphasized either efficiency or being prosocial. The content of the following computer-mediated discussion was coded for efficiency and prosocial related words. Figure 11.2 shows some of the results. Norms had more impact on anonymous groups than on groups that were not anonymous. Anonymous CMC groups used more efficiency-related words with an efficiency norm and used more prosocial words with a prosocial norm. Identifiable groups complied less with group norms and even tended to show the opposite pattern, perhaps because group members in that condition wanted to differentiate themselves from the group to emphasize their individuality.

In sum, CMC has certain advantages as compared to FTF communication, but also some clear disadvantages, one being that it is less efficient. Further, tasks in which group members are more interdependent are performed less well when using CMC than when using FTF discussions. Finally, anonymity in CMC may decrease social influence, but when group members' social identity is salient may also increase conformity to social norms.

Other media

CMC is less "rich" (or "leaner") than some of the other means of communication, such as videoconferencing or teleconferencing. These media are speech-based and therefore also confer paralinguistic cues. Video provides at least some nonverbal cues as well. Furthermore, because speaking is faster than typing, these media generally are more

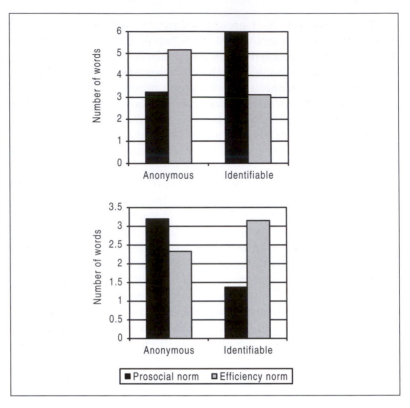

FIGURE 11.2.
Number of efficiency-related words (top) and number of prosocial words (bottom) used in the discussions (data from Postmes *et al.*, 2001). In anonymous groups, members conformed to group norms, whereas in identifiable groups they showed the opposite pattern.

efficient than CMC in terms of speed of communication. Several issues around these media have received attention.

First, researchers have investigated the differences between FTF communication and other media in the "flow" of the conversation. What is generally found is that FTF communication is less formal and more spontaneous than other types of communication. For example, speaking turns are longer and interruptions occur less often in teleconferencing (audio only) as compared to FTF communication (e.g., Beattie & Barnard, 1979; Rutter & Stephenson, 1977). One reason is that nonverbal cues, such as direction of gaze, are used to regulate the discussion, and turn-taking is harder to regulate without these visual cues. Furthermore, nonverbal cues are also used to check the interpretation of messages (e.g., nodding one's head). One consequence of missing these nonverbal cues is that both speakers and listeners more often check whether the listener has correctly understood a message in teleconferencing as compared to FTF discussions (Doherty-Sneddon *et al.*, 1997). In this respect, videoconferencing should have some advantages. However, also in videoconferencing speech is more formal and people more often check the interpretation of messages than in FTF communication (Doherty-Sneddon *et al.*, 1997; O'Connaill, Whittaker, & Wilbur, 1993). This might partly be due to unfamiliarity with this medium (Van der Kleij, 2007).

Second, in terms of performance, an early review of the literature suggested that there are few differences between FTF, audio only, and audio-video communication in task performance (Williams, 1977). For example, Chapanis, Ochsman, Parrish, and Weeks (1972) found no differences in performance on a problem-solving task between an audio only and an FTF condition. Similarly, Williams (1975) found no differences in performance between an audio only, an audio-video, and an FTF condition in a brainstorming task. More recently, Hambley, O'Neill, and Kline (2007) performed an experiment in which they compared the effectiveness of FTF communication with videoconferencing and chat. Groups of three or four members performed a problem-solving exercise (finding the optimal sequence in which to carry out 20 different activities). Hambley *et al.* found no differences in performance among the different conditions, although it should be noted that they gave chat groups more time for the task (50 min) than FTF and video groups (35 min); therefore chat groups were in fact less efficient, needing more time to reach a similar level of performance. Thus, the differences between different media, according to these results, are rather small, and all media that allow for verbal communication (i.e., speech) appear to perform equally well.

However, as was the case with CMC, the effectiveness of different media might depend on the group's task. The tasks reviewed above were problem-solving and brainstorming tasks, and in these tasks CMC also performs relatively well. Williams (1977), for example, argued that tasks that involve conflicts (e.g., differences of opinions) may show larger differences between FTF and teleconferencing or videoconferencing. A theoretical perspective on this issue is given by *media richness theory* (Daft & Lengel, 1986). This theory argues that media richness should match the requirements of the task. More specifically, the effectiveness of media depends on the "equivocality" of the task, which refers to the degree to which different interpretations of task-relevant information are possible. When information is more equivocal, it is argued, richer media are needed to communicate accurately about the meaning of information. When equivocality is low, leaner media will also be effective.

Although the theory sounds quite plausible, it has not received much support. For example, Dennis and Kinney (1998) performed an experiment in which dyads had to work on a task that was low in equivocality (solving puzzles) and one in which equivocality was high (making judgments while the dyad members had different information). They also varied media richness on two dimensions: presence of visual cues (comparing a condition with audio only to an audio-video condition) and immediacy of feedback (whether participants could immediately respond to each other or not). Media richness theory would predict that the richer media would work better, especially on the task high in equivocality. However, Dennis and Kinney found no effects of media richness on the quality of performance. They did find effects on the time required to solution. This time was shorter with richer media, but this was especially the case for the task low in equivocality, while the effects of media richness were smaller for the task high in equivocality. This contradicts media richness theory, which would have predicted that with more equivocal tasks richer media should be more advantageous.

In all, these results suggest that there are no large differences between FTF, audio, and audio-video communication in terms of group performance. In particular, it seems that adding a video-channel has limited effects. Some studies have found effects on socio-emotional reactions of group members, such as increased satisfaction and mutual liking with richer media (e.g., Dennis & Kinney, 1998), but these effects have not been found consistently (e.g., Burgoon et al., 2002). However, the picture is likely to be much more complex than this. Effects of media richness are likely to depend on many factors such as the level of and distribution of expertise among group members, the type of task, task difficulty, and amount of interdependence among group members. At present there simply are not sufficient studies to draw clear conclusions.

Virtual teams

Working in virtual teams has become more prevalent in recent years. For example, Hertel, Geister, and Konradt (2005) reported that 20 per cent of German managers spend most of their time in virtual teams, and Kanawattanachai and Yoo (2002) even reported that more than 60 per cent of professional employees work in teams that are characterized by some degree of "virtuality." However, what exactly do we mean when we talk about "virtual teams"?

Several authors have argued that there is no clear black-and-white distinction between regular and virtual teams, but that *virtuality* can be seen as a dimension on which teams vary (e.g., Gibson & Gibbs, 2006; Griffith, Sawyer, & Neale, 2003). Several characteristics have been associated with virtuality, such as geographic dispersion, electronic dependence, structural dynamism, and national diversity (Gibson & Gibbs, 2006). Geographic dispersion is an important characteristic, from which the other characteristics are derived. For example, as teams are more dispersed they are more dependent on electronic communication (meeting face to face becomes harder) and are more likely to be nationally diverse (consisting of members from different nations). However, this association is not one-on-one: Team members working in the same location might also rely heavily on electronic communication (e.g., email) and may consist of members from different countries (e.g., expatriates).

The most important reason to use virtual teams is that members can be assigned to these teams based on expertise rather than geographical location. One consequence of this might also be that the team boundaries become more variable, as members enter the team when their expertise is required and leave when their input is no longer needed. Because of this, structural dynamism – the frequency with which membership, roles, and relations among members change – can also be seen as one of the features underlying virtuality. Because direct face-to-face interaction and stable membership contribute to group entitativity, these characteristics make virtual teams less entitative than regular work teams (Chapter 1).

The main advantage of virtual teams thus lies in the possibility to recruit experts irrespective of their geographical location. According to the general framework introduced in Chapter 3, this would increase the team's potential performance to the degree that this expertise is needed for the team's task. Indeed, virtual teams are not and cannot be used for simple production tasks, but rather are used for tasks in which having different areas of expertise is likely to be helpful (e.g., innovative tasks; Gibson & Gibbs, 2006). However, whether the team's potential is realized will depend on effective group processes. Unfortunately, virtual teamwork has a number of features that might distract from effective group processes, and it is to these problems (and how to deal with them) that we now turn.

Problems in virtual teams

There are several challenges when one is working in or with virtual teams (for overviews Hertel et al., 2005; Martins, Gilson, & Maynard, 2004). We will address three issues: the problem of "common ground," the development of trust, and problems with monitoring and control of virtual teams. Also, issues of how to manage virtual teams will be discussed.

One problem that faces virtual teams is the development of "common ground." Problems and miscommunication may arise when team members lack *mutual knowledge*: "knowledge that the communicating parties share in common and know they share" (Cramton, 2001, p. 346). Having mutual knowledge facilitates communication because it allows people to formulate their messages with an awareness of what the other party does and does not know. Mutual knowledge is established when people have had similar experiences (e.g., talked to the same person, have been in the same place), when they explicitly communicate knowledge, but also through knowledge of group membership (Krauss & Fussell, 1990). For example, when you know that someone also is a psychology student, you will presume that this person has some knowledge in common with you.

The problem facing virtual teams is that it is harder to establish common knowledge, firstly because (due to geographical distance and cultural differences) team members will usually not have similar experiences. Furthermore, information about many issues is often not explicitly communicated, such as information about local holidays and customs, available equipment and support, or the presence of competing demands on someone's time. What will happen in these cases is that group members will "fill in" missing knowledge based on their own situation or based on the other's group membership. This can cause problems, especially when errors or misinterpretations cannot easily be discovered or rectified, which often is the case when using asynchronous communication (e.g., email) or media low in media richness (without immediate or clear feedback on the interpretation of messages).

In a qualitative study among 13 virtual teams, Cramton (2001) identified several types of problem that can arise. The first is a lack of knowledge about local conditions. For example, when team members do not know the local situation of other members they might interpret a late reaction as laziness, when in fact there were technical difficulties or someone was on a holiday. A second problem was that often messages were not communicated to the whole team, and team members wrongly assumed that everybody was aware of a certain issue. Third, team members often differed in their judgment of how important certain information was, which sometimes led to irritation because of slow or sloppy replies from people who interpreted something as unimportant. Cramton argued that with a lack of common knowledge team members have a tendency to attribute actions of others to their disposition (e.g., a sloppy personality), rather than (more accurately) to differences in the situation they are in. In turn, this may lead to dislike, ineffective team processes, and distrust.

Trust is the second issue that has received attention. Trust is important in teams, including virtual teams, because it allows members to participate in risky activities (such as putting much effort into a task) that they cannot control or monitor and where they may be disappointed by the actions of others (e.g., when others are not putting in much effort; free-riding, Chapter 5). Trust may be harder to establish in virtual teams than in traditional teams, because members will interact less frequently, do not always have sufficient mutual knowledge, and cannot easily monitor each other's behavior. Nevertheless, Jarvenpaa and Leidner (1999) found, in a qualitative study, that some virtual teams quickly developed a sense of trust (and others did not), in particular when they communicated a lot about social issues (e.g., hobbies) and when members were enthusiastic about their task. However, they found that trust could also quickly disappear, especially when teams failed to establish an effective way to coordinate their activities (e.g., when there were unclear roles and communication was unpredictable).

Other researchers have suggested that an initial face-to-face meeting to get a team started may stimulate the development of trust (e.g., Kraut, Galegher, & Egido, 1988). Wilson, Straus, and McEvily (2006) have argued that trust develops slower in virtual teams than in face-to-face teams, because virtual teams are slower at exchanging social and personal information (e.g., because they are more task-focused than focused on interpersonal issues). However, precisely the exchange of social information is needed to build trust. In their study, three-person teams worked together in three meetings over a period of three weeks. There were several conditions: In the FFF condition the three meetings were all face to face; in the FEE condition the first meeting was face to face but the others were computer-mediated, and in the EEE condition all meetings were computer-mediated. Trust was measured every week. Wilson *et al.* found that trust developed more quickly in the teams that started with a face-to-face meeting. However, even in the EEE condition, where no face-to-face meetings took place, eventually trust did increase. Thus, it appears that trust can be boosted with an initial face-to-face meeting, but that it will also gradually develop in teams that never meet face to face (see also Alge, Wiethoff, & Klein, 2003).

A third problem of virtual teams is difficulties with monitoring and control. Obviously, when team members work in different parts of the world it is very hard to monitor their behavior ("are they working?") but also to control their behavior. This presents a problem for team leaders: How can they effectively lead a team while not able to observe team members? One solution might be to use performance monitoring systems, such as computer software that monitors employees' behavior (e.g., online and offline time, working pace) or watching team members with a webcam. However, direct performance monitoring can lead to stress and dissatisfaction, and team members may not like or accept that someone is constantly looking over their shoulders (e.g., Aiello & Kolb, 1995). Further, performance monitoring can lead to social facilitation and inhibition effects (Chapter 4) and worse performance on more difficult and demanding tasks, especially for less skilled employees (Aiello & Svec, 1993).

Another option would be to give virtual teams much autonomy, and perhaps even not to appoint a formal leader (see also Chapter 9). Some research suggests that this might be a better strategy (e.g., Vickery, Clark, & Carlson, 1999). A related construct that has recently been studied is *team empowerment*, defined as "an increased task motivation that is due to team members' collective, positive assessment of their organizational tasks" (Kirkman, Rosen, Tesluk, & Gibson, 2004, p. 176). According to Kirkman *et al.*, team empowerment entails that the team feels capable of performing its task, that the team has high autonomy, and that the task the team performs is meaningful and important. In a study among 35 virtual teams in the tourism industry, Kirkman *et al.* found that team empowerment led to better team performance (e.g., higher client satisfaction).

However, the question is how managers might stimulate team empowerment. Hertel, Konradt, and Orlikowski (2004) argued that group member motivation to contribute to virtual team performance (cf. empowerment) depends on team members' evaluation of team goals as important, the perceived indispensability of their contributions (i.e., the perception that one's contribution is really needed for the group to succeed), their self-efficacy (i.e., the belief that effort will lead to high performance), and their trust in the other members. These motivational factors, in turn, depend on different types of interdependence. Hertel *et al.* argued that managers should create goal interdependence by setting clear and fair goals, design the team task in such a way that members are highly task-interdependent, and work with team-based rewards (i.e., create outcome interdependence). These factors indeed affected team member motivation and this in turn influenced team performance. It therefore appears that certain management practices (e.g., goal-setting and the use of team-based rewards) can motivate or empower members of virtual teams, which in turn results in higher team performance.

In sum, virtual teams have the main advantage that team members need not be collocated, but "virtuality" also creates certain problems, including misunderstandings due to lack of mutual knowledge, lack of trust, and the inability to monitor and control team members' behaviors. These problems may all lead to process losses and the result might be that virtual teams perform below their potential (see Chapter 3). Many of these problems might, however, be prevented or counteracted. For example, an initial face-to-face kick-off meeting may contribute to the emergence of trust. Furthermore, empowering teams through certain management practices might be very effective, and more effective than strict performance monitoring.

Chapter summary

(1) Recent developments in ICT have had important consequences for working in groups, as they allow geographically dispersed groups to collaborate using electronic media. The advantage is that groups can be composed of members with relevant exper-tise, independent of geographical location, which contributes to their potential performance.

(2) Different media differ in media richness, referring to the degree to which a medium contains cues regarding the meaning of messages and provides immediate feedback so that the inter-pretation of a message can be checked.

(3) Computer-mediated communication (CMC) is low in media richness but has certain advantages, such as parallel access and more equal participation. However, disadvantages such as slower task progress and information overload reduce the effec-tiveness of CMC. Especially in tasks that require much coordi-nation of group members, such as decision making, CMC is less effective than face-to-face (FTF) communication. This difference is smaller for tasks requiring less coordination (e.g., brainstorm-ing and problem-solving).

(4) Anonymity in CMC may lead to less conformity, but might actually increase conformity when group members' social identity is salient.

(5) Mediated speech-based communication (audio or audio-video) is more formal than FTF communication. There seem to be no big differences in task performance between groups using these different media.

(6) Virtuality is a dimension on which teams vary, and consists of geographical dispersion, electronic dependence, structural dynamism, and national diversity. Virtual teams are less entitative than face-to-face teams.

(7) Virtual teams face certain problems, including a lack of mutual knowledge, a slower development of trust, and an inability to monitor and control team members. However, teams can reach high levels of performance when management practices, such as goal-setting and a team-based reward system, lead to team empowerment and high motivation of team members.

Exercises

(1) In this chapter we have discussed how developments in ICT have affected group-based work. What other developments in society affect working in groups? What kind of developments might be expected in the future?

(2) Suppose typing were as fast as speaking. Would you still expect performance differences between CMC and FTF communication (e.g., on decision-making tasks)? Why would this be the case?

(3) Which task factors might determine whether videoconferencing is more effective than audio-only communication? How would you test your prediction?

(4) Goal-setting and team-based rewards can improve the effective functioning of virtual teams. Can you think of other things a manager could do to improve the performance of virtual teams?

Further reading

General

Driskell, J. E., Radtke, P. H., & Salas, E. (2003). Virtual teams: The effects of technological mediation on team performance. *Group Dynamics: Theory, Research and Practice, 7*, 297–323.

On computer-mediated communication

Straus, S. G., & McGrath, J. E. (1994). Does the medium matter? The interaction of task type and technology on group performance and member reactions. *Journal of Applied Psychology, 79,* 87–97.

On virtual teams

Hertel, G., Geister, S., & Konradt, U. (2005). Managing virtual teams: A review of current empirical work. *Human Resource Management Review, 15,* 69–95.

Glossary

additive tasks: Potential performance of the group is determined by the sum or the average of individual performances (e.g., filling envelopes).

advocacy: Group members' tendency to defend their initial *preference* during group discussion, by mentioning information that is consistent rather than inconsistent with this preference.

audience paradigm: Participants work on a task while others (may) observe them.

Big Five: Widely accepted way to organize personality traits on five dimensions: neuroticism, extraversion, openness to experience, agreeableness, and conscientiousness.

bottom-up effects: Occur when characteristics at the individual level determine outcomes at the group level.

boundary-spanning: Activities that group members perform to manage their relation with the environment of the group.

brainstorming: Creative problem-solving method in which quantity of ideas is emphasized.

co-action paradigm: Participants work on similar tasks alongside each other.

cognitive dissonance theory: Argues that people find it uncomfortable when two cognitions or cognition and behavior are inconsistent (dissonant) and are likely to change their cognitions or behaviors to reduce dissonance.

cognitive stimulation: Occurs when access to others' ideas leads to process gains because people can build on these ideas.

cohesion (or "cohesiveness"): The force that binds members to the group and induces them to stay with the group.

collective induction: Tasks of this type ask of a group to induce a general rule from available evidence.

commitment: The degree to which a member identifies with the group and its goals and wishes to maintain group membership.

common good dilemma: Members of a social collective (e.g., a group) can contribute resources to establish a common good. If enough people contribute, the common good will be provided to all members of the collective, regardless of whether they contributed or not.

Common Ingroup Identity Model: Argues that *ingroup bias* will be reduced when groups have a common superordinate identity: when members of two groups perceive that both belong to a larger overarching group.

common knowledge effect: Shared information has a bigger impact on group choice than unshared information.

conflict: The process resulting from tensions between team members because of real or perceived differences.

conjunctive tasks: Potential performance of the group depends on the least capable member (e.g., mountain-climbing).

consideration: Leader behaviors that indicate respect and trust, and communicate that leaders value good relationships with followers; often associated with democratic decisions.

contact hypothesis: Argues that direct positive contact between people from different groups will reduce prejudice and *ingroup bias*. This reduction in bias is expected especially under certain optimal *contact conditions*: when the groups have equal status, have common goals, when intergroup cooperation is present, and with support from authorities, law, or custom.

contingency theory of leadership: Argues that the effectiveness of leadership styles depends on the situation: *initiating structure* is preferred under very favorable or unfavorable circumstances while *consideration* is preferred under moderately favorable circumstances.

conversion theory: Theory that argues that *minority influence* has effects that are qualitatively different from those of *majority influence*: majority influence is more likely to lead to *public compliance*, whereas minority influence is more likely to lead to *private acceptance*.

coordination loss: Occurs when group members do not combine their (potential) contributions in an optimal way.

cross-training: An instructional strategy in which each team member is trained in the duties of his or her teammates.

demonstrability (of a task): Underlying property of the decision-making task continuum ranging from *judgmental* to *intellective tasks*, referring to the degree to which a solution can be demonstrated as correct using a verbal or mathematical conceptual system.

depersonalization: A shift from seeing people as individuals to seeing them as group members.

discontinuity effect: The finding that intergroup behavior in a *mixed-motive situation* is less cooperative than interpersonal behavior.

discretionary tasks: In discretionary tasks there is no fixed way in which individual contributions are transformed into outcomes, but this is up to (the discretion of) the group (e.g., in a rock band).

disjunctive tasks: In disjunctive tasks potential performance of the group is determined by the best member (e.g., a math problem).

disparity: Concerns group *diversity* along a vertical continuum of valued social assets, such as power, pay, and status.

distraction conflict theory: Argues that the presence of others leads to an attentional conflict potentially leading to *social facilitation* or *inhibition* effects.

diversity: Characteristic of a social grouping that reflects the degree to which objective or subjective differences exist between group members.

downward matching: Tendency to be as productive as the least productive member of the group.

drive theory: Argues that the mere presence of others serves to increase generalized drive and arousal, which leads to a higher likelihood that people emit a dominant response.

emergent states: Properties of teams that are typically dynamic in nature and vary as a function of team context, inputs, processes, and outcomes.

entitativity: The degree to which a collection of persons is perceived as being bonded together in a coherent unit.

eureka tasks: Problem type with the property that when someone finds the solution this is immediately recognized as correct by others.

evaluation apprehension: Fear of being evaluated negatively by others.

exchange theory: Argues that social relations take the form of social exchange processes in which material and psychological goods are exchanged.

expectancy-value theory: Argues that motivation is a multiplicative function of three factors: expectancy (the belief that effort will lead to performance), instrumentality (the belief that performance will lead to positive outcomes), and value (the evaluation of outcomes on a positive–negative dimension).

expectation states theory: Argues that status differences within a group result from different expectations that group members have about each other.

faultline: Hypothetical dividing lines that may split a group into subgroups based on one or more attributes.

free-riding: A reduction in effort that occurs when group members feel their effort is dispensable.

group polarization: The phenomenon that on any judgmental dimension groups after a group discussion tend to shift to the pole that their members favored initially.

group socialization: The efforts of the group to assimilate new members to existing group *norms* and practices.

groupthink: A mode of thinking that people engage in when they are deeply involved in a cohesive ingroup, when members' strivings for unanimity override their motivation to appraise alternative courses of action realistically.

hidden profile: (Experimental) situation in which the correct solution of a problem is initially hidden and can only be detected when group members exchange their unshared information.

informational social influence: People conform to others because they accept information obtained from others as evidence about reality.

ingroup bias: The tendency to treat and evaluate members of one's own group more favorably than members of other groups.

initiating structure: Leader behaviors that ensure that followers perform their jobs and that role ambiguity and conflict are minimized, and involves giving directions and making autocratic decisions.

initiation: The *role transition* of entry into a group, often accompanied by some ritual.

input-process-output (IPO) model: According to this model, input variables (such as group size and composition, organizational climate, or leadership) affect group processes (e.g., information-sharing, conflict) and these in turn determine group output (e.g., performance).

intellective tasks: Problems or decisions for which there exists a *demonstrably* correct answer within a verbal or mathematical conceptual system.

interaction anxiousness: The degree to which various interaction situations arouse anxiety and stress.

interaction process analysis (IPA): A formal observational measurement system devised by Bales for coding the interactions of members of small groups.

interpersonal cohesion: The attraction of group members to the group based on mutual liking of group members.

judgmental tasks: Evaluative, behavioral or aesthetic judgments for which no *demonstrable* correct answer exists.

Köhler effect: Group members work harder because they fear that the group would otherwise fail because of them;

this is especially true for low-ability people.

KSAs: Abbreviation of knowledge, skills, and abilities as the basic resources of group members.

laissez-faire **leadership**: Non-leadership or lack of leader behavior.

leadership: A process of social influence in which one person is able to enlist the aid and support of others in the accomplishment of a common task.

leniency bias: The finding that in jury decisions pro-acquittal factions are more influential than pro-conviction factions.

majority influence: Occurs when a larger subgroup produces conformity in a smaller subgroup.

management teams: Coordinate and provide direction to sub-units under their jurisdiction and are responsible for the overall performance of those sub-units.

media richness: The degree to which a medium contains cues regarding the meaning of messages and provides immediate feedback so that the interpretation of the message can be checked.

media richness theory: Argues that media richness should match the group task and that tasks higher in equivocality require richer media.

minority influence: A smaller subgroup produces change in a larger subgroup.

mixed-motive situations: Situations characterized by the presence of both incentives to cooperate and incentives to compete with others (or other groups).

motivation loss: Occurs when members are not optimally motivated, and therefore exert less effort than would be possible or needed for optimal performance.

Multifactor Leadership Questionnaire (MLQ): Questionnaire that is widely used to measure *transactional* and *transformational leadership*.

multilevel systems: Groups are multilevel systems because individuals (lower level) are part of the group (higher level), and because there are specific relations among these levels (*top-down* and *bottom-up effects*).

mutual knowledge: Knowledge that the communicating parties share in common and know they share.

need to belong: The human predisposition to form and maintain stable, strong and positive relationships with others.

nominal groups: Are groups in name only and consist of members who work individually and whose contributions are pooled.

normative social influence: People conform to the expectations of others to obtain positive evaluations.

norms: Implicit rules that prescribe which behaviors and opinions are and are not appropriate in the context of a social group.

outcome interdependence: The degree to which group members are mutually dependent to obtain certain outcomes.

parallel teams: Exist parallel to an organization, and perform functions that the regular organization is not equipped to perform well.

persuasive arguments theory: Argues that *group polarization* is the result of hearing new and valid arguments in favor of the group's position during discussion.

potential performance: What a group could potentially achieve given group member resources and task demands.

preference: An inclination of an individual to select one option from a set of response alternatives.

private acceptance: A real change in one's private opinion that is likely to persist (e.g., because of having been convinced by arguments).

process gain: Occurs when the actual performance of a group is above its *potential performance*.

process loss: Occurs when the actual performance of a group is below its *potential performance*.

production blocking: Negative effect on group performance arising because group members must wait for their turn before they can enter their contribution (e.g., in *brainstorming*).

project teams: Time-limited teams that work at one-time outputs, typically a new product or service.

public compliance: A change in behavior without changing one's private beliefs.

relationship conflict: *Conflicts* about personal taste, political preferences, values, and interpersonal style.

Ringelmann effect: Inverse relation between group size and individual performance (e.g., in rope-pulling).

role: Set of behaviors associated with a certain position in the group.

role transition: A change in the relation between a group member and a group.

sampling bias: Shared information (information that was available to all group members before the discussion) has higher probability to be mentioned during discussion than unshared information.

self-categorization theory: Argues that people divide others and themselves into social categories and that this leads to *depersonalization*. One consequence of self-categorization is that people behave more in line with the *norms*, values and customs of their group.

self-efficacy: Expectation that reflects a person's belief that he/she is capable of performing a required behavior.

self-efficacy theory: Argues that *social facilitation* occurs when people have high self-efficacy and positive outcome expectations while *social inhibition* occurs when people have low self-

efficacy and negative outcome expectations.

separation: Concerns group diversity in terms of position or opinion (a horizontal continuum).

shared leadership: An *emergent state* that results from the distribution of leadership influence across multiple team members.

social comparison theory: Argues that people have a tendency to compare their abilities, performance, opinions, and preferences with those of others in order to validate them.

social compensation: Occurs when people work harder on a task because they expect that other group members will perform poorly and final performance of the group will depend on them.

social decision scheme (SDS): A decision rule that specifies how group compositions (in terms of preferences) are turned into a group decision (e.g., majority wins, truth wins).

social decision scheme theory: Formal (mathematical) theory that specifies the relations among individual preferences, group compositions and group decisions.

social facilitation: Effect that individual performance improves in the presence of others.

social identity: That part of the self-concept that derives from group membership combined with the value and significance of that membership.

social identity model of deindividuation effects (SIDE): Argues that anonymity may increase social influence when group membership is salient, because anonymity reduces cues to individual identity.

social identity theory: Argues that people's identity in part consists of group membership (*social identity*) and that people strive for a positive social identity. This leads to a tendency to distinguish one's own group positively from other groups and (among others) to *ingroup bias*.

social inhibition: Effect that individual performance deteriorates in the presence of others.

social loafing: The reduction of effort when working in a group as compared to when working alone due to a lack of evaluability of individual contributions.

socio-emotional behaviors: Behaviors during group interactions that are directed at interpersonal relations.

speaking hierarchy: Hierarchy within a group based on who talks most.

staffing level: Degree to which the actual number of group members is similar to the ideal number of group members.

sucker effect: A reduction of effort in order to prevent being exploited by *free-riding* fellow group members.

task behaviors: Behaviors during group interactions that are directed at task completion.

task cohesion: The shared commitment of group members to the group task.

task conflict: *Conflicts* about the distribution of resources, procedures, and policies, and judgments and interpretation of facts.

task interdependence: The degree to which group members are mutually dependent on one another to accomplish their tasks.

team: A collection of individuals who are interdependent in their tasks, who share responsibility for outcomes, who see themselves and are seen by others as an intact social entity embedded in one or more social systems (for example, business unit or the corporation), and who manage their relationships across organizational boundaries.

team empowerment: An increased task motivation that is due to team members' collective, positive assessment of their organizational tasks.

team mental model: Organized knowledge structures that allow team members to interact with each other and perform the team's task.

team processes: Members' interdependent acts that convert inputs to outcomes through cognitive, verbal, and behavioral activities directed toward organizing task work to achieve collective goals.

top-down effects: Characteristics at the group level influence group members' behavior, thoughts and feelings.

transactional leadership: Leader behavior that focuses on reward contingencies and exchange relations: Leaders influence their followers by rewarding high performance and reprimanding mistakes and substandard performance.

transactive memory: A system in which group members know which other members have what information.

transformational leadership: Leader behaviors that aim to stimulate followers to move beyond immediate self-interest, and strive towards a higher collective purpose, mission or vision. Leaders accomplish this by developing, intellectually stimulating, and inspiring their followers.

variety: Group diversity in terms of kind or category, primarily in terms of information, knowledge, or expertise.

virtuality: A dimension on which teams may vary depending on geographical location (collocated–dispersed), national diversity (homogeneous–diverse), electronic dependency (low–high), and structural dynamism (low–high).

work teams: Continuing work units responsible for producing goods or providing services.

References

Abrams, D., Wetherell, M., Cochrane, S., Hogg, M. A., & Turner, J. C. (1990). Knowing what to think by knowing who you are: Self-categorization and the nature of norm formation, conformity and group polarization. *British Journal of Social Psychology, 29,* 97–119.

Aiello, J., & Kolb, K. (1995). Electronic performance monitoring and social context: Impact on productivity and stress. *Journal of Applied Psychology, 80,* 339–353.

Aiello, J. R., & Svec, C. M. (1993). Computer monitoring and work performance: Extending the social facilitation framework to electronic presence. *Journal of Applied Social Psychology, 23,* 537–548.

Aldag, R. J., & Fuller, S. R. (1993). Beyond fiasco: A reappraisal of the groupthink phenomenon and a new model of group decision processes. *Psychological Bulletin, 11,* 533–552.

Alge, B. J., Wiethoff, C., & Klein, H. J. (2003). When does the medium matter? Knowledge-building experiences and opportunities in decision-making teams. *Organizational Behavior and Human Decision Processes, 91,* 26–37.

Allport, F. (1920). The influence of the group upon association and thought. *Experimental Psychology, 3,* 159–182.

Allport, G. W. (1954). *The nature of prejudice.* Reading, MA: Addison-Wesley.

Amabile, T. M. (1983). *The social psychology of creativity.* New York: Springer-Verlag.

Amiot, C. E., Terry, D. J., & Callan, V. J. (2007). Status, equity and social identification during an intergroup merger: A longitudinal study. *British Journal of Social Psychology, 46,* 557–577.

Ancona, D. G., & Bresman, H. (2006). Begging, borrowing, and building on ideas from the outside to create pulsed innovation inside teams. In L. L. Thompson & H. S. Choi (Eds.), *Creativity and innovation in organizational teams* (pp. 183–198). Hillsdale, NJ: Lawrence Erlbaum Associates.

Ancona, D. G., & Caldwell, D. F. (1988). Beyond task and maintenance: Defining external functions in groups. *Group and Organization Studies, 13,* 468–494.

Ancona, D. G., & Caldwell, D. F. (1992). Bridging the boundary: External activity and performance in organizational teams. *Administrative Science Quarterly, 37,* 634–665.

Aronson, E., & Mills, J. (1959). The effects of severity of initiation on liking for a group. *Journal of Abnormal and Social Psychology, 59,* 177–181.

Asch, S. E. (1951). Effects of group pressure upon the modification and distortion of judgments. In H. Guetzkow (Ed.), *Groups, leadership and men* (pp. 177–190). Pittsburgh, PA: Carnegie.

Asch, S. E. (1952). *Social psychology.* Englewood Cliffs, NJ: Prentice Hall.

Asch, S. E. (1955). Opinions and social pressure. *Scientific American, 193*, 31–35.

Asch, S. E. (1956). Studies of independence and submission to group pressure: I. A minority of one against a unanimous majority. *Psychological Monographs, 70* (9) (whole no. 417).

Bales, R. F. (1950). *Interaction process analysis: A method for the study of small groups*. Chicago: University of Chicago Press.

Bales, R. F. (1953). The equilibrium problem in small groups. In T. Parson, R. F. Bales, & E. A. Shils (Eds.), *Working papers in the theory of action* (pp. 444–476). New York: The Free Press.

Bales, R. F., & Slater, P. E. (1955). Role differentiation in small decision-making groups. In T. Parson & R. F. Bales (Eds.), *Family, socialization, and interaction process* (pp. 259–306). Glencoe, IL: Free Press.

Baltes, B. B., Dickson, M. W., Sherman, M. P., Bauer, C. C., & LaGanke, J. S. (2002). Computer-mediated communication and group decision-making: A meta-analysis. *Organizational Behavior and Human Decision Processes, 87*, 156–179.

Bandura, A. (1977). Self-efficacy: Toward a unifying theory of behavioral change. *Psychological Review, 84*, 191–215.

Baron, R. S. (1986). Distraction-conflict theory: Progress and problems. In L. Berkowitz (Ed.), *Advances in experimental social psychology* (Vol. 19, pp. 1–40). Ontario, Canada: Elsevier.

Baron, R. S. (2005). So right it's wrong: Groupthink and the ubiquitous nature of polarized group decision making. In M. P. Zanna (Ed.), *Advances in experimental social psychology* (Vol. 37, pp. 219–253). San Diego, CA: Elsevier.

Baron, R. S., Moore, D. L., & Sanders, G. S. (1978). Distraction as a source of drive in social facilitation research. *Journal of Personality and Social Psychology, 36*, 816–824.

Baron, R. S., Vandello, J. A., & Brunsman, B. (1996). The forgotten variable in conformity research: Impact of task importance on social influence. *Journal of Personality and Social Psychology, 71*, 915–927.

Bartis, S., Szymanski, K., & Harkins, S. G. (1988). Evaluation and performance: A two-edged knife. *Personality and Social Psychology Bulletin, 14*, 242–251.

Bass, B. M. (1985). *Leadership and performance beyond expectations*. New York: Free Press.

Bass, B. M. (1998). *Transformational leadership: Industry, military, and educational impact*. Mahwah, NJ: Erlbaum.

Bass, B. M. (1999). Two decades of research and development in transformational leadership. *European Journal of Work and Organizational Psychology, 8*, 9–32.

Bass, B. M., & Avolio, B. J. (1990a). The implications of transactional and transformational leadership for individual, team, and organizational development. In R. W. Woodman & W. A. Passmore (Eds.), *Research in organizational change and development* (Vol. 4, pp. 231–272). Greenwich, CT: JAI Press.

Bass, B. M., & Avolio, B. J. (1990b). *Manual for the multifactor leadership questionnaire*. Palo Alto, CA: Consulting Psychologists Press.

Bass, B. M., Avolio, B. J., Jung, D. I., & Berson, Y. (2003). Predicting unit performance by assessing transformational and transactional leadership. *Journal of Applied Psychology, 88*, 207–218.

Baumeister, R. F. (1984). Choking under pressure: Self-consciousness and paradoxical effects of incentives on skillful performance. *Journal of Personality and Social Psychology, 46*, 610–620.

Baumeister, R. F., & Leary, M. R. (1995). The need to belong: Desire for interpersonal attachments as a fundamental human motivation. *Psychological Bulletin, 117,* 497–529.

Beattie, G. W., & Barnard, P. J. (1979). The temporal structure of natural telephone conversations. *Linguistics, 17,* 213–230.

Beersma, B., & De Dreu, C. K. W. (2005). Conflict's consequences: Effects of social motives on postnegotiation creative and convergent group functioning and performance. *Journal of Personality and Social Psychology, 89,* 358–374.

Berger, J., Rosenholtz, S. J., & Zelditch, M., Jr. (1980). Status organizing processes. In A. Inkeles, N. J. Smelser, & R. Turner (Eds.), *Annual review of sociology* (pp. 479–508). Palo Alto, CA: Annual Reviews.

Berkman, L. F., & Syme, S. L. (1979). Social networks, host-resistance, and mortality: 9-year follow-up-study of Alameda residents. *American Journal of Epidemiology, 109,* 186–204.

Berscheid, E., & Reis, H. T. (1998). Attraction and close relationships. In D. T. Gilbert, S. T. Fiske, & G. Lindzey (Eds.), *The Handbook of Social Psychology* (4th ed., pp. 193–281). New York: McGraw-Hill.

Bettencourt, B. A., Brewer, M. B., Croak, M. R., & Miller, N. (1992). Cooperation and the reduction of intergroup bias: The role of reward structure and social orientation. *Journal of Experimental Social Psychology, 28,* 301–319.

Blascovich, J., Mendes, W. B., Hunter, S. B., & Salomon, K. (1999). Social "facilitation" as a challenge and threat. *Journal of Personality and Social Psychology, 77,* 68–77.

Blickensderfer, E., Cannon-Bowers, J. A., & Salas, E. (1998). Cross training and team performance. In J. A. Cannon-Bowers & E. Salas (Eds.), *Making decisions under stress: Implications for individual and team training* (pp. 299–311). Washington, DC: American Psychological Association.

Boen, F., Vanbeselaere, N., Brebels, L., Huybens, W., & Millet, K. (2007). Post-merger identification as a function of pre-merger identification, relative representation, and premerger status. *European Journal of Social Psychology, 37,* 380–389.

Bond, C. F. (1982). Social facilitation: A self-presentational view. *Journal of Personality and Social Psychology, 42,* 1042–1050.

Bond, C. F., Jr., & Titus, L. J. (1983). Social facilitation: A meta-analysis of 241 studies. *Psychological Bulletin, 94,* 265–292.

Bowlby, J. (1958). The nature of a child's tie to his mother. *International Journal of Psycho-analysis, 39,* 350–373.

Brandon, D. P., & Hollingshead, A. B. (2004). Transactive memory systems in organizations: Matching tasks, expertise, and people. *Organization Science, 15,* 633–644.

Brewer, M. B. (1979). In-group bias in the minimal intergroup situation: A cognitive-motivational analysis. *Psychological Bulletin, 86,* 307–324.

Brickner, M. A., Harkins, S. G., & Ostrom, T. M. (1986). Effects of personal involvement: Thought-provoking implications for social loafing. *Journal of Personality and Social Psychology, 51,* 763–769.

Brown, R. (1974). Further comment on the risky shift. *American Psychologist, 29,* 468–470.

Burgoon, J. K., Bonito, J. A., Ramirez, A., Jr., Dunbar, N. E., Kam, K., & Fischer, J. (2002). Testing the interactivity principle: Effects of mediation, propinquity, and verbal and nonverbal modalities in interpersonal interaction. *Journal of Communication, 52,* 657–677.

Burke, C. S., Stagl, K. C., Klein, C., Goodwin, G. F., Salas, E., & Halpin, S. M. (2006). What type of leadership behaviors are functional in teams? A meta-analysis. *Leadership Quarterly, 17,* 288–307.

Burns, J. M. (1978). *Leadership.* New York: Harper & Row.

Burnstein, E., & Vinokur, A. (1977). Persuasive argumentation and social comparison as determinants of attitude polarization. *Journal of Experimental Social Psychology, 13,* 315–332.

Byrne, D. (1971). *The attraction paradigm.* New York: Academic Press.

Camacho, L. M., & Paulus, P. B. (1995). The role of social anxiousness in group brainstorming. *Journal of Personality and Social Psychology, 68,* 1071–1080.

Campbell, D. T. (1958). Common fate, similarity, and other indices of the status of aggregates of persons as social entities. *Behavioral Science, 3,* 14–25.

Cannon-Bowers, J. A., & Salas, E. (1990). *Cognitive psychology and team training: Shared mental models in complex systems.* Paper presented at the Annual Meeting of the Society of Industrial and Organizational Psychology, Miami, FL.

Cannon-Bowers, J. A., Salas, E., & Converse, S. A. (1990). Cognitive psychology and team training: Shared mental models in complex systems. *Human Factors Society Bulletin, 33,* 1–4.

Cannon-Bowers, J. A., Salas, E., & Converse, S. A. (1993). Shared mental models in expert team decision making. In N. J. Castellan, Jr. (Ed.), *Current issues in individual and group decision making* (pp. 221–246). Hillsdale, NJ: Lawrence Erlbaum Associates.

Carson, J. B., Tesluk, P. E., & Marrone, J. A. (2007). Shared leadership in teams: An investigation of antecedent conditions and performance. *Academy of Management Journal, 50,* 1217–1234.

Carver, C. S., & Scheier, M. F. (1981). *Attention and self-regulation: A control theory approach to human behavior.* New York: Springer-Verlag.

Chaiken, S., & Stangor, S. (1987). Attitudes and attitude change. *Annual Review of Psychology, 38,* 575–630.

Chapanis, A., Ochsman, R. B., Parrish, R. N., & Weeks, G. D. (1972). Studies in interactive communication: The effects of four communication modes on the behavior of teams during cooperative problem-solving. *Human Factors, 14,* 487–509.

Chemers, M. M. (2000). Leadership research and theory: A functional integration. *Group Dynamics: Theory, Research, and Practice, 4,* 27–43.

Chen, S. C. (1937). Social modification of the activity of ants in nest-building. *Physiological Zoology, 10,* 420–436.

Chirumbolo, A., Livi, S., Mannetti, L., Pierro, A., & Kruglanski, A. W. (2004). Effects of need for closure on creativity in small group interactions. *European Journal of Personality, 18,* 265–278.

Choi, H. S., & Levine, J. M. (2004). Minority influence in work teams: The impact of newcomers. *Journal of Experimental Social Psychology, 40,* 273–280.

Choi, H. S., & Thompson, L. (2005). Old wine in a new bottle: Impact of membership change on group creativity. *Organizational Behavior and Human Decision Processes, 98,* 121–132.

Cini, M. A., Moreland, R. L., & Levine, J. M. (1993). Group staffing levels and responses to prospective and new members. *Journal of Personality and Social Psychology, 65,* 723–734.

Cohen, S., & Bailey, D. (1997). What makes teams work: Group effectiveness research from the shop floor to the executive suite. *Journal of Management, 23,* 239–290.

Collaros, P. A., & Anderson, L. R. (1969). Effect of perceived expertise upon creativity members of brainstorming groups. *Journal of Applied Psychology, 53,* 159–163.

Cooper, W. H., Gallupe, R. B., Pollard, S., & Cadsby, J. (1998). Some liberating effects of anonymous electronic brainstorming. *Small Group Research, 29,* 147–178.

Costa, P. T., Jr., & McCrae, R. R. (1988). Personality in adulthood: A six-year longitudinal study of self-reports and spouse ratings on the NEO Personality Inventory. *Journal of Personality and Social Psychology, 54,* 853–863.

Cottrell, N. B. (1972). Social facilitation. In C. G. McClintock (Ed.), *Experimental Social Psychology* (pp. 185–236). New York: Holt.

Cottrell, N. B., Wack, D. L., Sekerak, G. J., & Rittle, R. H. (1968). Social facilitation of dominant responses by the presence of an audience and the mere presence of others. *Journal of Personality and Social Psychology, 9,* 245–250.

Cramton, C. (2001). The mutual knowledge problem and its consequences in dispersed collaboration. *Organizational Science, 12,* 346–371.

Dabbs, J. M., Jr., & Ruback, R. B. (1987). Dimensions of group process: Amount and structure of vocal interaction. In L. Berkowitz (Ed.), *Advances in experimental social psychology* (Vol. 20, pp. 123–169). San Diego, CA: Academic Press.

Daft, R. L., & Lengel, R. H. (1986). Organizational information requirements, media richness and structural design. *Management Science, 32,* 554–571.

Davis, J. H. (1973). Group decision and social interaction: A theory of social decision schemes. *Psychological Review, 80,* 97–125.

De Dreu, C. K. W., De Vries, N. K., Franssen, H., & Altink, W. M. M. (2000). Minority dissent in organizations: Factors influencing the willingness to dissent. *Journal of Applied Social Psychology, 30,* 2451–2466.

De Dreu, C. K. W., Nijstad, B. A., & Van Knippenberg, D. (2008). Motivated information processing in group judgment and decision making. *Personality and Social Psychology Review, 12,* 22–49.

De Dreu, C. K. W., & Weingart, L. R. (2003). Task versus relationship conflict and team effectiveness: A meta analysis. *Journal of Applied Psychology, 86,* 741–749.

Dennis, A. R., George, J. F., Jessup, L. M., Nunamaker, J. F., & Vogel, D. (1988). Information technology to support electronic meetings. *Management Information Systems Quarterly, 12,* 591–624.

Dennis, A. R., & Kinney, S. T. (1998). Testing media richness theory in the new media: The effects of cues, feedback, and task equivocality. *Information Systems Research, 9,* 256–274.

Dennis, A. R., & Valacich, J. S. (1993). Computer brainstorms: More heads are better than one. *Journal of Applied Psychology, 78,* 531–537.

Dennis, A. R., & Williams, M. L. (2003). Electronic brainstorming: Theory, research, and future directions. In P. B. Paulus & B. A. Nijstad (Eds.), *Group creativity: Innovation through collaboration* (pp. 160–178). New York: Oxford University Press.

Deutsch, M. (1949). A theory of co-operation and competition. *Human Relations, 2,* 129–152.

Deutsch, M., & Gerard, H. B. (1955). A study of normative and informational social influences upon individual judgment. *Journal of Abnormal and Social Psychology, 51,* 629–636.

DeRosa, D. M., Smith, C. L., & Hantula, D. A. (2007). The medium matters: Mining the long-promised merit of group interaction in creative idea generation tasks in a meta-analysis of the electronic group brainstorming literature.

Computers in Human Behavior, 23, 1549–1581.

Diehl, M., & Stroebe, W. (1987). Productivity loss in brainstorming groups: Toward the solution of a riddle. *Journal of Personality and Social Psychology, 53,* 497–509.

Diehl, M., & Stroebe, W. (1991). Productivity loss in idea generating groups: Tracking down the blocking effect. *Journal of Personality and Social Psychology, 61,* 392–403.

Dobbins, G. H., Long, W. S., Dedrick, E. J., & Clemons, T. C. (1990). The role of self-monitoring and gender on leader emergence: A laboratory and field study. *Journal of Management, 16,* 609–618.

Doherty-Sneddon, G., Anderson, A., O'Malley, C., Langton, S., Garrod, S., & Bruce, V. (1997). Face-to-face and video mediated communication: A comparison of dialogue structure and task performance. *Journal of Experimental Psychology: Applied, 3,* 105–125.

Dovidio, J. F., Gaertner, S. L., & Saguy, T. (2007). Another view of "we": Majority and minority group perspectives on a common ingroup identity. In W. Stroebe & M. Hewstone (Eds.), *European review of social psychology* (Vol. 18, pp. 296–330). Hove, UK: Psychology Press.

Dovidio, J. F., Gaertner, S. L., Validizic, A., Matoka, K., Johnson, B., & Frazier, S. (1997). Extending the benefit of recategorization: Evaluations, self-disclosure, and helping. *Journal of Experimental Social Psychology, 33,* 401–442.

Driskell, J. E., & Mullen, B. (1990). Status, expectations, and behaviour: A meta-analytic review and test of the theory. *Personality and Social Psychology Bulletin, 16,* 541–553.

Driskell, J. E., Radtke, P. H., & Salas, E. (2003). Virtual teams: The effects of technological mediation on team performance. *Group Dynamics: Theory, Research and Practice, 7,* 297–323.

Dugosh, K. L., Paulus, P. B., Roland, E. J., & Yang, H. (2000). Cognitive stimulation in brainstorming. *Journal of Personality and Social Psychology, 79,* 722–735.

Eagly, A. H., & Chaiken, S. (1993). *The psychology of attitudes.* New York: Harcourt Brace Jovanovich.

Edmondson, A. (1999). Psychological safety and learning behavior in work teams. *Administrative Science Quarterly, 44,* 350–383.

Edwards, B. D., Day, E. A., Arthur, W., Jr., & Bell, S. T. (2006). Relationships among team ability composition, team mental models, and team performance. *Journal of Applied Psychology, 91,* 727–736.

Eisenberger, N. I., Lieberman, M. D., & Williams, K. D. (2003). Does rejection hurt? An fMRI study of social exclusion. *Science, 302,* 290–292.

Esser, J. K. (1998). Alive and well after 25 years: A review of groupthink research. *Organizational Behavior and Human Decision Processes, 73,* 116–141.

Esser, J. K., & Lindoerfer, J. L. (1989). Groupthink and the space shuttle *Challenger* accident: Toward a quantitative analysis. *Journal of Behavioral Decision Making, 2,* 167–177.

Everett, J. J., Smith, R. E., & Williams, K. D. (1992). Effects of team cohesion and identifiability on social loafing in relay swimming performance. *International Journal of Sport Psychology, 23,* 311–324.

Faure, C. (2004). Beyond brainstorming: Effects of different group procedures on selection of ideas and satisfaction with the process. *Journal of Creative Behavior, 38,* 13–34.

Festinger, L. (1950). Informal social communication. *Psychological Review, 57,* 271–282.

Festinger, L. (1954). A theory of social comparison processes. *Human Relations, 7*, 117–140.

Festinger, L. (1957). *A theory of cognitive dissonance*. Palo Alto, CA: Stanford University Press.

Fiedler, F. E. (1964). A contingency model of leadership effectiveness. In L. Berkowitz (Ed.), *Advances in experimental social psychology* (Vol. 1, pp. 149–190). New York: Academic Press.

Fiedler, F. E. (1967). *A theory of leadership effectiveness*. New York: McGraw-Hill.

Flowers, M. (1977). A laboratory test of some implications of Janis's groupthink hypothesis. *Journal of Personality and Social Psychology, 1*, 288–299.

Fodor, E. M., & Smith, T. (1982). The power motive as an influence on group decision making. *Journal of Personality and Social Psychology, 42*, 178–185.

Freese, L., & Cohen, B. P. (1973). Eliminating status generalization. *Sociometry, 36*, 177–193.

Gaertner, S. L., & Dovidio, J. F. (2000). *Reducing intergroup bias: The common ingroup identity model*. Philadelphia: Psychology Press.

Gaertner, S. L., Dovidio, J. F., Rust, M. C., Nier, J. A., Banker, B. S., Ward, C. M., *et al.* (1999). Reducing intergroup bias: Elements of intergroup cooperation. *Journal of Personality and Social Psychology, 76*, 388–402.

Gallupe, R. B., Bastianutti, L., & Cooper, W. H. (1991). Unblocking brainstorms. *Journal of Applied Psychology, 76*, 137–142.

Gallupe, R. B., Cooper, W. H., Grisé, M., & Bastianutti, L. M. (1994). Blocking electronic brainstorms. *Journal of Applied Psychology, 79*, 77–86.

Gates, M. F., & Allee, W. C. (1933). Conditioned behavior of isolated and groups of cockroaches on a simple maze. *Journal of Comparative Psychology, 15*, 331–358.

George, J. M. (1990). Personality, affect, and behavior in groups. *Journal of Applied Psychology, 75*, 107–116.

Gibson, C. B., & Gibbs J. L. (2006). Unpacking the concept of virtuality: The effects of geographic dispersion, electronic dependence, dynamic structure, and national diversity on team innovation. *Administrative Science Quarterly, 51*, 451–495.

Giessner, S. R., & Mummendey, A. (2008). United we win, divided we fail? Effects of cognitive representations and performance feedback on merging groups. *European Journal of Social Psychology, 38*, 412–435.

Giessner, S. R., Viki, G. T., Otten, S., Terry, D. J., & Täuber, S. (2006). The challenge of merging: Merger patterns, premerger status, and merger support. *Personality and Social Psychology Bulletin, 32*, 339–352.

Gigone, D., & Hastie, R. (1993). The common knowledge effect: Information sharing and group judgment. *Journal of Personality and Social Psychology, 65*, 959–974.

Gigone, D., & Hastie, R. (1997). The impact of information in small group choice. *Journal of Personality and Social Psychology, 72*, 132–140.

Goncalo, J. A., & Staw, B. M. (2006). Individualism–collectivism and group creativity. *Organizational Behavior and Human Decision Processes, 100*, 96–109.

Gordon, J. (1992). Work teams: How far have they come? *Training*, Oct., 59–65.

Greitemeyer, T., & Schulz-Hardt, S. (2003). Preference-consistent evaluation of information in the hidden profile paradigm: Beyond group-level explanations for the dominance of shared information in group decisions. *Journal of Personality and Social Psychology, 84*, 322–339.

Griffith, T. L., Sawyer, J. E., & Neale, M. A. (2003). Virtualness and knowledge in teams: Managing the love triangle of organizations, individuals, and information technology. *MIS Quarterly, 27*, 265–287.

Groff, B. D., Baron, R. S., & Moore, D. L. (1983). Distraction, attentional conflict, and drivelike behavior. *Journal of Experimental Social Psychology, 19*, 359–380.

Guerin, B. (1983). Social facilitation and social monitoring: A test of three models. *British Journal of Social Psychology, 22*, 203–214.

Guerin, B. (1986). Mere presence effects in humans: A review. *Journal of Experimental Social Psychology, 22*, 38–77.

Hackman, J. R. (1987). The design of work teams. In J. L. Lorsch (Ed.), *Handbook of Organizational Behavior* (pp. 315–342). Englewood Cliffs, NJ: Prentice Hall.

Hains, S. C., Hogg, M. A., & Duck, J. M. (1997). Self-categorization and leadership: Effects of group prototypicality and leader stereotypicality. *Personality and Social Psychology Bulletin, 23*, 1087–1100.

Halpin, A. W., & Winer, B. J. (1957). A factorial study of the leader behavior descriptions. In R. M. Stogdill & A. E. Coons (Eds.), *Leader behavior: Its description and measurement* (pp. 39–51). Columbus: Ohio State University, Bureau of Business Research.

Hambley, L. A., O'Neill, T. A., & Kline, T. J. B. (2007). Virtual team leadership: The effects of leadership style and communication medium on team interaction styles and outcomes. *Organizational Behavior and Human Decision Processes, 103*, 1–20.

Harkins, S. (1987). Social loafing and social facilitation. *Journal of Experimental Social Psychology, 23*, 1–18.

Harkins, S. G., & Jackson, J. M. (1985). The role of evaluation in eliminating social loafing. *Personality and Social Psychology Bulletin, 11*, 457–465.

Harrison, D. A., & Klein, K. J. (2007). What's the difference? Diversity constructs as separation, variety, or disparity in organizations. *Academy of Management Review, 32*, 1199–1228.

Hastie, R., & Kameda, T. (2005). The robust beauty of the majority rule. *Psychological Review, 112*, 494–508.

Hastie, R., Penrod, S. D., & Pennington, N. (1983). *Inside the jury*. Cambridge, MA: Harvard University Press.

Hertel, G., Deter, C., & Konradt, U. (2003). Motivation gains in computer-mediated work groups. *Journal of Applied Social Psychology, 33*, 2080–2105.

Hertel, G., Geister, S., & Konradt, U. (2005). Managing virtual teams: A review of current empirical work. *Human Resource Management Review, 15*, 69–95.

Hertel, G., Kerr, N. L., & Messé, L. A. (2000). Motivation gains in performance groups: Paradigmatic and theoretical developments on the Köhler effect. *Journal of Personality and Social Psychology, 79*, 580–601.

Hertel, G., Konradt, U., & Orlikowski, B. (2004). Managing distance by interdependence: Goal setting, task interdependence, and team-based rewards in virtual teams. *European Journal of Work and Organizational Psychology, 13*, 1–28.

Hewstone, M., Rubin, M., & Willis, H. (2002). Ingroup bias. *Annual Review of Psychology, 53*, 575–604.

Hinsz, V. B., Tindale, R. S., & Vollrath, D. A. (1997). The emerging conceptualization of groups as information processors. *Psychological Bulletin, 121*, 43–64.

Hofstede, G. (1980). *Culture's consequences: International differences in work-related values*. Beverly Hills, CA: Sage.

Hogg, M. A. (2001). A social identity theory of leadership. *Personality and Social Psychology Review, 5*, 184–200.

Hogg, M. A., & Abrams, D. (1993). Towards a single process uncertainty reduction model of social motivation in groups. In M. A. Hogg and D. Abrams (Eds.), *Group motivation: Social psychological perspectives* (pp. 173–190). New York: Harvester-Wheatsheaf.

Hogg, M. A., Martin, R., Epitropaki, O., Mankad, A., Svensson, A., & Weeden, K. (2005). Effective leadership in salient groups: Revisiting leader–member exchange theory from the perspective of social identity theory of leadership. *Personality and Social Psychology Bulletin, 31*, 991–1004.

Homan, A. C., van Knippenberg, D., van Kleef, G. A., & De Dreu, C. K. W. (2007). Bridging faultlines by valuing diversity: Diversity beliefs, information elaboration, and performance in diverse work groups. *Journal of Applied Psychology, 92*, 1189–1199.

Homma, M., Tajima, K., & Hayashi, M. (1995). The effects of misperception of performance in brainstorming groups. *Japanese Journal of Experimental Psychology, 34*, 221–231.

Hsu, F. L. K. (1970). *Americans and Chinese.* New York: Doubleday.

Huguet, P., Galvaing, M. P., Monteil, J. M., & Dumas, F. (1999). Social presence effects in the Stroop task: Further evidence for an attentional view of social facilitation. *Journal of Personality and Social Psychology, 77*, 1011–1025.

Ilgen, D. R., Hollenbeck, J. R., Johnson, M., & Jundt, D. (2005). Teams in organizations: From I-P-O models to IMOI models. *Annual Review of Psychology, 56*, 517–543.

Ingham, A. G., Levinger, G., Graves, J., & Peckham, V. (1974). The Ringelmann effect: Studies of group size and group performance. *Journal of Experimental Social Psychology, 10*, 371–384.

Innes, J. M., & Young, R. F. (1975). The effect of presence of an audience, evaluation apprehension, and objective self awareness on learning. *Journal of Experimental Social Psychology, 11*, 35–42.

Isenberg, D. J. (1986). Group polarization: A critical review and meta-analysis. *Journal of Personality and Social Psychology, 50*, 1141–1151.

Jackson, J. M., & Williams, K. D. (1985). Social loafing on difficult tasks: Working collectively can improve performance. *Journal of Personality and Social Psychology, 49*, 937–942.

James, K., & Cropanzano, R. (1994). Dispositional group loyalty and individual action for the benefit of an ingroup: Experimental and correlational evidence. *Organizational Behavior and Human Decision Processes, 60*, 179–205.

James, K., & Greenberg, J. (1989). In-group salience, intergroup comparison, and individual performance and self-esteem. *Personality and Social Psychology Bulletin, 15*, 604–616.

Janis, I. L. (1972). *Victims of groupthink.* Boston: Houghton-Mifflin.

Janis, I. L. (1982). *Victims of groupthink* (2nd ed.). Boston: Houghton-Mifflin.

Jarvenpaa, S. L., & Leidner, D. E. (1999). Communication and trust in global virtual teams. *Organization Science, 10*, 791–815.

Jehn, K. (1994). Enhancing effectiveness: An investigation of advantages and disadvantages of value based intragroup conflict. *The International Journal of Conflict Management, 5*, 223–238.

Jehn, K. (1995). A multimethod examination of the benefits and detriments of intragroup conflict. *Administrative Science Quarterly, 40*, 256–282.

Jehn, K., Northcraft, G. B., & Neale, M. A. (1999). Why differences make a difference: A field study of diversity, conflict, and performance in workgroups. *Administrative Science Quarterly, 44,* 741–762.

Judge, T. A., Bono, J. E., Ilies, R., & Gerhardt, M. W. (2002). Personality and leadership: A qualitative and quantitative review. *Journal of Applied Psychology, 87,* 765–780.

Judge, T. A., & Piccolo, R. F. (2004). Transformational and transactional leadership: A meta-analytic test of their relative validity. *Journal of Applied Psychology, 89,* 755–768.

Judge, T. A., Piccolo, R. F., & Ilies, R. (2004). The forgotten ones? The validity of consideration and initiating structure in leadership research. *Journal of Applied Psychology, 89,* 36–51.

Kahneman, D., & Tversky, A. (1972). Subjective probability: A judgment of representativeness. *Cognitive Psychology, 3,* 430–454.

Kameda, T., Ohtsubo, Y., & Takezawa, M. (1997). Centrality in sociocognitive networks and social influence: An illustration in a group decision-making context. *Journal of Personality and Social Psychology, 73,* 296–309.

Kanawattanachai, P., & Yoo, Y. (2002). Dynamic nature of trust in virtual teams. *Journal of Strategic Information Systems, 11,* 187–213.

Kane, A. A., Argote, L., & Levine, J. M. (2005). Knowledge transfer between groups via personnel rotation: Effects of social identity and knowledge quality. *Organizational Behavior and Human Decision Processes, 96,* 46–71.

Kaplan, M. F., & Miller, L. E. (1987). Group decision making and normative versus information influence: Effects of type of issue and assigned decision rule. *Journal of Personality and Social Psychology, 53,* 306–313.

Karakowsky, L., & Siegel, J. P. (1999). The effects of proportional representation and gender orientation of the task on emergent leadership behavior in mixed gender work groups. *Journal of Applied Psychology, 84,* 620–631.

Karau, S. J., & Williams, K. D. (1993). Social loafing: A meta-analytic review and theoretical integration. *Journal of Personality and Social Psychology, 65,* 681–706.

Karau, S. J., & Williams, K. D. (1997). The effects of group cohesiveness on social loafing and social compensation. *Group dynamics: Theory, Research, and Practice, 1,* 156–168.

Keller, R. T. (2001). Cross-functional project groups in research and new product development: Diversity, communications, job stress, and outcomes. *Academy of Management Journal, 44,* 547–555.

Kelly, J. R., & Loving, T. (2004). Time pressure and group performance: Exploring underlying processes in the attentional focus model. *Journal of Experimental Social Psychology, 40,* 185–198.

Kent, R. L., & Moss, S. E. (1994). Effects of sex and gender role on leader emergence. *Academy of Management Journal, 37,* 1335–1346.

Kerr, N. L. (1983). Motivation losses in small groups: A social dilemma analysis. *Journal of Personality and Social Psychology, 45,* 819–828.

Kerr, N. L., & Bruun, S. E. (1981). Ringelmann revisited: Alternative explanations for the social loafing effect. *Personality and Social Psychology Bulletin, 7,* 224–231.

Kerr, N. L., & Bruun, S. E. (1983). Dispensability of member effort and group motivation losses: Free-rider effects. *Journal of Personality and Social Psychology, 44,* 78–94.

Kerr, N. L., MacCoun, R. J., & Kramer, G. P. (1996). Bias in judgment: Comparing individuals and groups. *Psychological Review, 103,* 687–719.

Kerr, N. L., Messé, L. A., Seok, D. H., Sambolec, E. J., Lount, R. B., & Park, E.

S. (2007). Psychological mechanisms underlying the Köhler motivation gain. *Personality and Social Psychology Bulletin, 33*, 828–841.

Kerr, N. L., & Tindale, R. S. (2004). Group performance and decision making. *Annual Review of Psychology, 55*, 623–655.

Kiesler, S., Siegel, J., & McGuire, T. W. (1984). Social psychological aspects of computer-mediated communication. *American Psychologist, 39*, 1123–1134.

Kiesler, S., Zubrow, D., Moses, A., & Geller, V. (1985). Affect in computer-mediated communication: An experiment in synchronous terminal-to-terminal discussion. *Human–Computer Interaction, 1*, 77–104.

Kirkman, B. L., Rosen, B., Tesluk, P. E., & Gibson, C. B. (2004). The impact of team empowerment on virtual team performance: The moderating role of face-to-face interaction. *Academy of Management Journal, 47*, 175–192.

Klein, K. J., & Kozlowski, S. W. J. (Eds., 2000). *Multilevel theory, research, and methods in organizations: Foundations, extensions, and new directions.* San Francisco: Jossey-Bass.

Klinger, E. (1969). Feedback effects and social facilitation of vigilance performance: Mere coaction versus potential evaluation. *Psychonomic Science, 14*, 161–162.

Köhler, O. (1926). Kraftleistungen bei Einzel und Gruppenarbeit [Physical performance in individual and group situations]. *Industrielle Psychotechnik, 3*, 274–282.

Köhler, O. (1927). Ueber den Gruppenwirkungsgrad der menschlichen Koerperarbeit und die Bedingungen optimaler Kollektivkraftreaktion [On group efficiency of physical labor and the conditions of optimal collective performance]. *Industrielle Psychotechnik, 4*, 209–226.

Kozlowski, S. W. J., & Klein, K. J. (2000). A multilevel approach to theory and research in organizations: Contextual, temporal, and emergent processes. In K. J. Klein & S. W. J. Kozlowski (Eds.), *Multilevel theory, research and methods in organizations: Foundations, extensions, and new directions* (pp. 3–90). San Francisco: Jossey-Bass.

Krauss, R. M., & Fussell, S. (1990). Mutual knowledge and communicative effectiveness. In J. Galegher & R. Kraut (Eds.), *Intellectual teamwork: Social and technological foundations of group work* (pp. 111–145). Hillsdale, NJ Lawrence Erlbaum Associates.

Kraut, R. E., Galegher, J., & Egido, C. (1988). Relationships and tasks in scientific collaboration. *Human–Computer Interaction, 3*, 31–58.

Kruger, J., Epley, N., Parker, J., & Ng, Z. W. (2005). Egocentrism over email: Can we communicate as well as we think? *Journal of Personality and Social Psychology, 89*, 925–936.

Kruglanski, A. W., Pierro, A., Mannetti, L, & De Grada, E. (2006). Groups as epistemic providers: Need for closure and the unfolding of group-centrism. *Psychological Review, 113*, 84–100.

Lamm, H., & Myers, D. G. (1978). Group-induced polarization of attitudes and behavior. In L. Berkowitz (Ed.), *Advances in experimental social psychology* (Vol. 2, pp. 147–195). New York: Academic Press.

Lamm, H., & Trommsdorff, G. (1973). Group versus individual performance on tasks requiring ideational proficiency (brainstorming): A review. *European Journal of Social Psychology, 3*, 361–388.

Larey, T. S., & Paulus, P. B. (1995). Individual and group goal setting in brainstorming groups. *Journal of Applied Social Psychology, 25*, 1579–1596.

Larey, T. S., & Paulus, P. B. (1999). Group preference and convergent tendencies in groups: A content analysis of group brainstorming performance. *Creativity Research Journal, 12,* 175–184.

Larson, J. R., Christensen, C., Abbott, A. S., & Franz, T. M. (1996). Diagnosing groups: Charting the flow of information in medical decision-making teams. *Journal of Personality and Social Psychology, 71,* 315–330.

Larson, J. R., Foster-Fishman, P. G., & Franz, T. M. (1998). Leadership style and the discussion of shared and unshared information in decision-making groups. *Personality and Social Psychology Bulletin, 24,* 482–495.

Larson, J. R., Foster-Fishman, P. G., & Keys, C. B. (1994). Discussion of shared and unshared information in decision-making groups. *Journal of Personality and Social Psychology, 67,* 446–461.

Latané, B. (1981). The psychology of social impact. *American Psychologist, 36,* 343–356.

Latané, B., Williams, K., & Harkins, S. (1979). Many hands make light the work: The causes and consequences of social loafing. *Journal of Personality and Social Psychology, 37,* 822–832.

Lau, D. C., & Murnighan, J. K. (1998). Demographic diversity and faultlines: the compositional dynamics of organizational groups. *Academy of Management Review, 23,* 325–340.

Lau, D. C., & Murnighan, J. K. (2005). Interactions with groups and subgroups: The effects of demographic faultlines. *Academy of Management Journal, 48,* 645–659.

Laughlin, P. R. (1980). Social combination process of cooperative problem solving groups at verbal intellective tasks. In M. Fishbein (Ed.), *Progress in social psychology* (Vol. 1, pp. 127–155). Hillsdale, NJ: Lawrence Erlbaum Associates.

Laughlin, P. R. (1999). Collective induction: Twelve postulates.

Organizational Behavior and Human Decision Processes, 80, 50–69.

Laughlin, P. R., & Adamopoulos, J. A. (1980). Social combination processes and individual learning for six-person cooperative groups on an intellective task. *Journal of Personality and Social Psychology, 38,* 941–947.

Laughlin, P. R., Bonner, B. L., & Altermatt, T. W. (1998). Collective versus individual induction with single multiple hypotheses. *Journal of Personality and Social Psychology, 75,* 1481–1489.

Laughlin, P. R., Bonner, B. L., & Miner, A. G. (2002). Groups perform better than the best individuals on letter-to-numbers problems. *Organizational Behavior and Human Decision Processes, 88,* 605–620.

Laughlin, P. R., & Ellis, A. L. (1986). Demonstrability and social combination processes on mathematical intellective tasks. *Journal of Experimental Social Psychology, 22,* 177–189.

Laughlin, P. R., Hatch, E. C., Silver, J. S., & Boh, L. (2006). Groups perform better than the best individuals on letter-to-numbers problems: Effects of group size. *Journal of Personality and Social Psychology, 90,* 644–651.

Laughlin, P. R., Kerr, N. L., Davis, J. H., Halff, H. M., & Marciniak, K. A. (1975). Group size, member ability, and social decision schemes on an intellective task. *Journal of Personality and Social Psychology, 31,* 522–535.

Laughlin, P. R., Kerr, N. L., Munch, M. M., & Haggarty, C. A. (1976). Social decision schemes of the same four-person groups on two different intellective tasks. *Journal of Personality and Social Psychology, 33,* 80–88.

Laughlin, P. R., & McGlynn, R. P. (1986). Collective induction: Mutual group and individual influence by exchange of hypotheses and evidence. *Journal of*

Experimental Social Psychology, 22, 567–589.

Laughlin P. R., & Shippy, T. A. (1983). Collective induction. *Journal of Personality and Social Psychology, 45,* 94–100.

Laughlin, P. R., VanderStoep, S. W., & Hollingshead, A. B. (1991). Collective versus individual induction: Recognition of truth, rejection of error, and collective information processing. *Journal of Personality and Social Psychology, 61,* 50–67.

Laughlin, P. R., Zander, M. L., Knievel, E. M., & Tan, K. T. (2003). Groups perform better than the best individuals on letter-to-numbers problems: Informative equations and effective strategies. *Journal of Personality and Social Psychology, 85,* 684–694.

Lawler, E. E., Mohrman, S. A., and Benson, G. S. (2001) *Organizing for high performance: The CEO report on employee involvement, TQM, reengineering, and knowledge management in Fortune 1000 Companies.* San Francisco: Jossey-Bass.

Lawler, E. E., III, Mohrman, S. A., & Ledford, G. E., Jr. (1995). *Creating high performance organizations: Practices and results of employee involvement and Total Quality Management in Fortune 1000 companies.* San Francisco: Jossey-Bass.

Le, B., & Agnew, C. R. (2003). Commitment and its theorized determinants: A meta-analysis of the investment model. *Personal Relationships, 10,* 37–57.

Leary, M. R. (1983). A brief version of the fear of negative evaluation scale. *Personality and Social Psychology Bulletin, 9,* 371–375.

Leary, M. R. (2004). *Introduction to behavioural research methods* (4th ed.). Boston: Pearson Education.

Levine, J. M. (1989). Reaction to opinion deviance in small groups. In P. B. Paulus (Ed.), *The psychology of group influence* (pp. 187–231). Hillsdale, NJ: Lawrence Erlbaum Associates.

Levine, J. M., & Moreland, R. L. (1990). Progress in small group research. *Annual Review of Psychology, 41,* 585–634.

Levine, J. M., & Moreland, R. L. (1994). Group socialization: Theory and research. In W. Stroebe & M. Hewstone (Eds.), *European review of social psychology* (Vol. 5, pp. 305–336). London: Wiley.

Lewin, K. (1948). *Resolving social conflicts.* New York: Harper and Row.

Lewis, K., Belliveau, M., Herndon, B., & Keller, J. (2007). Group cognition, membership change and performance: Investigating the benefits and detriments of collective knowledge. *Organizational Behavior and Human Decision Processes, 103,* 159–178.

Li, J., & Hambrick, D. C. (2005). Factional groups: A new vantage on demographic faultlines, conflict, and disintegration in work teams. *Academy of Management Journal, 48,* 794–813.

Liang, D. W., Moreland, R., & Argote, L. (1995). Group versus individual training and group performance: The mediating role of transactive memory. *Personality and Social Psychology Bulletin, 21,* 384–393.

Lickel, B., Hamilton, D. L., & Sherman, S. J. (2001). Elements of a lay theory of groups: Types of groups, relational styles, and the perception of group entitativity. *Personality and Social Psychology Review, 5,* 129–140.

Lickel, B., Hamilton, D. L., Wieczorkowska, G., Lewis, A., Sherman, S. J., & Uhles, A. N. (2000). Varieties of groups and the perception of group entitativity. *Journal of Personality and Social Psychology, 78,* 223–246.

Lim, B. C., & Klein, K. J. (2006). Team mental models and team performance: A field study of the effects of team mental model similarity and accuracy. *Journal of Organizational Behavior, 27,* 403–418.

Lim, B. C., & Ployhart, R. E. (2004). Transformational leadership: Relations to the five-factor model and team performance in typical and maximum contexts. *Journal of Applied Psychology, 89,* 610–621.

Lodewijkx, H. F. M., & Syroit, J. E. M. M. (1997). Severity of initiation revisited: Does severity of initiation increase the attractiveness of real groups? *European Journal of Social Psychology, 27,* 275–300.

Lord, R. G., De Vader, C. L., & Alliger, G. M. (1986). A meta-analysis of the relation between personality traits and leadership perceptions: An application of validity generalization procedures. *Journal of Applied Psychology, 71,* 402–410.

Lorge, I., Fox, D., Davitz, J., & Brenner, M. (1958). A survey of studies contrasting the quality of group performance and individual performance. *Psychological Bulletin, 55,* 337–371.

Lount, R. B., & Phillips, K. W. (2007). Working harder with the out-group. The impact of social category diversity on motivation gains. *Organizational Behavior and Human Decision Processes, 103,* 214–224.

Lount, R. B., Park, E. S., Kerr, N. L., Messé, L. A., & Seok, D. H. (2008). Evaluation concerns and the Köhler effect: The impact of physical presence on motivation gains. *Small Group Research, 39,* 795–812.

MacCoun, R. J. (1990). The emergence of extralegal bias during jury deliberation. *Criminal Justice and Behavior, 17,* 303–314.

MacCoun, R. J., & Kerr, N. L. (1988). Asymmetric influence in mock jury deliberation: Jurors' bias for leniency. *Journal of Personality and Social Psychology, 54,* 21–33.

Mackie, D. M. (1986). Social identification effects in group polarization. *Journal of Personality and Social Psychology, 50,* 720–728.

Marks, M. A., Mathieu, J. E., & Zaccaro, S. J. 2001. A temporally based framework and taxonomy of team processes. *Academy of Management Review, 26,* 356–376.

Marks, K. L., & Mirvis, P. (1985). Merger syndrome: Stress and uncertainty. *Mergers and Acquisitions, 20,* 50–55.

Marks, M. A., Sabella, M. J., Burke, C. S., & Zaccaro, S. J. (2002). The impact of cross-training on team effectiveness. *Journal of Applied Psychology, 87,* 3–13.

Marques, J. M., Yzerbyt, V. Y., & Leyens, J. P. (1988). The "black sheep effect": Extremity of judgments towards ingroup members as a function of identification. *European Journal of Social Psychology, 18,* 1–16.

Martins, L. L., Gilson, L. L., & Maynard, M. T. (2004). Virtual teams: What do we know and where do we go from here? *Journal of Management, 30,* 805–835.

Mathieu, J. E., Heffner, T. S., Goodwin, G. F., Salas, E., & Cannon-Bowers, J. A. (2000). The influence of shared mental models on team process and performance. *Journal of Applied Psychology, 85,* 273–283.

McCann, J. E., & Gilkey, R. (1988). *Creating and managing successful mergers and acquisitions.* Englewood Cliffs, NJ: Prentice Hall.

McCrae, R. R., & Costa, P. T., Jr. (1997). Personality trait structure as a human universal. *American Psychologist, 52,* 509–516.

McGrath, J. E. (1984). *Groups: Interaction and performance.* Englewood Cliffs, NJ: Prentice Hall.

McLeod, P. L., Baron, R. S., Marti, M. W., & Yoon, K. (1997). The eyes have it: Minority influence in face-to-face and computer-mediated group discussions.

Journal of Applied Psychology, 82, 706–718.

Messé, L. A., Hertel, G., Kerr, N. L., Lount, R. B., & Park, E. S. (2002). Knowledge of partner's ability as a moderator of group motivation gains: An exploration of the Köhler discrepancy effect. *Journal of Personality and Social Psychology, 82,* 935–946.

Milliken, F. J., Bartel, C. A., & Kurtzberg, T. R. (2003). Diversity and creativity in work groups. In P. B. Paulus & B. A. Nijstad (Eds.), *Group creativity: Innovation through collaboration* (pp. 32–62). New York: Oxford University Press.

Milliken, F. J., & Martins, L. L. (1996). Searching for common threads: Understanding the multiple effects of diversity in organizational groups. *Academy of Management Review, 21,* 402–433.

Moorhead, G., & Montanari, J. R. (1986). An empirical investigation of the groupthink phenomenon. *Human Relations, 39,* 399–410.

Moreland, R. L. (1987). The formation of small groups. In C. Hendrick (Ed.), *Group processes* (pp. 80–110). Newbury Park, CA: JAI Press.

Moreland, R. L., Hogg, M. A., & Hains, S. C. (1994). Back to the future: Social psychological research on groups. *Journal of Experimental Social Psychology, 30,* 527–555.

Moreland, R. L., & Levine, J. M. (1982). Socialization in small groups: Temporal changes in individual-group relations. In L. Berkowitz (Ed.), *Advances in experimental social psychology* (vol. 15, pp. 137–192). New York: Academic Press.

Moreland, R. L., & Levine, J. M. (1992). Problem identification by groups. In S. Worchel, W. Wood, & J. A. Simpson (Eds.), *Group process and productivity* (pp. 17–47). Newbury Park, CA: Sage.

Moscovici, S. (1980). Toward a theory of conversion behavior. In L. Berkowitz (Ed.), *Advances in Experimental Social Psychology* (vol. 13, pp. 209–239). New York: Academic Press.

Moscovici, S., Lage, E., & Naffrechoux, M. (1969). Influence of a consistent minority on the responses of a majority in a color perception task. *Sociometry, 32,* 365–380.

Moscovici, S., & Zavalloni, M. (1969). The group as a polarizer of attitudes. *Journal of Personality and Social Psychology, 12,* 125–135.

Mottola, G. R., Bachman, B. A., Gaertner, S. L., & Dovidio, J. F. (1997). How groups merge: The effects of merger integration patterns on anticipated commitment to the merged organization. *Journal of Applied Social Psychology, 27,* 1335–1358.

Mullen, B., Anthony, T., Salas, E., & Driskell, E. (1994). Group cohesion and quality of decision-making: An integration test of the groupthink hypothesis. *Small Group Research, 25,* 189–204.

Mullen, B., & Copper, C. (1994). The relation between group cohesiveness and performance: An integration. *Psychological Bulletin, 115,* 210–227.

Mullen, B., Johnson, C., & Salas, E. (1991). Productivity loss in brainstorming groups: A meta-analytic integration. *Basic and Applied Social Psychology, 65,* 219–225.

Munkes, J., & Diehl, M. (2003). Matching or competition? Performance comparison in an idea generation task. *Group Processes & Intergroup Relations, 6,* 305–320.

Murnighan, J. K., & Conlon, D. E. (1991). The dynamics of intense work groups: A study of British string quartets. *Administrative Science Quarterly, 36,* 165–186.

Nemeth, C. J. (1986). Differential contributions of majority and minority influence. *Psychological Review, 93,* 23–32.

Nemeth, C. J., & Kwan, J. (1985). Originality of word associations as a function of majority and minority influence. *Social Psychology Quarterly, 48,* 277–282.

Nemeth, C. J., & Nemeth-Brown, B. (2003). Better than individuals? The potential benefits of dissent and diversity for group creativity. In P. B. Paulus & B. A. Nijstad (Eds.), *Group creativity: Innovation through collaboration* (pp. 63–84). Oxford, UK: Oxford University Press.

Nemeth, C. J., & Ormiston, M. (2007). Creative idea generation: Harmony versus stimulation. *European Journal of Social Psychology, 37,* 524–535.

Newcomb, T. M. (1956). The prediction of interpersonal attraction. *American Psychologist, 11,* 575–586.

Nijstad, B. A. (1995). *Het geheel groter dan de som der delen? Productiviteitswinst in brainstormgroepen* [The whole larger than the sum of the parts? Productivity gains in brainstorming groups]. Unpublished master's thesis, Utrecht University, The Netherlands.

Nijstad, B. A., & Paulus, P. B. (2003). Group creativity: common themes and future directions. In P. B. Paulus & B. A. Nijstad (Eds.), *Group creativity: Innovation through collaboration* (pp. 326–339). New York: Oxford University Press.

Nijstad, B. A., Rietzschel, E. F., & Stroebe, W. (2005). Four principles of group creativity. In L. Thompson & H. S. Choi (Eds.), *Creativity and innovation in organizational teams* (pp. 161–179). Hillsdale, NJ: Lawrence Erlbaum Associates.

Nijstad, B. A., & Stroebe, W. (2006). How the group affects the mind: A cognitive model of idea generation in groups. *Personality and Social Psychology Review, 10,* 186–213.

Nijstad, B. A., Stroebe, W., & Lodewijkx, H. F. M. (2002). Cognitive stimulation and interference in groups. Exposure effects in an idea generation task. *Journal of Experimental Social Psychology, 38,* 535–544.

Nijstad, B. A., Stroebe, W., & Lodewijkx, H. F. M. (2003). Production blocking and idea generation: Does blocking interfere with cognitive processes? *Journal of Experimental Social Psychology, 39,* 531–548.

Nijstad, B. A., Stroebe, W., & Lodewijkx, H. F. M. (2006). The illusion of group productivity: A reduction of failures explanation. *European Journal of Social Psychology, 36,* 31–48.

Nijstad, B. A., Van Vianen, A. E. M., Stroebe, W., & Lodewijkx, H. F. M. (2004). Persistence in brainstorming: Exploring stop rules in same-sex groups. *Group Processes and Intergroup Relations, 7,* 195–206.

Nunamaker, J. F., Applegate, L. M., & Konsynski, B. R. (1988). Computer-aided deliberation: Model management and group decision support. *Journal of Operations Research, 36,* 826–848.

O'Connaill, B., Whittaker, S., & Wilbur, S. (1993). Conversations over video-conferences: An evaluation of the spoken aspects of video-mediated communication. *Human–Computer Interaction, 8,* 389–428.

Olson, M. (1965). *The logic of collective action: Public goods and the theory of groups.* Cambridge, MA: Harvard University Press.

Orbell, J., & Dawes, R. (1981). Social dilemmas. In G. M. Stephenson & J. M. Davis (Eds.), *Progress in applied social psychology* (pp. 37–65). New York: Wiley.

Osborn, A. F. (1953). *Applied imagination.* New York: Scribner's.

Osborn, A. F. (1957). *Applied imagination* (2nd ed.). New York: Scribner's.

Ouwerkerk, J. W., de Gilder, D., & de Vries, N. K. (2000). When the going gets tough, the tough get going: Social identification and individual effort in intergroup competition. *Personality and Social Psychology Bulletin, 26,* 1550–1559.

Park, W. W. (2000). A comprehensive empirical investigation of the relationships among variables of the groupthink model. *Journal of Organizational Behavior, 21,* 873–887.

Parker, K. (1988). Speaking turns in small group interaction: A context-sensitive event sequence model. *Journal of Personality and Social Psychology, 54,* 965–971.

Parnes, S. J., & Meadow, A. (1959). Effects of "brainstorming" instructions on creative problem solving by trained and untrained subjects. *Journal of Educational Psychology, 50,* 171–176.

Paulus, P. B., & Dzindolet, M. T. (1993). Social influence processes in group brainstorming. *Journal of Personality and Social Psychology, 64,* 575–586.

Paulus, P. B., Dzindolet, M. T., Poletes, G., & Camacho, L. M. (1993). Perception of performance in group brainstorming: The illusion of productivity. *Personality and Social Psychology Bulletin, 19,* 78–89.

Paulus, P. B., Larey, T. S., & Ortega, A. H. (1995). Performance and perceptions of brainstormers in an organizational setting. *Basic and Applied Social Psychology, 17,* 249–265.

Paulus, P. B., & Nijstad, B. A. (2003). *Group creativity: Innovation through collaboration.* New York: Oxford University Press.

Paulus, P. B., & Yang, H. (2000). Idea generation in groups: A basis for creativity in organizations. *Organizational Behavior and Human Decision Processes, 82,* 76–87.

Pelled, L. H., Eisenhardt, K. M., & Xin, K. R. (1999). Exploring the black box: An analysis of work group diversity, conflict, and performance. *Administrative Science Quarterly, 44,* 1–28.

Pemberton, M. B., Insko, C. A., & Schopler, J. (1996). Memory for and experience of differential competitive behavior of individuals and groups. *Journal of Personality and Social Psychology, 71,* 953–966.

Pessin, J. (1933). The comparative effects of social and mechanical stimulation on memorizing. *American Journal of Psychology, 48,* 263–270.

Peters, L. H., Hartke, D. D., & Pohlmann, J. T. (1985). Fiedler's contingency theory of leadership: An application of the meta-analysis procedures of Schmidt and Hunter. *Psychological Bulletin, 97,* 274–285.

Pettigrew, T. F. (1998). Intergroup contact theory. *Annual Review of Psychology, 49,* 65–85.

Pettigrew, T. F., & Tropp, L. R. (2006). A meta-analytic test of intergroup contact theory. *Journal of Personality and Social Psychology, 90,* 751–783.

Podsakoff, P. M., MacKenzie, S. B., & Ahearne, M. (1997). Moderating effects of goal acceptance on the relationship between group cohesiveness and productivity. *Journal of Applied Psychology, 82,* 974–983.

Postmes, T., Spears, R., & Cihangir, S. (2001). Quality of decision making and group norms. *Journal of Personality and Social Psychology, 80,* 918–930.

Postmes, T. R., Spears, R., & Lea, M. (1998). Breaching or building social boundaries? SIDE-effects of computer-mediated communication. *Communication Research, 25,* 689–715.

Postmes, T., Spears, R., Sakhel, K., & De Groot, D. (2001). Social influence in computer-mediated communication: The effects of anonymity on group behavior. *Personality and Social Psychology Bulletin, 27,* 1243–1254.

Pruitt, D. G. (1971). Choice shifts in group discussion: An introductory review. *Journal of Personality and Social Psychology, 20*, 339–360.

Pugh, M., & Wahrman, R. (1983). Neutralizing sexism in mixed-groups: Do women have to be better than men? *American Journal of Sociology, 88*, 746–762.

Rabbie, J. M., & Horowitz, M. (1969). Arousal of ingroup-outgroup bias by a chance win or loss. *Journal of Personality and Social Psychology, 13*, 269–277.

Report of the Presidential Commission on the Space Shuttle Challenger Accident (Rogers Commission). (1986). Washington, DC. Retrieved February 27, 2009, from http://history.nasa.gov/rogersrep/genindex.htm

Ridgeway, C. L. (2001). Social status and group structure. In M. A. Hogg & S. Tindale (Eds.), *Blackwell handbook of social psychology: Group processes* (pp. 352–375). Oxford: Blackwell.

Ridley, M. (1996). *The origins of virtue.* London: Viking.

Rietzschel, E. F., Nijstad, B. A., & Stroebe, W. (2006). Productivity is not enough: A comparison of interactive and nominal brainstorming groups on idea generation and selection. *Journal of Experimental Social Psychology, 42*, 244–251.

Rietzschel, E. F., Nijstad, B. A., & Stroebe, W. (2007). Relative accessibility of domain knowledge and creativity: The effects of knowledge activation on the quantity and originality of generated ideas. *Journal of Experimental Psychology, 43*, 933–946.

Rietzschel, E. F., Nijstad, B. A., & Stroebe, W. (in press). Idea selection after individual brainstorming: Choosing between originality and impact. *British Journal of Psychology.*

Ringelmann, M. (1913). Recherches sur les moteurs animés: Travail de l'homme.

Annales de l'Insitut National Agronomique, 12, 1–40.

Rusbult, C. E., & Farrell, D. (1983). A longitudinal test of the investment model: The impact on job satisfaction, job commitment, and turnover of variations in rewards, costs, alternatives, and investments. *Journal of Applied Psychology, 68*, 429–438.

Rutter, D. T., & Stephenson, G. M. (1977). The role of visual communication in social interaction. *Current Anthropology, 20*, 124–125.

Saavedra, R. P., Earley, P. C., & Van Dyne. L. (1993). Complex interdependence in task-performing groups. *Journal of Applied Psychology, 78*, 61–72.

Sanders, G. S., & Baron, R. S. (1975). The motivation effects of distraction on task performance. *Journal of Personality and Social Psychology, 32*, 956–963.

Sanders, G. S., & Baron, R. S. (1977). Is social comparison irrelevant for producing choice shifts? *Journal of Experimental Social Psychology, 13*, 303–314.

Sanders, G. S., Baron, R. S., & Moore, D. L. (1978). Distraction and social comparison as mediators of social facilitation effects. *Journal of Experimental Social Psychology, 14*, 291–303.

Sanna, L. J. (1992). Self-efficacy theory: Implications for social facilitation and social loafing. *Journal of Personality and Social Psychology, 62*, 774–786.

Sanna, L. J., & Parks, C. D. (1997). Group research trends in social and organizational psychology: What happened to intragroup research? *Psychological Science, 8*, 261–267.

Sanna, L. J., & Shotland, R. L. (1990). Valence of anticipated evaluation and social facilitation. *Journal of Experimental Social Psychology, 26*, 82–92.

Sawyer, J. E., Houlette, M. A., & Yeagley, E. L. (2006). Decision performance and diversity structure: Comparing faultlines in convergent, crosscut, and racially homogeneous groups. *Organizational Behavior and Human Decision Processes, 99*, 1–15.

Sawyer, R. K. (2006). *Explaining creativity: The science of human innovation*. New York: Oxford University Press.

Schachter, S. (1951). Deviation, rejection and communication. *Journal of Abnormal and Social Psychology, 46*, 190–207.

Schaubroeck, J., Lam, S. S., & Cha, S. E. (2007). Embracing transformational leadership: Team values and the impact of leader behavior on team performance. *Journal of Applied Psychology, 92*, 1020–1030.

Scholten, L., Van Knippenberg, D., Nijstad, B. A., & De Dreu, C. K. W. (2007). Motivated information processing and group decision-making: Effects of process accountability on information processing and decision quality. *Journal of Experimental Social Psychology, 43*, 539–552.

Schulz-Hardt, S., Brodbeck, F. C., Mojzisch, A., Kerschreiter, R., & Frey, D. (2006). Group decision making in hidden profile situations: Dissent as a facilitator for decision quality. *Journal of Personality and Social Psychology, 91*, 1080–1093.

Seta, J. J. (1982). The impact of comparison processes on coactors' task performance. *Journal of Personality and Social Psychology, 42*, 281–291.

Shaw, M. E. (1932). A comparison of individuals and small groups in the rational solution of complex problems. *American Journal of Psychology, 44*, 491–504.

Shepperd, J. A. (1993). Productivity loss in performance groups: A motivation analysis. *Psychological Bulletin, 113*, 67–81.

Shepperd, J. A., & Taylor, K. M. (1999). Social loafing and expectancy-value theory. *Personality and Social Psychology Bulletin, 25*, 1147–1158.

Sherif, M. (1935). A study of some social factors in perception. *Archives of Psychology, 27* (187), 1–60.

Sherif, M. (1936). *The psychology of social norms*. New York: Harper.

Sherif, M. (1966). *Group conflict and co-operation*. London: Routledge and Kegan.

Sherif, M., Harvey, O. J., White, B. J., Hood, W. R., & Sherif, C. W. (1961). *Intergroup conflict and cooperation: The Robbers Cave experiment*. Norman, OK: University Book Exchange, University of Oklahoma.

Sherif, M., & Sherif, C. W. (1969). *Social psychology*. New York: Harper and Row.

Simonton, D. K. (2004). Group artistic creativity: Creative clusters and cinematic success in feature films. *Journal of Applied Social Psychology, 34*, 1494–1520.

Slater, P. E. (1955). Role differentiation in small groups. *American Sociological Review, 20*, 300–310.

Smith, B. N., Kerr, N. A., Markus, M. J., & Stasson, M. F. (2001). Individual differences in social loafing: Need for cognition as a motivator in collective performance. *Group Dynamics: Theory, Research, and Practice, 5*, 150–158.

Smith, S. (1985). Groupthink and the hostage rescue mission. *British Journal of Political Science, 15*, 117–123.

Somech, A. (2006). The effects of leadership style and team process on performance and innovation in functionally heterogeneous teams. *Journal of Management, 32*, 132–157.

Spears, R., Lea, M., & Lee, S. (1990). De-individuation and group polarization in computer-mediated communication. *British Journal of Social Psychology, 29*, 121–134.

Stasser, G. (1988). Computer simulation as a research tool: The DISCUSS model of group decision making. *Journal of Experimental Social Psychology, 24*, 393–422.

Stasser, G. (1999). A primer of social decision theory: Models of group influence, competitive model-testing, and prospective modeling. *Organizational Behavior and Human Decision Processes, 80,* 3–20.

Stasser, G. (1999). The uncertain role of unshared information in collective choice. In L. Thompson & J. Levine (Eds.), *Shared knowledge in organizations* (pp. 49–69). Mahwah, NJ: Lawrence Erlbaum Associates.

Stasser, G., & Birchmeier, Z. (2003). Group creativity and collective choice. In P. B. Paulus & B. A. Nijstad (Eds.), *Group creativity: Innovation through collaboration* (pp. 85–109). New York: Oxford University Press.

Stasser, G., Kerr, N. L., & Davis, J. H. (1989). Influence processes and consensus models in decision-making groups. In P. B. Paulus (Ed.), *Psychology of group influence* (pp. 279–326). Hillsdale, NJ: Lawrence Erlbaum Associates.

Stasser, G., & Stewart, D. (1992). Discovery of hidden profiles by decision-making groups: Solving a problem versus making a judgment. *Journal of Personality and Social Psychology, 63,* 426–434.

Stasser, G., Stewart, D. D., & Wittenbaum, G. M. (1995). Expert roles and information exchange during discussion: The importance of knowing who knows what. *Journal of Experimental Social Psychology, 31,* 244–265.

Stasser, G., Taylor, L. A., & Hanna, C. (1989). Information sampling in structured and unstructured discussion of three- and six-person groups. *Journal of Personality and Social Psychology, 57,* 67–78.

Stasser, G., & Titus, W. (1985). Pooling of unshared information in group decision making: Biased information sampling during discussion. *Journal of Personality and Social Psychology, 48,* 1467–1478.

Stasser, G., & Titus, W. (1987). Effects of information load and percentage of shared information on the dissemination of unshared information during group discussion. *Journal of Personality and Social Psychology, 53,* 81–93.

Stasser, G., & Vaughan, S. I. (1996). Models of participation during face-to-face unstructured discussion. In E. H. Witte & J. H. Davis (Eds.), *Understanding group behavior: Consensual action by small groups* (Vol. 1, pp. 165–192). Mahwah, NJ: Lawrence Erlbaum Associates.

Stasser, G., Vaughan, S. I., & Stewart, D. D. (2000). Pooling unshared information: The benefits of knowing how access to information is distributed among group members. *Organizational Behavior and Human Decision Processes, 82,* 102–116.

Steiner, I. D. (1972). *Group process and productivity.* New York: Academic Press.

Stephan, F. F., & Mishler, E. G. (1952). The distribution of participation in small groups: An exponential approximation. *American Sociological Review, 17,* 598–608.

Sternberg, R. J., & Lubart, T. I. (1999). The concept of creativity: Prospects and paradigms. In R. J. Sternberg (Ed.), *Handbook of creativity* (pp. 3–15). Cambridge, UK: Cambridge University Press.

Stewart, D. D., & Stasser, G. (1995). Expert role assignment and information sampling during collective recall and decision making. *Journal of Personality and Social Psychology, 69,* 619–628.

Stogdill, R. M. (1972). Group productivity, drive, and cohesiveness. *Organizational Behavior and Human Performance, 81,* 26–43.

Stoner, J. A. F. (1961). *A comparison of individual and group decisions involving risk.* Unpublished master's thesis,

Massachusetts Institute of Technology, Cambridge, MA.

Stouten, J., De Cremer, D., & Van Dijk, E. (2005). All is well that ends well, at least for proselfs: Emotional reactions to equality violation as a function of social value orientation. *European Journal of Social Psychology, 35*, 767–783.

Straus, S. G., & McGrath, J. E. (1994). Does the medium matter? The interaction of task type and technology on group performance and member reactions. *Journal of Applied Psychology, 79*, 87–97.

Stroebe, W., & Diehl, M. (1994). Why groups are less effective than their members: On productivity losses in idea-generating groups. In W. Stroebe & M. Hewstone (Eds.), *European Review of Social Psychology* (Vol. 5, pp. 271–303). London: Wiley.

Stroebe, W., Diehl, M., & Abakoumkin, G. (1992). The illusion of group effectivity. *Personality and Social Psychology Bulletin, 18*, 643–650.

Stroebe, W., Diehl, M., & Abakoumkin, G. (1996). Social compensation and the Koehler effect: Toward a theoretical explanation of motivation gains in group productivity. In E. Witte & J. H. Davis (Eds.), *Understanding group behavior* (Vol. 2, pp. 37–65). Mahwah, NJ: Lawrence Erlbaum Associates.

Stroebe, W., & Frey, B. S. (1982). Self-interest and collective action: The economics and psychology of public goods. *British Journal of Social Psychology, 21*, 121–137.

Strube, M. J., Miles, M. E., & Finch, W. H. (1981). The social facilitation of a simple task: Field tests of alternative explanations. *Personality and Social Psychology Bulletin, 7*, 701–707.

Sutton, R. I., & Hargadon, A. (1996). Brainstorming groups in context: Effectiveness in a product design firm. *Administrative Science Quarterly, 41*, 685–718.

Taggar, S. (2002). Individual creativity and group ability to utilize creative resources: A multilevel model. *Academy of Management Journal, 45*, 315–330.

Taggar, S., Hackett, R., & Saha, S. (1999). Leadership emergence in autonomous work teams: Antecedents and outcomes. *Personnel Psychology, 52*, 899–926.

Tajfel, H. (1981). *Human groups and social categories.* Cambridge, UK: Cambridge University Press.

Tajfel, H. (1982). Instrumentality, identity, and social comparisons. In H. Tajfel (Ed.), *Social identity and intergroup relations* (pp. 483–507). Cambridge: Cambridge University Press.

Tajfel, H., Billig, M., Bundy, R., & Flament, C. (1971). Social categorization and intergroup behaviour. *European Journal of Social Psychology, 1*, 149–178.

Tajfel, H., & Turner, J. (1979). An integrative theory of intergroup conflict. In W. G. Austin & S. Worchel (Eds.), *The social psychology of intergroup relations* (pp. 33–47). Monterey, CA: Brooks/Cole.

Tajfel, H., & Turner, J. C. (1986). The social identity theory of intergroup behaviour. In S. Worchel & W. G. Austin (Eds.), *Psychology of intergroup relations* (pp. 7–24). Chicago: Nelson Hall.

Tajfel, H., & Wilkes, A. L. (1963). Classification and quantitative judgement. *British Journal of Psychology, 54*, 101–114.

Taylor, D. W., Berry, P. C., & Block, C. H. (1958). Does group participation when using brainstorming facilitate or inhibit creative thinking? *Administrative Science Quarterly, 3*, 23–47.

Terry, D. J. (2003). A social identity perspective on organizational mergers: The role of group status, permeability, and similarity. In M. J. Platow, N. Ellemers, A. S. Haslam, & D. van Knippenberg (Eds.), *Social identity at work: Developing theory for organizational* practice (pp. 223–240). New York: Psychology Press.

Tetlock, P. E. (1979). Identifying victims of groupthink from public statements of decision makers. *Journal of Personality and Social Psychology, 37,* 1314–1324.

Tetlock, P. E., Peterson, R. S., McGuire, C., Chang, S., & Feld, P. (1992). Assessing political group dynamics: A test of the groupthink model. *Journal of Personality and Social Psychology, 21,* 318–326.

Thibaut, J. W., & Kelley, H. H. (1959). *The social psychology of groups.* New York: Wiley.

Tindale, R. S. (1993). Decision errors made by individuals and groups. In N. Castellan, Jr. (Ed.), *Individual and group decision making: Current issues* (pp. 109–124). Hillsdale, NJ: Lawrence Erlbaum Associates.

Todd, A. R., Seok, D., Kerr, N. L., & Messé, L. A. (2006). Social compensation: Fact or social comparison artifact? *Group Processes & Intergroup Relations, 9,* 431–442.

Travis, L. E. (1925). The effect of a small audience upon eye-hand coordination. *Journal of Abnormal Social Psychology, 29,* 142–146.

Triandis, H. C. (1989). The self and social behavior in differing cultural contexts. *Psychological Review, 96,* 506–520.

Triplett, N. (1898). The dynamogenic factors in pacemaking and competition. *American Journal of Psychology, 9,* 507–533.

Tuckman, B. W. (1965). Developmental sequence in small groups. *Psychological Bulletin, 63,* 384–399.

Tuckman, B. W., & Jensen, M. A. C. (1977). Stages of small group development reconsidered. *Group and Organizational Studies, 2,* 419–427.

Turner, J. C. (1982). Toward a cognitive redefinition of the social group. In H. Tajfel (Ed.), *Social identity and intergroup behavior* (pp. 15–40). Cambridge, UK: Cambridge University Press.

Turner, J. C., Hogg, M. A., Oakes, P. J., Reicher, S. D., & Wetherell, M. S. (1987). *Rediscovering the social group: A self-categorization theory.* Oxford, UK: Blackwell.

Turner, M. E., Pratkanis, A. R., Probasco, P., & Leve, C. (1992). Threat, cohesion, and group effectiveness: Testing a social identity maintenance perspective on groupthink. *Journal of Personality and Social Psychology, 63,* 781–796.

Tversky, A., & Kahneman, D. (1974). Judgment in uncertainty: Heuristics and biases. *Science, 185,* 1124–1131.

Tversky, A., & Kahneman, D. (1983). Extensional versus intuitive reasoning: The conjunction fallacy in probability judgment. *Psychological Review, 90,* 293–315.

Valacich, J. S., Dennis, A. R., & Connolly, T. (1994). Idea generation in computer-based groups: A new ending to an old story. *Organizational Behavior and Human Decision Processes, 57,* 448–467.

Valacich, J. S., Dennis, A. R., & Nunamaker J. F., Jr. (1992). Group size and anonymity effects on computer-mediated idea generation. *Small Group Research, 2,* 49–73.

Van der Kleij, R. (2007). *Overcoming distance in virtual teams: Effects of communication media, experience, and time pressure on distributed teamwork.* Doctoral dissertation, University of Amsterdam.

Van der Vegt, G. S., Emans, B. J. M., & Van de Vliert, E. (2000). Affective responses to intragroup interdependence and job complexity. *Journal of Management, 26,* 633–655.

Van der Vegt, G. S., & Van de Vliert, E. (2002). Intragroup interdependence and effectiveness: Review and proposed directions for theory and practice. *Journal of Managerial Psychology, 17,* 50–67.

Van Knippenberg, D., De Dreu, C. K. W., & Homan, A. C. (2004). Work group diversity and group performance: An integrative model and research agenda. *Journal of Applied Psychology, 89,* 1008–1022.

Van Knippenberg, D., van Knippenberg, B., Monden, L., & de Lima, F. (2002). Organizational identification after a merger: A social identity perspective. *British Journal of Social Psychology, 41,* 233–252.

Van Knippenberg, D., & Schippers, M. C. (2007). Work group diversity. *Annual Review of Psychology, 58,* 515–541.

Van Leeuwen, E., Van Knippenberg, D., & Ellemers, N. (2003). Continuing and changing group identities: The effects of merging on social identification and intergroup bias. *Personality and Social Psychology Bulletin, 29,* 679–690.

Vickery, C. M., Clark, T. D., & Carlson, J. R. (1999). Virtual positions: An examination of structure and performance in ad hoc workgroups. *Information Systems Journal, 9,* 291–312.

Volpe, C. E., Cannon-Bowers, J. A., Salas, E., & Spector, P. (1996). The impact of cross-training on team functioning: An empirical examination. *Human Factors, 38,* 87–100.

Vroom, V. H. (1964). *Work and motivation.* New York: Wiley.

Vroom, V., & Yetton, P. (1973). *Leadership and decision making.* Pittsburgh, PA: University of Pittsburgh Press.

Wageman, R. (1995). Interdependence and group effectiveness. *Administrative Science Quarterly, 40,* 145–180.

Weber, B., & Hertel, G. (2007). Motivation gains of inferior members: A meta-analytic review. *Journal of Personality and Social Psychology, 93,* 973–993.

Webber, S. S., & Donahue, L. M. (2001). Impact of highly and less job-related diversity on work group cohesion and performance: A meta-analysis. *Journal of Management, 27,* 141–162.

Wegner, D. M. (1986). Transactive memory: A contemporary analysis of the group mind. In B. Mullen & G. R. Goethals (Eds.), *Theories of group behavior* (pp. 185–208). New York: Springer-Verlag.

West, M. A. (1990). The social psychology of innovation in groups. In: M. A. West & J. L. Farr (Eds.), *Innovation and creativity at work: Psychological and organizational strategies* (pp. 309–333). Chichester, UK: Wiley.

Wheelan, S. A. (1994). *Group processes: A developmental perspective.* Needham Heights, MA: Allyn & Bacon.

Wheelan, S. A., Davidson, B., & Tilin, F. (2003). Group development across time: Reality or illusion? *Small Group Research, 34,* 223–245.

Wilder, D. A., & Allen, V. L. (1977). Social comparison, self-evaluation, and conformity to the group. In J. M. Suls, & R. L. Miller (Eds.). *Social comparison processes. Theoretical and empirical perspectives* (pp. 187– 208). Washington, DC: Hemisphere Publishing.

Wildschut, T., Insko, C. A., & Gaertner, L. (2002). Intragroup social influence and intergroup competition. *Journal of Personality and Social Psychology, 82,* 975–992.

Wildschut, T., Pinter, B., Vevea, J. L., Insko, C. A., & Schopler, J. (2003). Beyond the group mind: A quantitative review of the interindividual–intergroup discontinuity effect. *Psychological Bulletin, 129,* 698–722.

Williams, E. (1975). Medium or message: Communications medium as a determinant of interpersonal evaluation. *Sociometry, 38,* 119–130.

Williams, E. (1977). Experimental comparisons of face-to-face and mediated communication: A review. *Psychological Bulletin, 84,* 963–976.

Williams, K. D. (2001). *Ostracism: The power of silence.* Philadelphia, PA: Psychology Press.

Williams, K. D., Cheung, C. K. T., & Choi, W. (2000). Cyberostracism: Effects of being ignored over the internet. *Journal of Personality and Social Psychology, 79,* 748–762.

Williams, K. D., Harkins, S., & Latané, B. (1981). Identifiability as a deterrent to social loafing: Two cheering experiments. *Journal of Personality and Social Psychology, 40,* 303–311.

Williams, K. D., & Karau, S. J. (1991). Social loafing and social compensation: The effects of expectations of co-worker performance. *Journal of Personality and Social Psychology, 61,* 570–580.

Williams, K., & O'Reilly, C. (1998). The complexity of diversity: A review of forty years of research. In D. Gruenfeld & M. Neale (Eds.), *Research on managing in groups and teams* (Vol. 20, pp. 77–140). Greenwich, CT: JAI Press.

Wilson, J. M., Straus, S. G., & McEvily, B. (2006). All in due time: The development of trust in computer-mediated and face-to-face teams. *Organizational Behavior and Human Decision Processes, 99,* 16–33.

Winquist, J. R., & Larson, J. R., Jr. (1998). Information pooling: When it impacts group decision making. *Journal of Personality and Social Psychology, 74,* 371–377.

Witte, E. H. (1989). Köhler rediscovered: The anti-Ringelmann effect. *European Journal of Social Psychology, 19,* 147–154.

Wittenbaum, G. M., Hubbell, A. P., & Zuckerman, C. (1999). Mutual enhancement: Toward an understanding of the collective preference for shared information. *Journal of Personality and Social Psychology, 77,* 967–978.

Wood, W., Lundgren, S., Ouellette, J. A., Busceme, S., & Blackstone, T. (1994). Minority influence: A meta-analytical review of social influence processes. *Psychological Bulletin, 115,* 323–345.

Zaccaro, S. (1984). Social loafing: The role of task attractiveness. *Personality and Social Psychology Bulletin, 10,* 99–106.

Zaccaro, S. J., & Lowe, C. A. (1988). Cohesiveness and performance on an additive task: Evidence for multidimensionality. *Journal of Social Psychology, 128,* 547–558.

Zaccaro, S. J., Rittman, A. L., & Marks, M. A. (2001). Team leadership. *Leadership Quarterly, 12,* 451–483.

Zajonc, R. B. (1965). Social facilitation. *Science, 149,* 269–274.

Zajonc, R. B. (1980). Compresence of group influence. In P. B. Paulus (Ed.), *Psychology of group influence* (pp. 35–60). Hillsdale, NJ: Lawrence Erlbaum Associates.

Zajonc, R. B., & Sales, S. M. (1966). Social facilitation of dominant and subordinate responses. *Journal of Experimental Social Psychology, 2,* 160–168.

Ziller, R. C. (1965). Toward a theory of open and closed groups. *Psychological Bulletin, 64,* 164–182.

Author index

Abakoumkin, G. 105, 115
Abbott, A. S. 138
Abrams, D. 10, 206
Adamopoulos, J. A. 153–155
Agnew, C. R. 10
Ahearne, M. 6, 13, 88
Aiello, J. R. 232
Aldag, R. J. 143
Alge, B. J. 231
Allee, W. C. 65
Allen, V. L. 32
Alliger, G. M. 188
Allport, F. 64, 66
Allport, G. W. 64, 210, 214
Altermatt, T. W. 157
Altink, W. M. M. 43
Amabile, T. M. 116
Amiot, C. E. 215
Ancona, D. G. 8, 57, 59, 196–197
Anderson, A. 226–227
Anderson, L. R. 106
Anthony, T. 143
Applegate, L. M. 111
Argote, L. 8, 55, 201–202, 210
Aronson, E. 22
Arthur, W., Jr. 178–179
Asch, S. E. 31–33, 39, 129
Avolio, B. J. 184–186

Bachman, B. A. 215
Bailey, D. 165–166, 168
Bales, R. F. 3, 27–28, 180
Baltes, B. B. 223
Bandura, A. 72
Banker, B. S. 212
Barnard, P. J. 226
Baron, R. S. 34, 37, 69–72, 76, 143, 224
Bartel, C. A. 175
Bartis, S. 104
Bass, B. M. 184–186
Bastianutti, L. 111
Bauer, C. C. 223
Baumeister, R. F. 8, 75

Beattie, G. W. 226
Beersma, B. 118
Bell, S. T. 178–179
Belliveau, M. 199–200
Benson, G. S. 188
Berger, J. 29, 188
Berkman, L. F. 9
Berry, P. C. 104
Berscheid, E. 169
Berson, Y. 186
Bettencourt, B. A. 211
Billig, M. 204
Birchmeier, Z. 123, 131, 144
Blackstone, T. 39–40
Blascovich, J. 68, 73
Blickensderfer, E. 179
Block, C. H. 104
Boen, F. 214
Boh, L. 157–158
Bond, C. F., Jr. 68–69, 75
Bonito, J. A. 228
Bonner, B. L. 157–158
Bono, J. E. 188–189
Bowlby, J. 9
Brandon, D. P. 8
Brebels, L. 214
Brenner, M. 150
Bresman, H. 8
Brewer, M. B. 169, 211
Brickner, M. A. 87
Brodbeck, F. C. 127, 136–137, 145
Brown, R. 37
Bruce, V. 226–227
Brunsman, B. 34
Bruun, S. E. 89–92
Bundy, R. 204
Burgoon, J. K. 228
Burke, C. S. 178–179, 183, 186
Burns, J. M. 184
Burnstein, E. 37
Busceme, S. 39–40
Byrne, D. 5, 169

Cadsby, J. 224
Caldwell, D. F. 57, 59, 196–197
Callan, V. J. 215
Camacho, L. M. 104–105, 108–109, 114–115
Campbell, D. T. 3, 5
Cannon-Bowers, J. A. 177–179
Carlson, J. R. 232
Carson, J .B. 191
Carver, C. S. 75
Cha, S. E. 187
Chaiken, S. 9, 35
Chang, S. 141, 143
Chapanis, A. 227
Chemers, M. M. 180
Chen, S. C. 65
Chirumbolo, A. 118
Choi, H. S. 23, 118, 199, 201, 203
Christensen, C. 138
Cihangir, S. 135
Cini, M. A. 23
Clark, T. D. 232
Clemons, T. C. 188
Cochrane, S. 206
Cohen, B. P. 30
Cohen, S. 165–166, 168
Collaros, P. A. 106
Conlon, D. E. 165–166
Connolly, T. 111
Converse, S. A. 177–178
Cooper, W. H. 111, 224
Copper, C. 6–7, 13–14, 55
Costa, P. R., Jr. 188
Cottrell, N. B. 69–70
Cramton, C. 230–231
Croak, M. R. 211
Cropanzano, R. 204

Dabbs, J. M., Jr. 29
Daft, R. L. 220, 227
Davidson, B. 28
Davis, J. H. 46, 123–124, 128, 153

Subject index

Experimental research 15–16
  and causality 15–16
  and manipulations 15
  quasi experiments 16
  and random assignment 15–16

Free riding 89–92, 93, 97, 99, 105–106, 231–232
  and dispensability 89–92 , 99, 176, 232

Group context 57–59, 195–218
Group development 26–28
Group output (evaluation of) 53–57
  and comparison standards 55–56
  and performance dimensions 53–55
  versus individual performance 56–57
Group polarization 35–38, 41, 161, 206–207, 211
  persuasive arguments theory of 37–38
  and self-categorization 206–207, 211
  and social comparisons 37–38
Group size 3, 7, 45, 46, 81–86, 105, 111–112, 114,
  150, 152, 162–163, 223,
Group socialization 19, 20–24, 199
  and commitment 21, 22, 23, 24
  and initiation rituals 21–22
  and role transitions 20
Group structure 3, 4, 26, 28–31; *see also* Roles; Status
Groups as multilevel systems 45–47, 119, 195
  and bottom-up effects 46–47, 48, 51
  and top-down effects 46, 57
Groupthink 1–2, 38, 140–144
  antecedents 140
  Bay of Pigs invasion and 1–2, 140
  case studies of 141–143
  Challenger disaster and 141, 142
  cohesion and 140, 143
  concurrence seeking and 1, 140
  Cuba crisis and 1–2, 140, 151
  definition of 1, 140
  experimental studies of 143–144
  leadership and 140, 143
  symptoms of 141

Idea generation *see* Brainstorming
Individualism–collectivism 100, 118, 187
Ingroup bias 201, 203–204, 209–214
Interaction anxiousness 108–109, 113
Interaction Process Analysis (IPA) 27, 28–29, 180
  and socio-emotional behaviors 27, 29, 180
  and task behaviors 27, 29, 180
Interdependence 4–5, 165, 168, 176–179, 180,
  207–208, 212, 222, 228, 232–233
  outcome 4–5, 176, 232
  task 4–5, 176, 177, 222, 232
Intergroup relations 203–216
  intergroup competition 204, 206, 207–209
  intergroup contact 210, 214

Judgment, errors and biases in 149, 159–163
  base-rate fallacy 159, 160, 161, 162
  conjunction error 159, 160, 161, 162
  and error correction 159, 161, 163
  and relative bias of groups 162–163
  and social decision schemes 162–163

Jury decision-making 37, 129–130, 163
  leniency bias in 129–130, 163

Köhler effect 93, 95–98, 99, 204
  and competition 96, 99
  and dispensability 97, 99
KSAs (knowledge, skills, abilities) 47–49; *see also*
  Member resources

Leadership 3, 19, 23, 26, 138–139, 140, 143–144, 167,
  175, 180–191, 196, 232–233
  consideration 180–183
  contingency theory of 181–183
  directive 143, 181, 183
  emergent leadership 187–190
  and information sharing 138–139, 180
  initiating structure 180–183
  and groupthink 140, 143–144
  laissez-faire 184–186
  Multi-factor leadership questionnaire 184–185
  participative 183
  shared leadership 191
  transactional 183–187
  transformational 183–187
  in virtual teams 232–233

Majority influence *see* Social influence
Media richness 220, 222, 227–228, 230
Member resources 48–50, 51, 53, 58–59, 123, 169,
  171, 173, 176, 199, 201, 202–203; *see also* KSAs
Membership change 5, 8, 118–119, 195, 198–203,
  229; *see also* Group socialization; Newcomers
Mergers 213–216
  merger integration patterns 215
  and status 214–215
Minority influence *see* Social influence
Mixed motive situations 208–209
Motivation gains *see* Process gains (*see also* Köhler
  effect; Social compensation)
Motivation losses *see* Process loss (*see also*
  Downward matching; Free riding; Social loafing;
  Sucker effect)

Need to belong 8–9, 10, 21
Newcomers 28, 199–203
Nominal groups 104–109, 111, 116–117, 157–158
Norms 4, 9, 10, 19, 22–25, 26, 31, 33, 92, 118, 206,
  224–226
  and deviance 23, 24, 25, 33, 206

Permeability 4–5, 7, 45
Potential performance 49–53, 81, 82, 104, 157, 169,
  199, 229
Problem-solving 46, 65, 126, 149–158, 167, 223,
  227
  collective induction 155–158
  and correction of errors 149–150, 157
  and social decision schemes 126, 150–154
Process gains 52–53, 56–57, 93, 95–96, 131, 157–158,
  169
  coordination gains 53
  motivation gains 53, 81, 93–98, 204; *see also* Köhler
  effect; Social compensation